*TO MY WIFE*

# MELVILLE AND THE COMIC SPIRIT

# MELVILLE

## and the

## Comic Spirit

EDWARD H. ROSENBERRY

Harvard University Press

Cambridge

1955

Library of Congress Catalog Card Number *55–10976*
Printed in the United States of America

# Preface

Contemporary criticism has found few subjects more attractive than the Anatomy of Melville, perhaps because few authors have so clearly needed its services or so obstinately resisted its definitions. The last word is never said on any great artist, and Melville criticism, for all its rapid growth, is still far too young to be in any immediate danger of superfluity. So long as there are fresh frames of reference in which to read Melville's extraordinary books, such commentaries as this will be more nearly first words than last.

The materials of the study are chiefly Melville's own writings. In drawing on these I have chosen to abandon the old limited edition of the Collected Works (London: Constable, 1922–24) in favor of the volumes so far published in the new standard edition of Hendricks House, and to supplement these with the best available reprints. In order to facilitate reference for readers using other editions than those listed in my bibliography, the notes specify both chapter and page in each citation of the nine major works discussed. A few major writings, notably "Benito Cereno," *Clarel*, and *Billy Budd*, are not discussed directly, since their close analysis is not germane to this study.

In addition to published works, I have examined manuscript materials, including marginalia in books which Melville owned. For access to these sources and permission to use them here I am indebted to the Harvard College Library, the Yale University Library, and the New York Public Library. Among the many librarians who have given me ready and indispensable aid, I am particularly grateful to Mrs. Delphine Okie Richardson of the

University of Pennsylvania Library, Mrs. Fannie Cox Hendrie of the Drexel Institute of Technology Library, Miss Ruth Alford of the University of Delaware Library, and my old friend William H. Bond, who turned up, to my pleasure and profit, among the other treasures in Harvard's Houghton Library. In the writing of this book I have received valuable assistance and suggestions from a number of scholars, among them Professors Sculley Bradley, Tyrus Hillway, Henry A. Murray, Walter Blair, and Elizabeth Foster. To these helpers, and especially to Professor Robert E. Spiller, who guided my interest in Melville into its first written form, I owe my escape from more shortcomings than appear in these pages. The debt to my wife, Elizabeth Allen Rosenberry, cannot be summed up, but it is what every woman knows.

E. H. R.

Newark, Delaware
March 1955

# CONTENTS

*Part Four*

# THE END OF COMEDY

# Introduction

In the first chapter of his first book, *Typee*, Herman Melville tells the story of a cannibal queen who electrified the French navy with an impulsive exhibition of her most intimate tattooing. It is a neatly spun yarn, which has attracted critical attention on the ground that "a great deal can be told about a writer from the first note he strikes." [1] Certainly the most obvious fact about Melville's first note is that it is a comic one. It was as a comic writer that he won his early fame and that he was still remembered when he had long outlived it. Forty years after *Typee* and *Omoo* Robert Louis Stevenson went to the South Seas with the conviction that he could write a better book on the subject than anyone else had done, but he added, "except Herman Melville, perhaps, who is a howling cheese." [2] And only a year before his virtually unnoticed death Melville was still accorded by *Harper's Magazine* a literary position of sorts among the minor humorists who had been active in the middle decades of the century. No other American writer has made so spectacular a recovery from oblivion as Herman Melville has done since then; yet only a few years ago someone felt it necessary to exhume that *Harper's* article as well, as a reminder to literary historians that "Melville was, among other things, a humorist." [3]

The twentieth century has made many things of Melville, but Stevenson's "howling cheese" is a forgotten man. An unnatural cleavage has developed between that merry figure and the tragic titan that has reached mythic proportions in modern criticism. Even the founder of the myth recognized that "when Melville sat down to write, always at his knee stood that chosen emissary of

Satan, the comic spirit: a demoniac familiar never long absent from his pages." [4] Yet what humor has not been missed in those pages has for the most part been ignored in the search for tragedy, or distorted in the special pursuit of autobiography or Freudian symbols or cryptic antagonisms. If Melville is as important and complex as our generation believes him to be, it seems a curious omission to overlook the one approach to him that is most strongly indicated by his earlier reputation and by that principle of psychology which seemed so elementary to Carlyle: "How much lies in laughter: the cipher-key, wherewith we decipher the whole man!"

Laughter is paradoxically hard to define. However, there are two aspects of it that help to explain the kind of usefulness Carlyle had in mind. One is its ambivalence: "In every case in which a man laughs humorously there is an element which, if his sensitivity were sufficiently exaggerated, would contain the possibility of tears." [5] Laughter is not the simple antithesis of tears; comedy and tragedy are not distinct except as attitudes. The tragic spirit looks for destiny and is blind to compromise; the comic spirit looks for adjustment, and the sense of humor, which is its principal organ, is a juggler of values. It detects an imbalance, an incongruity, and plays with the discrepant values it exposes. Sometimes the discrepancy delights, sometimes it offends. The idea of "play" involves a multitude of human activities, from day-dreaming to Russian roulette, and its mood may range from sentimental euphoria to grim hysteria. Comedy, in other words, is "too complex to be merely funny." [6] What Meredith called "thoughtful laughter" is what Melville chiefly saw in his favorite comic authors, Rabelais and Shakespeare. As *Mardi* abundantly proves, he never shared the common delusion about Rabelais "that laughter is incompatible with true seriousness," and his mature artistry reflects what has been said of Shakespeare, that "there may even be an air of open sadness" about his humor that at times becomes "melancholy, sardonic, or frankly bitter." [7]

The tone of an author's "play" will vary sharply with his personal reaction to a given situation at a given moment. That is a second key to the importance of laughter. If it is true that "humor, of all human qualities, lies closest to the heart," [8] then we ought to find some reward in exploring the comic impulses of a great artist. Students of Shakespearean comedy have declared that "we owe to humor, that sometimes transparent veil which the author casts over his face, one of the least uncertain revelations of his essential personality," and that "if his comedy is indeed instinctive it is possible we may learn more of Shakespeare's very self from his comic than from his tragic scenes." [9] In its forms and uses Melville's comic art was a sometimes sedulous imitation of Shakespeare and others, but in its essential attitude it was instinctive as theirs had been. The vision his art reflects was colored by that peculiarly personal diffraction which he called his "infirmity of jocularity," referring half-apologetically to its habit of spontaneous intrusion upon otherwise sober matters.[10] Irrepressible as a limp or a tic, and as distinctive, the sense of humor must always be an "infirmity" in the sense that its ultimate springs are not art or tradition but the intimate orientations of personality.

At the source of Melville's literary comedy was a warm and robust personality. His life at sea had taught him that there were no substitutes for good health and good nature, "both first-rate things," he later remarked to Evert Duyckinck, "but not universally to be found." [11] And when he read Cervantes in 1855, he marked Don Quixote's praise of Sancho Panza for being "good-natured, without which no knowledge is of any value." Despite the mythic identification of Melville with the tragic "isolatoes" he created, he had a life-long passion for the comforts of friendship and conviviality, founded about equally on a love of talk and a love of sharing his animal enthusiasms for food and drink. As a young sailor a shipmate remembered him as good for five servings of leathery "duff," and thirty years later his appetite for breakfast was still "clamorous at an hour too early for any rational household to satisfy." [12] Settled near Hawthorne in the Berkshires, Melville's notion of entertaining his famous neighbor was "getting him up in my snug room here, & discussing the Universe with a bottle of brandy & cigars." If there was any fault in Hawthorne, it was "something lacking . . . to the plump sphericity of the man. . . . He doesn't patronize the butcher — he needs roast-beef, done rare." [13] Even in the trying days after the completion of *The Confidence-Man* Duyckinck could note in his diary: "Good talk — Herman warming like an old sailor over the supper." [14] Sailor after sailor in his books warmed himself in the same way:

"I never felt so bad yet, but I could eat a good dinner." "If you can get nothing better out of the world, get a good dinner out of it, at least." [15]

But humor is not all cakes and ale; the Hawthorne who lacked "plump sphericity" could be praised for that very lack:

> What a wild moonlight of contemplative humor bathes that Old Manse! . . . No rollicking rudeness, no gross fun fed on fat dinners, and bred in the lees of wine, — but a humor so spiritually gentle, so high, so deep, and yet so richly relishable, that it were hardly inappropriate in an angel. It is the very religion of mirth. . .[16]

There was a doubleness in Melville's nature which he never ceased to relish, and sometimes to tease people with. His comment on a photograph of himself sent to an old friend in 1885 is typical:

> What the deuce makes him look so serious, I wonder. I thought he was of a gay and frolicsome nature, judging from a little rhyme of his about a Kitten, which you once showed me. But is this the same man? Pray explain the inconsistency, or I shall begin to suspect your venerable friend of being a two-faced old fellow and not to be trusted.[17]

He was indeed a two-faced old fellow and his humor looked, as humor must, in two directions. No reader of *Mardi* or *Pierre* need be told of the special piquancy a paradox or an incongruity held for Melville. Even his unstudied journals speak clearly of the sense of ambivalence that informed his observations as a traveler. His reaction to the "Quixotism" of Christian missions in Palestine is in fact a capsule version of the Melvillian comic idea: "half melancholy, half farcical — like all the rest of the world." [18]

From *Mardi* to the end of his professional literary career in 1856 it was Melville's principal artistic struggle to achieve a synthesis of those halves that should contain the whole truth of life. He gave it up then, but he had succeeded perhaps better than he knew, certainly better than the world knew. In the course of the single decade in which his major work was done he explored the full range of comedy, expanding its possibilities until he had a masterpiece, then mining its polar reaches until he had exhausted the vein. The progress of that exploration tells the story of a maturing art. It is a complex story, but not hopelessly so if the range of comedy explored is seen in terms of the modes or categories it comprises.

Broadly, the growth of Melville's comic artistry may be measured by its cumulative advance through four theoretical and somewhat arbitrary phases. The first, which we may label the *jocular-hedonic*, is instantly translatable into the simple idea of fun; more literally, joking in the most light-hearted vein merely for the shared pleasure involved. It is the most instinctive manifestation of humor. It has no axes to grind, no subtle overtones to convey. It is an unreflecting expression of the native play-spirit of the individual and his folk tradition. Next in the scale of artistic complexity is the *imaginative-critical* type of comedy, more literary in its origins, more sophisticated in its tone, more ulterior in its motives. This is the mode which enables the artist to increase the suggestive power of his comedy by enlarging the orbit of its implications. His object may be the favorable insights of humor or the unfavorable insights of satire. His interest in any case has passed beyond laughter — usually without sacrificing it — to the more serious business of casting balances and judging values. A third phase, the *philosophical-psychological*, is concerned neither with laughter nor with critical reflections on the passing scene, but with the ambiguous nature of values themselves, the interrelations of comedy and tragedy, and the bearing of both problems on the life of man. It is a stage which represents the artist's search for a balanced view of himself and his world. Finally, in the *dramatic-structural* phase, the artist who has mastered the other three deploys his comic forces to expose the vital interplay of character and situation and performs the successful act of creation that fuses the disparate elements of comedy and tragedy into a balanced work of art. As organic functions, these phases are not mutually exclusive, nor was Melville's exploration of the gamut always conscious and orderly. But his work, read in these terms, takes on an illuminating pattern of progress and retrogression, success and failure.

The pattern is roughly pyramidal. Drawing on the fresh appeal of his exotic adventures, Melville established his reputation with a series of four semi-autobiographical romances which are predominantly comic in the jocular-hedonic vein. The first two, *Typee* and *Omoo*, show few symptoms of deviation from that basic character. The two later romances, *Redburn* and *White-Jacket*, on the other hand, reveal tendencies toward an expanded compass which is all the more remarkable for the negligent haste in which they were written. The explanation of the change, of course, lies in the intervening composition of *Mardi*, a momentous experimental failure, which moves from the bluff, happy-go-lucky air of *Typee* and *Omoo* to that critical and introspective attitude from which *Redburn* and *White-Jacket* represent only a partial return. *Mardi* was a premature bid for greatness, from which temporary retreat was inevitable, but its prematurity is a showcase of embryonic art. Laid out in order in its pages and almost completely unintegrated are the records of Melville's successive sallies through the first three phases of his ripening comic art. Beginning in the familiar mood of picaresque gaiety, *Mardi* shifts abruptly to the bookish laughter of its "world of mind," and culminates in the hysterical ambiguity of its diabolical comic vision. Although *Redburn* and *White-Jacket* taught Melville essential disciplines in organization, thematic counterpoint, and the achievement of credibility, he correctly lumped them in his mind with the Polynesian romances as things of relative simplicity. When he came to *Moby-Dick* he built upon the more ambitious structure of *Mardi*, its true predecessor by the inner logic of artistic growth.

*Moby-Dick*, not surprisingly, stands at the apex of this pyramidal pattern. Here, for the first time in his career — and the last time on a major scale — Melville was master of all four modes of comic art, each deepened by the experience of prior books, and all enriched by their own organic intermingling. His native exuberance reached an epic robustiousness, his poetic wit mined a multitude of meanings from the most unpromising materials, his comic vision steadied as he found the sanative balance between primitive and demonic laughter, and his profound grasp of the human comedy showed at last that he had both "swum through libraries and sailed through oceans." [19] After *Moby-Dick* his great talent declined, in scope if not in vigor. Of the three novels and the score of essays and stories that concluded his professional authorship, perhaps only "Bartleby," in its brief and muted way, displays the full range of his comic genius.

To say that Melville retreated down the comic scale he had ascended would be an oversimplification, since the stages through which he had so clearly marched in *Mardi* forever lost their elemental independence in *Moby-Dick*. Yet the pattern of decline emerges, symmetrical though blurred, in the succession of special interests, below the dramatic-structural plane, which he exploited in the unbalanced writings that followed. His principal absorption, a philosophical-psychological one, was the grimly amusing problem of ambiguities, particularly the ambiguity of comedy itself and the dilemma in which it involves the artist between the dark and bright views of life. In the imaginative-critical vein, he turned his invention and wit to primarily satiric purposes in a war of ideas that reached its stunning climax in *The Confidence-Man*. And finally he made a partial return toward the purely playful laughter of his earliest books, a tendency culminating in a remarkable valedictory burst of native humor coloring all the work of 1856.

But the end of *The Confidence-Man* is darkness and silence, and its folk laughter is less a resurgence than an echo, muffled and diffused by its accretion of thoughtful overtones. In its broad sweep, Melville's career as a comic artist is well symbolized in the image of Balzac, a favorite author of his later years: "As children only do we laugh, and when we travel onward laughter sinks down and dies out like the light of an oil-lit lamp." The symbolism is strikingly like Melville's own. It is indeed the laughter of children that we hear in his earliest books:

> *The small, merry laughter it is*
> *Of the sons and daughters of the tattooed.*[20]

And it is precisely the light of an oil-lit lamp that dies as "The Cosmopolitan Increases in Seriousness" in the last chapter of *The Confidence-Man*. The birth and death of the comic spirit in Melville's art lies in between.

*Part One*

# THE SMALL, MERRY LAUGHTER

# 1

# The Comic Matter

The story of Melville's literary comedy begins in the racy and circumstantial pages of his first four adventure stories — *Typee, Omoo, Redburn,* and *White-Jacket.* The old delusion that these books are faithful self-portraits of the artist as a young man has been dispelled, but they remain collectively the most reliable portrait of the man as a young artist that we are likely to get. Whatever their departures from literal autobiography, they have a broad common foundation in the actual experiences of their roving author. In his reactions to certain preposterously altered orders of life across the world from Lansingburgh, New York, we can see his sense of humor most instinctively reflecting the values that color the elemental chiaroscuro of fact and fancy.

I

There is no reason to question Melville's sincerity when he wrote in the Preface to *Typee* that matters in that book were stated "just as they occurred." Like the author of *Huckleberry Finn,* "there was things which he stretched, but mainly he told the truth." If it was not quite the "unvarnished truth" he claimed it to be, it was at least the brand of truth that came naturally to his countrymen in reporting wonders. Fact, on the frontier, was fabulous in itself; the men who dealt with it had to become a little fabulous too. The national humor that flowered in writers like Melville and Twain got its distinctive character when the frontier, as Albert Bigelow Paine has said, "even with its hardships and its tragedies, was little more than a vast primal joke;

when all frontiersmen were obliged to be laughing philosophers in order to survive the stress of its warfares." [1]

Melville's adventures before the mast in the 1840's were so fraught with crudity, privation, and danger that one's hair rises at the thought of the reality behind many of his casual and ludicrous descriptions. Yet, like scores of budding Western humorists around their prairie campfires, Melville learned on midnight watches before the flaring try-works how whalemen "narrated to each other their unholy adventures, their tales of terror told in words of mirth." [2] After three years of practice in sharing horrors with his shipmates and matching their mountainous comic lies about them, he was marvelously equipped to shock the mere "state-room sailors" he turned to entertain in his books. With relish he recalled the great tobacco famine on the *Highlander*, which the crew combatted by renovating their "chaws" in the ship's oven, then combing dark corners for discarded plugs, and finally settling for the "cheese-like" yarn of old ship's cable, a delicacy marred only by the tar "with which the flavour of all ropes is more or less vitiated." There is no dread, only a wry exhilaration, in his description of the nauseous *Julia*, whose forecastle was "like the hollow of an old tree going to decay" and was so overrun with cockroaches and rats that "the business of eating and drinking was better done in the dark than in the light of day." [3] "Lucky for us Melville makes it fantastic," D. H. Lawrence has remarked. "It must have been pretty sordid." Like the fantasy-makers of the West of whom Constance Rourke tells us, Melville had swung "from an impinging terror to a gross and often brutal comedy." [4]

The variety of terrors and hardships which Melville turned to comic account in his early books extends over a considerable range. One thinks of the "midnight misgivings" of Tommo and Toby at their first cannibal campfire, of the battle with the "small swordfish" that were the Polynesian mosquitoes, of the incredible obstacles to sleep in both the Navy and the merchant marine, of the perils of shaving, either with a dull blade in a rocking storm or with a shark's tooth in a cannibal hut. But the unmistakable keynote in Melville's comedy of hardship is a gastronomic one. The bias is evident in both the rope-yarn episode and the account of the *Julia*'s vermin. The cannibal scare of Tommo and Toby adds to this element the terror of death; but at bottom, and quite overtly as the scene progresses, the central point of attack is the digestive sensibility. When it becomes clear that the Typees are planning to feed rather than eat their guests, a new and even more plausible horror replaces the old:

"I say, Tommo, you are not going to eat any of that mess there, in the dark, are you? Why, how can you tell what it is?"

"By tasting it, to be sure," said I, masticating a morsel that Kory-Kory had just put in my mouth; "and excellently good it is too, very much like veal."

"A baked baby, by the soul of Captain Cook!" burst forth Toby, with amazing vehemence; "veal! why there never was a calf on the island till you landed."[5]

"Emetics and luke-warm water!" Melville remarks in our stead. "What a sensation in the abdominal regions!"

No qualms disturb the playfulness with which he damns the miserable fare he had managed to thrive on as a sailor. Evert Duyckinck, after reading about the grim larder of the *Dolly*, wrote to Hawthorne that Melville had actually preferred "the society of cannibals to the interminable casks of corned beef and impracticable bread which so afflicted his imagination in the hold of that vessel." It might easily have seemed so from the description in the fourth chapter of *Typee*, but, as another writer of sea stories observed with British understatement, "Melville romances somewhat when he approaches the galley; and you are scarcely sure that he means all he says."[6] The mess of the *Julia*, on which the fictional Melville escaped from Nukuheva, was evidently worse than that of the ship that had brought him there, but its only literary effect is a heightened humor. The pork "looked as if preserved in iron rust"; the beef gave rise to a "story of a horse's hoof with the shoe on having been fished up out of the pickle"; the biscuits were "hard little gunflints, honey-combed through and through, as if the worms usually infesting this article on long tropical voyages, had, in boring after nutriment, come out at the antipodes without finding anything." The Liverpool packet on which young Redburn sailed may have had less appalling food, but the coffee it served is described with compensatory eloquence. Generally cold, and inexhaustible in its variety of bad flavors, it was prepared by an unhygienic Negro cook who was never seen to wash but once, "and that was at one of his own soup pots." Standard fare on all ships was a concoction called *duff*, "made of flour and water, and of about the consistence of an underdone brick." [7]

The zenith — or nadir — of Melville's gastronomic humor, the episode that comes closest to turning "impinging terror" into "gross and brutal comedy," is the story of the practical joke played on Surgeon Cuticle by the wardroom officers in *White-Jacket.*

> Once [it begins] when they had some sago pudding for dinner, and Cuticle chanced to be ashore, they made up a neat parcel of this bluish-white, firm, jelly-like preparation, and placing it in a tin box, carefully sealed with wax, they deposited it on the gun-room table, with a note, purporting to come from an eminent physician in Rio, . . . begging leave to present the scientific Senhor Cuticle — with the donor's compliments — an uncommonly fine specimen of a cancer.[8]

Readers of *White-Jacket* will recall, and nonreaders of *White-Jacket* will imagine, how the story proceeds from there. It is not the business of this study to pronounce on Melville's taste; but it is interesting to note that he did draw the line somewhere. Speaking in *Redburn* of the self-medications of sailors, he mentions that they have been known to take "calomel off Cape Horn and still remain on duty," in which connection "some really frightful stories might be told; but I forbear."

The devouring of the ambiguous sago pudding is a practical joke at the expense of Surgeon Cuticle; the routine ship's diet of "salt horse," "shot soup," and "choice old water" is a practical joke at the expense of the author. Present in any case is a comic victim — the "sucker" or "goat" who has traditionally paid the bill for American laughter. When a man took on the immense challenge of the frontier, it was well for him to be the first to see the humor in his temerity. In Sculley Bradley's words, "If you could not laugh at [dangers and routine catastrophes] or at yourself in the role of the sucker, you were doomed." [9] As a sailor, Melville learned that priceless secret of self-preservation; as a writer, he never ceased to apply it, though with a gradual shift in emphasis that reflects the evolution of his mind and art.

Self-ridicule, in the halcyon atmosphere of *Typee, Omoo, Redburn,* and *White-Jacket,* is for the most part purely jocular. The richest vein occurs in *Redburn*, not unnaturally, since the theme of the book is the practical education of a greenhorn. But the attitude is maintained as consistently, if with less concentration, in the other narratives. One strongly anti-romantic episode in *Omoo* is characteristic of Melville's gleeful exposures of his own punctured pride. Languishing in the stocks of a makeshift Tahitian prison, Melville and his fellow mutineers from the *Julia* are mortified by a stream of native sight-seers and particularly by one light-minded beauty, who laughs and points at each successive absurdity sprawled before her. Melville determines to stifle her ridicule with a show of manly dignity.

Ere her glance fell upon me, I had, unconsciously, thrown myself into the most graceful attitude I could assume, leaned my head upon my hand, and summoned up as abstracted an expression as possible. Though my face was averted, I soon felt it flush, and knew that the glance was on me: deeper and deeper grew the flush, and not a sound of laughter.

Delicious thought! she was moved at the sight of me. I could stand it no longer, but started up. Lo! there she was; her great hazel eyes rounding and rounding in her head, like two stars, her whole frame in a merry quiver, and an expression about the mouth that was sudden and violent death to anything like sentiment.[10]

In some such light-hearted vein Melville treats every instance in which he appears in these books as the traditional "goat" — every instance, that is, but one. The occasion is young Redburn's departure from home on a river boat, a ragged, hungry pauper, armed with a fowling piece to be pawned for sea-togs, and a single dollar to pay his boat fare. He becomes a "goat" when he discovers that the fare has gone up to two dollars and that he is reduced to still more abject disgrace before his fashionable fellow-travelers, who have already been eyeing his patches askance.

I stood their gazing some time, but at last could stand it no more. I pushed my seat right up before the most insolent gazer, a short fat man, with a plethora of cravat around his neck, and fixing my gaze on his, gave him more gazes than he sent. This somewhat embarrassed him, and he looked around for someone to take hold of me; but no one coming, he pretended to be very busy counting the gilded wooden beams overhead. I then turned to the next gazer, and clicking my gun-lock, deliberately presented the piece at him.

Upon this, he oversat his seat in his eagerness to get beyond my range, for I had him point-blank, full in the left eye; and several persons starting to their feet, exclaimed that I must be crazy. So I was at that time; for otherwise I know not how to account for my demoniac feelings. . ."[11]

It is the first dramatic instance we have of the peculiar perversity of humor which Melville so suggestively labels for us as "demoniac." The episode is striking here because of its singularity in the midst of a sunnier humor, but it was destined to cast a long shadow after it.

2

Around the central self-portrait Melville's memory drew, with comic distortion, the myriad figures that had peopled his transposed frontier world. Fortunately, Melville's forte, like every true humorist's, was the human comedy, and it is to the enduring humor of his portraiture, more than anything else, that the survival of his "popular" novels is due. The raw material was perfect, and the artist evidently knew what it was good for. "At sea a fellow comes out," he wrote to Duyckinck years later. "Salt water is like wine, in that respect." [12] The young Melville simply capitalized on a matchless opportunity to study all kinds of men under the influence of both salt water and wine, frequently both at once. The resulting gallery is heavy in rogues, most of them at sea and most of them drunk, but some merely at sea or merely drunk, and a few even on land and sober.

These last, a gentle, well-modulated minority, are for the most part little more than quaint, as Kory-Kory and Marheyo in *Typee*, or "Captain Bob," the gormandizing Tahitian jailer in *Omoo*. The white members of the category are even less exciting to the extent to which they lack novelty. One thinks of Zeke and Shorty, the potato farmers of Imeeo in the latter book, pretty much the undifferentiated Yankee and Cockney, with even their stereotyped characteristics clumsily and, one feels, half-heartedly sketched. In the earlier book, one thinks of Toby himself, an important figure, intimately known and closely drawn, yet entirely forgettable. The best that has been said of him critically is that he is "a sort of sailor Sancho Panza . . . a diverting personage,"

and even this is too generous an analogy. Despite Melville's obvious affection for the man, and specifically for his "dry sarcastic
humour," Toby is allotted only enough real breath for a few isolated outbursts of comic truculence.[13]

Perhaps Toby is merely out of his element. The fact is that
until Ahab, Melville created no memorable character without the
aid of the comic spirit, and the comic spirit lived on brine and
alcohol. "Rope Yarn" in *Omoo* is out of his element too, but he
is more interesting than Toby because he is a landsman at sea
rather than a seaman on land. His brief portrait achieves the delicate balance between ridicule and sympathy that constitutes true
humor. "Alas! for the land-lubber at sea," says Melville, temper-
ing the blast to his shorn lamb. "He is the veriest wretch the
watery world over. And such was Rope Yarn; of all land-lubbers,
the most lubberly and the most miserable." The specification of
his miseries is pure fun; yet we never lose sight of the well-meaning, rather pathetic human being turned "goat" by circumstance
and his own infirmities of character. Perhaps the secret of the
compassion which transforms the caricature is that Ropey's chief
infirmity is Melville's cardinal virtue: "The ex-baker would have
fared far better, had it not been for his heart, which was soft and
underdone. A kind word made a fool of him; and hence most of
the scrapes he got into." [14]

*Redburn*, despite Melville's apparent contempt for it, is anything but "beggarly" [15] in the caliber of its salt-fed comic portraiture. One searches very nearly in vain, before *Moby-Dick*, for
anything surpassing the sure, full-bodied artistry displayed in the
sketches of the cook, the steward, and Jack Blunt. The *Highlander*'s cook takes on a more memorable charm than his coffee
and his grooming would suggest. Behind an imposing façade of
doormat, knocker, and name-plate, the devout "Mr. Thompson"
presides with sovereign dignity over his stove-filled cubicle, earnestly poring over a greasy Bible as he stirs his pots, but occasionally forgetting his piety with a high sea running in his firebox.
His boon companion is the mulatto steward, an ex-Broadway
barber named Lavender, who perfumes his hair, affects a glass
"diamond" and a turban, reads sentimental novels, and wears cast-
off clothing "in the height of exploded fashions." It is the incon-
testable hand of an artist that brings these two together to finish

their own portraits by the mutual illumination of their humors:

And sometimes Mr. Thompson would take down his Bible, and read a chapter for the edification of Lavender, whom he knew to be a sad profligate and gay deceiver ashore; addicted to every youthful indiscretion. He would read over to him the story of Joseph and Potiphar's wife; and hold Joseph up to him as a young man of excellent principles, whom he ought to imitate, and not be guilty of his indiscretion any more. And Lavender would look serious, and say that he knew it was all true — he was a wicked youth, he knew it — he had broken a good many hearts, and many eyes were weeping for him even then, both in New York, and Liverpool, and London, and Havre. But how could he help it? He hadn't made his handsome face, and fine head of hair, and graceful figure. It was not *he*, but the others, that were to blame; for his bewitching person turned all heads and subdued all hearts, wherever he went. And then he would look very serious and penitent, and go up to the little glass, and pass his hands through his hair, and see how his whiskers were coming on.[16]

Jack Blunt, who comes in for a somewhat fuller treatment in the next chapter, is that rare gift to the humorist, the happy sucker. A devotee of fortune-telling, "Balm of Paradise" hair oil, miscellaneous quack pills, and mathematical horoscopes, Blunt is also God's gift to the confidence man; but the gentle whimsicality with which Melville here handles both the fleecer and the fleeced stands in striking contrast to the acerbity of the book he was one day to write on that special theme.

Some of the sly urbanity that tempered Melville's comic portraiture, as well as a specific character here and there, such as the schoolmaster in *White-Jacket*, he may have owed to Irving. Certainly he delighted in Irving's carousing Dutchmen, those "horrible quaffers of new cider, and arrant braggarts in their liquor," for he marked the description when he read the *Knickerbocker History of New York*. A sturdy quaffer himself, Melville had a special genius for the delineation of tosspots, a long succession of whom sat, or swayed, for their sketches in the course of his travels. A few of these are scattered about the various lands Melville visited: for instance, the enormous Liverpool bar-fly, Bob Still, "that brewery of a toper"; and Father Murphy, the bluff Irish priest at Papeetee, who attracted an uncommon number of Protestant friends by his habit of entertaining with "four square flasks, which, somehow or other, always contained just enough to need emptying." Most of them, naturally, are sailors, defined in *Redburn* as men whose "reminiscences of travel are only a dim recollection of a chain of tap-rooms surrounding the globe." [17]

The majority of Melville's sailors are dedicated drinkers. Some are the heroic type who, like Mad Jack of the *Neversink*, seem to have been "suckled at a puncheon." Some are the narcotic type, maintaining, like the pilot at Nukuheva, "that interesting state of intoxication when a man is amiable and helpless." All are men of little discretion and no shame at all; according to Redburn's prim characterization, they "only blush after the third bottle." The degree of their dedication may have been a matter of sober regret to Melville. He suggests as much in his assertion that the Navy was an "asylum for drunkards . . . driven back to the spirit-tub and the gun-deck by [their] old hereditary foe, the ever-devilish god of grog." [18] As an artist, however, he wrung a good deal of excellent comedy from it. Writing of those very man-of-war's men he pitied for their addiction, he made a good thing of the occasion when the grog gave out on the *Neversink*. Deprived of their daily tot, the crew suffered an alarming slump in morale until ten curiously stiff and sweet-smelling fellows were laid out in the brig to sleep off a mysterious drunkenness, and it became known below decks that the ship's store was amply supplied with Eau de Cologne.

The news spread far and wide among the men, being only kept secret from the officers and underlings, and that night the long, crane-necked Cologne bottles jingled in out-of-the-way corners and by-places, and, being emptied, were sent flying out of the ports. With brown sugar, taken from the mess-chests, and hot water begged from the galley-cooks, the men made all manner of punches, toddies, and cocktails, letting fall therein a small drop of tar, like a bit of brown toast, by way of imparting a flavour. . . Next day, fore and aft, the whole frigate smelled like a lady's toilet. . .[19]

Even Melville's own disapproval of intemperance is turned to comic account in *Redburn*, where he portrays himself as a member of the "Juvenile Total Abstinence Association," driven to apostasy by being seasick among a crew well stocked with the standard cure, "which they had brought along to sea with them, *to taper off with*, as they called it."

The most notable concentration of these tosspots is found in
*Omoo*, of all Melville's books the most rakish and uninhibited.
The *Julia* was generously provided with "Pisco," a Peruvian concoction which could reduce a weakened man to delirium, but
which barely sustained Chips the carpenter and Bungs the cooper,
who "from time to time effected a burglarious entry" into the
hold where it was kept.

Bungs was a man after a bar-keeper's own heart. Drinking steadily,
until just manageably tipsy, he contrived to continue so; getting neither
more nor less inebriated, but, to use his own phrase, remaining "just
about right." When in this interesting state, he had a free lurch in his
gait, a queer way of hitching up his waistbands, looked unnecessarily
steady at you when speaking, and, for the rest, was in very tolerable
spirits.

Setting the pace for Chips and Bungs was Jermin, the mate, who
"abhorred all weak infusions, and cleaved manfully to strong
drink. At all times he was more or less under the influence of it."

Sometimes, when rather flustered from his potations, he went stag-
gering about deck, instrument to eye, looking all over for the sun —
a phenomenon which any sober observer might have seen right overhead. How upon earth he contrived, on some occasions, to settle his
latitude, is more than I can tell. The longitude he must either have
obtained by the rule of three, or else by special revelation. . .
The mate, however, in addition to his "dead reckoning," pretended
to ascertain his meridian distance from Bow bells by an occasional
lunar observation. . . The operation generally requires two observers
to take sights, at one and the same time.
Now, though the mate alone might have been thought well calculated for this, inasmuch as he generally saw things double, the
doctor was usually called upon to play a sort of second quadrant to
Jermin's first; and what with the capers of both, they used to furnish a
good deal of diversion. The mate's tremulous attempts to level his
instrument at the star he was after, were comical enough. For my own
part, when he *did* catch sight of it, I hardly knew how he managed
to separate it from the astral host revolving in his own brain.

Later, having miraculously made anchor off Papeetee, Jermin
continued his earnest tippling ashore.

Toward sunset the mate came off, singing merrily, in the stern of
his boat; and in attempting to climb up the side, succeeded in going
plump into the water. He was rescued by the steward, and carried
across the deck with many moving expressions of love for his bearer.[20]

These figures and others like them contribute as much as any single factor to the irresponsible charm for which *Omoo* is famous. But the book needed a drinker who was more than a drinker to bind its collection of quips, yarns, and thumbnail sketches into a coherent work of art. Melville gave it the unity of humorous impression it needed by draping it with becoming looseness about the gaunt and whimsical frame of Doctor Long Ghost, his greatest comic creation and one of the funniest characters in our literature. Critics have praised him in the broadest terms, as a veritable "picaresque library," and "the prototype of Stevenson's great adventurers." "This long and bony Scotsman" was D. H. Lawrence's favorite Melville character — "not a mere ne'er-do-well," but "a man of humorous desperation, throwing his life ironically away." Such a figure seems almost a wish-image for the creator of Taji, Ishmael, Pierre, and other ironic discarders of life; at least, as Matthiessen has seen, "the kind of life he relishes is epitomized in the portrait of Doctor Long Ghost." [21]

Long Ghost is as near as Melville came to creating a full-fledged American folk hero or comic demigod. It is of course a fruitless question whether he knew he was creating one, but his introductory sketch of the doctor certainly argues the conscious artist in this respect.

His early history, like that of many other heroes, was enveloped in the profoundest obscurity; though he threw out hints of a patrimonial estate, a nabob uncle, and an unfortunate affair which sent him a-roving.

His personal appearance was remarkable. He was over six feet high — a tower of bones, with a complexion absolutely colorless, fair hair, and a light, unscrupulous grey eye, twinkling occasionally with the very devil of mischief. . . And from whatever high estate Doctor Long Ghost might have fallen, he had certainly at some time or other spent money, drank Burgundy, and associated with gentlemen.

As for his learning, he quoted Virgil, and talked of Hobbes of Malmesbury, besides repeating poetry by the canto, especially Hudibras. He was, moreover, a man who had seen the world. In the easiest way imaginable he could refer to an amour he had in Palermo, his lion hunting before breakfast among the Caffres, and the quality of the coffee to be drunk in Muscat; and about these places, and a hundred others, he had more anecdotes than I can tell of. Then such mellow old songs as he sang, in a voice so round and racy, the real juice of sound. How such notes came forth from his lank body was a constant marvel.[22]

Such romantic additions as learning and aristocratic background are reconciled to the American folk tradition by making Long Ghost a militant democrat. Though he had begun the voyage as the captain's companion, he soon disagreed with him, "drove home an argument with his fist, and left the captain on the floor literally silenced." Overnight he becomes the forecastle champion and thereafter serves as a convenient foil for the stuffy representatives of authority and respectability — Captain Guy, Consul Wilson, Doctor Johnson.

One quality helping to offset his atypical literacy and sophistication in the eyes of the *hoi polloi* is his elementary taste for practical jokes. With Long Ghost aboard, the ship's cook was accustomed to finding wet logs in his hammock, old boots in his soup pots, "and sometimes cakes of pitch candying in his oven." On one occasion the doctor realized the dream of the practical joker, which is to turn another practical joker's prank against him. When, late one night, a sailor on watch slipped below and hitched a rope to a sleeping shipmate with the intention of hoisting him screaming to a yardarm, Long Ghost surreptitiously shifted the rope around the man's own sea-chest, which was forthwith yanked aloft with a bang and a clatter, leaving the owner of the box "looking aghast at its scattered contents, and with one wandering hand taking the altitude of a bump on his head."

Though possessed of a kind of unstable ingenuity, Long Ghost is essentially shiftless. He is an avowed enemy of work and devotes most of what energy he has to defeating its claims upon him. At sea this was fairly simple: having quarreled with the captain, he "sent in a written resignation as the ship's doctor, gave himself out as a passenger for Sydney, and took the world quite easy." Ashore, however, the pursuit of indolence was beset with problems. Once released from the sheltering "Calabooza," he and Melville were driven to hire themselves out as laborers on a potato farm, where, presented with hoes and an unmistakable invitation to be useful, they found themselves "in a scrape." But Long Ghost is constructed in the finest tradition of the American comic hero: he is a "trickster" and functions most brilliantly in a scrape. By blinding his unlettered employers with his suavity and erudition, soon "the doctor was considered nothing short of a prodigy." He could read a book upside down, do sums in his head, discourse upon the mysteries of navigation, and converse in "such imposing phrases, that, upon one occasion, they actually remained uncovered while he talked." Deciding that he was worth more "as a man of science than as a mere ditcher," they ended by inviting him to do the cooking, the only form of labor for which he had shown any inclination. "In gastronomic affairs," Melville tells us, "my friend was something of an artist."

As a rule, however, the epicurean waged an unequal struggle with the beachcomber in Long Ghost and he was content to live beneath his standards in preference to working for his meat — or drink. For Long Ghost shares with all of Melville's rogues, and with the picaresque hero in general, a strong taste for liquor. In the case of free liquor it is both a strong and an indiscriminate taste. When Melville rejected a hospitable islander's home brew as "very crude, and strong as Lucifer," Long Ghost not only drank it but "began to wax sociable over it."

It was a curious sight. Every one knows, that, so long as the occasion lasts, there is no stronger bond of sympathy and good feeling among men than getting tipsy together, and how earnestly, nay, movingly, a brace of worthies thus employed will endeavor to shed light upon and elucidate their mystical ideas!

Fancy Varvy and the doctor, then; lovingly tippling, and brimming over with a desire to become better acquainted; the doctor politely bent upon carrying on the conversation in the language of his host, and the old hermit persisting in trying to talk English. The result was, that between the two, they made such a fricassee of vowels and consonants, that it was enough to turn one's brain.

The next morning, on waking, I heard a voice from the tombs. It was the doctor, solemnly pronouncing himself a dead man. He was sitting up, with both hands clasped over his forehead, and his pale face a thousand times paler than ever.[23]

True to his sybaritic nature, and again true to the tradition of the comic hero, Long Ghost is a man of active libido. "With a pleasant companion, he was forever strolling inland, ostensibly to collect botanical specimens." His brand of botany is specified at a native dinner party where he was primarily interested in "a sort of fruit of which gentlemen of the sanguine temperament are remarkably fond; namely, the ripe cherry lips of Miss Day-born, who stood looking on." Among these Tahitian belles the amorous trickster adapts himself with the chameleon-like instinct of his

breed: he "increased their enjoyment, by assuming the part of a
Merry Andrew. Yet his cap and bells never jingled but to some
tune; and while playing the Tom-fool, I more than suspected that
he was trying to play the rake." On the other hand, turning his
versatile talent on a melancholy expatriate who had been jilted
by a local coquette, "Doctor Long Ghost was all sympathy. 'Bill,
my good fellow,' said he, tremulously, 'let *me* go and talk to her.' "

Yet, despite his aggressiveness and tactical ingenuity, the doctor
is never permitted the dignity of a victorious affair. He is to the
end a comically unsuccessful lover. In this respect he is a nice
combination of the trickster and the sucker. On one occasion, in
a particularly secluded and primitive community, he and Melville
persuaded the girls to stage a "hevar," a "genuine pagan fan-
dango." The climax of this voluptuous ceremony was an orgiastic
affair called the "Lory-Lory" — "the dance of the back-sliding
girls of Tamai" — during which Long Ghost was restrained with
considerable difficulty. He spent most of the next day hunting
the dancers, and when, after all that stimulation and effort, he
finally "pressed one rather hard, she all at once turned upon him,
and, giving him a box on the ear, told him to 'hanree perrar!' (be
off with himself)." To the comic hero, however, rebuff is a form
of challenge, and Long Ghost is never really defeated until his
disastrous encounter with the thorn-wielding Loo near the end of
the book. The strategic advances and fractured Polynesian with
which the doctor attempts to bridge the gap between his heated
desire and the cool disdain of his quarry make a fitting climax to
his literary career and one of the rarest comic scenes Melville
ever wrote.


3

Sex, the universal joke, is a recurrent theme in the writing of
Melville's jocular-hedonic period. It appears most unreservedly
in *Omoo*, under the combined influence of Long Ghost and the
free-and-easy mores of the islands, where "the best dress in court-
ing is motley" and the courtesies of hospitality may be extended
by a native hostess "to a degree altogether superfluous." Even in
the absence of these priming influences its persistence reflects the
normality of Melville's masculine bias and adds to the comic zest

of his early books. In *Pierre* he was to take on a new gravity in dealing with intersexual relations, but until then his literary women were no more than a piquant diversion. Melville on his canoeing excursions in *Typee* sounds a good deal like Long Ghost on his botanical ones: "But I was ever partial to what is termed in the *Young Men's Own Book* — 'the society of virtuous and intelligent young ladies;' and in the absence of the mermaids, the amusement became dull and insipid." Thus we are introduced to the famous *affaire* Fayaway, which, notwithstanding its theatrical romanticism and careful narrative propriety, is essentially a gambol on the part of a Male Animal frankly stimulated by a young lady's smoking, standing naked in a canoe, and otherwise wearing a dress which "began at the waist, and terminated sufficiently far above the ground to reveal the most bewitching ankle in the universe."

Elsewhere the rovings of the healthy masculine eye are chronicled in an even more clearly picaresque mood. When, in *Omoo*, the author caught sight of a beautiful girl on horseback, he promptly enlisted Long Ghost, identified the young lady as the wife of an English planter ("happy dog"), and undaunted by that intelligence, put in an appearance at the plantation with a view to making her acquaintance. There they were graciously entertained by the lady's husband, who appealed to their secondary weaknesses by offering them fresh melons filled with sherry. "Now this was extremely polite in Mr. Bell," says Melville, keeping his eye on the ball; "still, we came to see *Mrs.* Bell." A similar incident in *Redburn*, allowing for a more appropriate naïveté in the telling, achieves its comic effect by the same subordination of lesser appetites. Attracted to an English cottage by three beautiful girls, young Redburn rises to the challenge of a suspicious mother and talks himself into an invitation to tea, where even the presence of fresh milk and "such buttered muffins [as] never were spread on the other side of the Atlantic" fails to deflect his interest. "There they sat — the charmers, I mean — eating those buttered muffins in plain sight. I wished I was a buttered muffin myself."

Melville's favorite use of sex was in constructing little vignettes of domestic comedy. In Chapter 80 of *Omoo* there is a memorable yarn about Pomaree, the termagant queen of Tahiti, and her henpecked consort, Tanee. Of the same order is the story of the promiscuous wench in the steerage of the *Highlander* who played to the binoculars ogling her from the cabin while her ineffectual husband, a tailor with musical propensities, fiddled and burned. The subject of polygamy is treated with almost anthropological gravity in *Typee*, but it is meat for the comic spirit when Melville turns to his globe-trotting sailors. White-Jacket's reverence for the bearded crewmen of the *Neversink* is spiced by the observation that "some of them might have been grandsires, with grandchildren in every port round the world," and Redburn's mock innocence is the perfect medium for reporting the convenient domestic arrangements of Max the Dutchman, a sailor on the Atlantic run, who had his laundry done by one wife in New York and by another in Liverpool.

Risqué stories are an uncharacteristic commodity in Melville's books, but there are two in this early group, both inserted into the opening chapter of *Typee* as highly colored illustrations of the hiatus in manners and morals between the civilized and pagan worlds. These stories, dependent on the shock effect of savage immodesty, have lost much of their comic bloom in the course of the last century; but there is enduring humor in their impaling of vulnerable sensibilities and their incongruous elegance of style. The island queen's public display of her private tattooing is still funny for the reaction of the scandalized French; and the natives' investigation of the mortality of the missionary's wife still amuses because it "so far overstepped the limits of good breeding as deeply to offend the lady's sense of decorum."

### 4

The story of the missionary's wife is characteristic of Melville's jauntiness on yet another subject — that of religion and its practitioners. His wry remark on the stripping of the lady — that "the gentle dame was not sufficiently evangelized to endure this" — pretty much epitomizes his attitude toward the professional proselytizers who brought Christianity to the islands. It is an attitude rarely free from asperity. A signal exception is the case of the bibulous Father Murphy, who earns his uniquely affectionate portrait through a characteristic certain to alienate any sober

Board of Missions. There is forbearance too in the report of services in the principal Protestant church of Tahiti, where the parishioners comported themselves like youngsters at a picnic and the pastor harangued them in one-syllable Tahitian about the wickedness of Catholics, Frenchmen, and drunken sailors, and the merits of Great Britain and large contributions to the pastor. Nothing of religious value was learned, of course; still, the sermon was comprehensible to its hearers and to that extent sensible. The comic spirit is less charitable to the chaplain of the *Neversink*, a "transcendental divine" who was in the habit of "addressing five hundred salt-sea sinners upon the psychological phenomena of the soul, and the ontological necessity of every sailor's saving it at all hazards." [24]

As for the general run of missionaries in Polynesia, they struck Melville as a shallow, opinionated, humorless, unrealistic, and frequently hypocritical lot, who did more harm than good in educating a simple people in the sins and rituals of a culture whose meaning and virtues they were incapable of grasping. So profoundly did he distrust the agents of formal theology, especially in the midst of what he considered natural innocence, that a good part of the time he could not bring himself to make light of them at all. When he could, the earnest disapproval in his mind converted the humor into satire. Even the clownish recital of his rebuff by the missionary families in Chapter 43 of *Omoo* is edged with a savage irony: he retreated in haste from their disdain "and scarcely drew breath until safely housed in the Calabooza." At the point in Shakespeare's *Twelfth Night* (IV, ii) where Maria directs Feste to masquerade as a curate, Melville marked in his copy the clown's reply: "I would I were the first that ever dissembled in such a gown." While in his Polynesian books he took care not to make any blanket accusations of hypocrisy against the missionaries, he plainly held them responsible for the kind of induced hypocrisy he lampooned in the native girl who told him she was " 'Mickonaree *ena*' (church member *here*) . . . laying her hand upon her mouth . . . her eyes and hands," but who gave him "to understand, by unmistakable gestures, that in certain other respects she was not exactly a 'mickonaree.' " In view of the many silly and evil things Melville is willing to impute seriously to missionaries throughout *Typee* and *Omoo*, it comes with peculiar comic force that the one thing he cannot bring himself to believe them responsible for is the depraved state of Tahitian millinery.[25]

When Raymond Weaver called Melville "the first Missionary Polynesia ever sent to Christendom," he was praising him for his achieved "sense that the savage and the Christian belong to the same order of nature." [26] It is the comic spirit that finds the common denominator and makes it felt without defining it. Even in the preposterous chapter on the rituals of the Typees — so uncannily like the style of burlesque Mark Twain was to make famous — it is possible to detect hints of the kind of satire on Christianity that was to become almost painfully explicit in *Mardi*. In *Typee* the overt tone is one of flippant neutrality:

For my own part, I am free to confess my almost entire inability to gratify any curiosity that may be felt with regard to the theology of the valley. I doubt whether the inhabitants themselves could do so. They are either too lazy or too sensible to worry themselves about abstract points of religious belief. While I was among them they never held any synods or councils to settle the principles of their faith by agitating them. An unbounded liberty of conscience seemed to prevail. Those who pleased to do so were allowed to impose implicit faith in an ill-favoured god with a bottle-nose and fat shapeless arms crossed upon his breast; whilst others worshipped an image which, having no likeness either in heaven or on earth, could hardly be called an idol. As the islanders always maintained a discreet reserve with regard to my own peculiar views on religion, I thought it would be excessively ill-bred in me to pry into theirs.[27]

Only at the end of the chapter, after we have been entertained with the ludicrous stories of Moa Artua and other underprivileged deities who "had to carry themselves '*pretty straight*' or suffer the consequences," do we catch the gently mocking echo:

In truth, I regard the Typees as a back-slidden generation. They are sunk in religious sloth, and require a spiritual revival. A long prosperity of breadfruit and coco-nuts has rendered them remiss in the performance of their higher obligations. The wood-rot malady is spreading among the idols — the fruit upon their altars is becoming offensive — the temples themselves need re-thatching — the tattooed clergy are altogether too light-hearted and lazy — and their flocks are going astray.

Through all the books of this group runs the same note of

puckish irreverence. *Omoo* is full of it; Long Ghost is virtually a personification of it. When in the course of his vagabondage he scents prolonged and liberal entertainment in the household of the devout Po-Po, he loses no time in making the most expedient impression:

> When all was ready, and the household looking on, Long Ghos devoutly clasping his hands over the fated pig, implored a blessing. Hereupon everybody present looked exceedingly pleased; Po-Po coming up, and addressing the doctor with much warmth; and Arfretee, regarding him with almost maternal affection, exclaimed delightedly, "Ah! mickonaree tata maitai!" in other words, "What a pious young man!" [28]

In *Redburn* the irreverence is made even more puckish by the abandonment of the sophisticated approach for an air of burlesque naïveté. The worldly ways of sailors are viewed through the shocked eyes of a youth brought up in the ways of his Sunday School and its subsidiaries, the Anti-Smoking Society and the Juvenile Total Abstinence Association.

> And I called to mind a sermon I had once heard in a church in behalf of sailors, when the preacher called them strayed lambs from the fold, and compared them to poor lost children, babes in the wood, orphans without fathers or mothers.
> And I remembered reading in a magazine, called the Sailors' Magazine, with a sea-blue cover, and a ship painted on the back, about pious seamen who never swore, and paid over all their wages to the poor heathen in India; and how that when they were too old to go to sea, these pious old sailors found a delightful home for life in the Hospital, where they had nothing to do, but prepare themselves for their latter end. And I wondered whether there were any such good sailors among my shipmates; and observing that one of them lay on deck apart from the rest, I thought to be sure he must be one of them: so I did not disturb his devotions: but I was afterwards shocked at discovering that he was only fast asleep, with one of the brown jugs by his side. [29]

In *White-Jacket* there is comic irreverence, though it is less puckish than grotesque, a kind of theological whimsy making ironic sport of Christian fatalism, or the concept of evil, or the ritual of absolution. Whatever the approach, the basic religious attitude in these early books is pretty accurately reflected by Long Ghost as, one day, he sat in a Tahitian chapel while Deacon Po-Po, holding the floor, "tossed his arms overhead, stamped, scowled, and glared, till he looked like the very Angel of Vengeance." " 'Deluded man!' sighed the doctor . . . 'I fear he takes the fanatical view of the subject.' "

After his time Long Ghost might have found cause to sigh over Melville, too. As early as *Mardi*, religion and other subjects of a philosophical cast were occasionally viewed with something like fanaticism, or at least very unlike the doctor's tolerant amusement. But the common stratum of material that underlay the autobiographical romances lent itself by and large to the jocular-hedonic air to which Melville was both inclined and committed in works of popular entertainment.

# 2

# The Comic Manner

To say that Melville was a writer of comedy is not to say that his method was that of the professional funnyman. He did not make habitual use of the entire bag of tricks upon which the avowed comedian draws in his single-minded pursuit of laughs. For example, he did not make any appreciable use of nonsequitur; he was usually interested in maintaining some direction through his laughter in which to continue beyond it. Insofar as it is a factor in his art, comedy is a device for clarifying and coloring thought. Or rather it is a set of devices, the character of which identifies an art as a kit of tools identifies a trade. Melville's kit, exposed for inventory, contains:

1. A set of basic mechanical contrivances for extracting the humor from things and leaving them transparent by (*a*) expanding them, (*b*) compressing them, (*c*) hitting them on the head.

2. A comparable set of styles for coloring the transparencies.

3. A personal miscellany consisting of some odd scraps of irony, a few unpolished whimsies of a metaphysical cast, and an unsystematic but growing collection of wedge-shaped puns.

## I

The first of the mechanical contrivances, exaggeration, comes in two distinct designs: an old and familiar one inherited from folklore, and a new one bearing the stamp of original manufacture. Melville leaned to the former with a natural and inevitable affinity. The frontier of which his sea and his seamen were an organic part was home to the national comic instinct; he was

writing in the heyday of such periodicals as the Crockett alma-
nacs and *The Spirit of the Times,* which gave literary currency
to the oral traditions of the tall tale; and he was an almost exact
contemporary of P. T. Barnum, a personification of the tall tale
who was not without direct influence on Melville's work.[1] All
the earmarks of frontier art-lying are upon the story of the
"Flying Whaleman," told in *Typee* to illustrate the "proverbial
longevity of Cape Horn whaling voyages," or the story Surgeon
Cuticle, in *White-Jacket,* is made to tell about the bullet that shot
a soldier in the Adam's Apple, "ran completely round the neck,
and, emerging from the same hole it had entered, shot the next
man in the ranks." Such tales of multiple shootings, usually of
wild game, had been current for years among frontier boasters,
and were evidently still good for a laugh as late as 1867, when
Bret Harte lampooned Natty Bumppo with an especially implausible version in one of his *Condensed Novels.*

Equally obvious is the folk origin of many expressions attributed to sailors, especially in *White-Jacket.* A "Down Easter" is
spoken of as living "so far eastward, you know, shippy, that they
have to pry up the sun with a handspike." Rounding the Horn,
"it was cold as *Blue Flujin,* where sailors say fire freezes." This
sort of thing cannot be said to lack imagination; but the folk
imagination tends to exaggerate quantitatively, as in the remark
of the sailors about the *Neversink's* long stay in Rio harbor —
"that our frigate would at last ground on the beef-bones daily
thrown overboard by the cooks." When the exaggeration is
qualitative — that is, figurative — it is likely to be coarse and
suggestive of little beyond the ludicrousness of its own incongruity. A Brazilian diplomat with a gigantic mustache is variously
pictured by Melville's sailors as "a rat with his teeth through a
bunch of oakum, or a St. Jago monkey peeping through a prickly-
pear bush." It is funny enough but pretty rudimentary as art.

When Melville stops reporting and starts inventing, he reveals
his own propensity toward the tall talk of his shipmates. The
famous jacket which made him the goat of the *Neversink* is exaggerated into a portable blotter against which his "heartless shipmates . . . used to stand" to dry themselves on wet days. The
equally impractical shooting-jacket of Redburn "grew smaller
and smaller, particularly after a rain, until at last I thought it

would completely exhale, and leave nothing but the bare seams, by way of a skeleton, on my back." How far Melville's art could refine the exaggerations of popular humor can be gauged by comparing the folk similes on the Brazilian diplomat with the author's own portrait of a French officer encountered in Tahiti: "This gentleman's head was a mere bald spot; his legs, sticks; in short, his whole physical vigor seemed exhausted in the production of one enormous mustache." The same kind of inspired suggestiveness appears in the picture of the cannibal king, Mehevi, trying to sing "by screwing all the features of his face into the end of his nose." At its best the art of exaggeration can bring even comic prose very close to poetry. Certainly in his own verse Melville never surpassed the brilliance of his vignette, in *Omoo*, of three wizened French priests whose hats were "so preposterously big, that, in putting them on, the reverend fathers seemed extinguishing themselves."

In the equal and opposite art of understatement he was quite as successful, but with a difference. His understatement is not spread abroad through his pages, like the exaggeration, in little auxiliary dabs and patches, nor does it lean so heavily on the precedents of popular humor. The character of Toby is about as close as Melville comes to the traditional understater of folklore, who gets his laughs by being casual in the teeth of terror. During the grueling descent of the precipice into the valley of Typee, with life hanging repeatedly at the end of a vine swaying limply over the abyss, Toby comes out "in his usual dry tone" with such remarks as, "Mate, do me the kindness not to fall until I get out of your way"; or, "As soon as you have diverted yourself sufficiently, I would advise you to proceed." Melville more commonly applies his understatement in situations where the humor lies in the narrator's pretense to knowing less than he knows. This is the pattern of comic irony upon which Mark Twain later all but took a patent.

Comic irony is not nearly so characteristic of Melville as of Twain; but it is so broadly the method of *Redburn* as to set one wondering whether young Sam Clemens might have read the book that in some ways so clearly anticipates his own treatment of boyhood. Though *Redburn* has nothing like the comic consistency of *Tom Sawyer* or *Huckleberry Finn*, and was not intended to have, it invites comparison with *Life on the Mississippi*, which it strongly resembles in the nature of its subject as well as in the proportion and placement of its comedy. Both books are funniest in the early chapters dealing with the education of a youthful greenhorn to the hardships and complexities of nautical life, and they are funny in a remarkably similar way. Like Twain, Melville achieves his humorous tone by playing a calculated naïveté against a background of sophisticated and sometimes brutal reality. "So I went to the chief mate, and told him I thought I would just step below, till this miserable wetting was over; for I did not have any water-proof boots, and an aunt of mine had died of consumption." If Mr. Bixby had been the mate, he would have felt his blood pressure rising with a sense of familiarity. The very rhythms of Redburn's idiocies are Twain to the life. In making one of his appallingly uninformed inquiries of a grizzled salt, he was "particular to address him in a civil and condescending way, so as to show him very plainly that I did not deem myself one whit better than he was, taking all things together, and not going into particulars." Sometimes Melville out-Twains Twain, though he is unlikely ever to get general credit for it. What reader would not first think of two other boys when faced with Redburn's description of his Sunday boots?

I never had a pair of boots that I liked better; I used to turn my toes out when I walked in them, unless it was night time, when no one could see me, and I had something else to think of; and I used to keep looking at them during church, so that I lost a good deal of the sermon.

Midway between the arts of exaggeration and understatement stands the rarer art, not of distorting reality in one direction or the other, but of applying tart correctives to distortions that already exist. At its best it is an art with a surgical finesse, resulting in a clean and unexpected penetration to truth. In most comic artists it is a technique so exclusively astringent as to come within the most limited meaning of the term "wit." But the young Melville wrote with such an abiding sense of the brotherhood of human error that his corrective wit was rarely unwarmed by the friendlier qualities of true humor. His first two books especially are rich in whimsical insights of an anthropological cast, such as the observation that the mineral water popular among the Nukuhevan aborigines was "sufficiently nauseous to have made the fortune of the proprietor, had the spa been situated in the midst of any civilized community." Most characteristically these insights take the form of deft, almost aphoristic, inversions which constitute another point of resemblance to Twain. The trustworthy members of the *Julia*'s crew are distinguished as being "of an inferior order of rascality." The Marquesans demonstrate their constitutional hardihood "in the quantity of sleep they can endure." And one delightful islander in particular "carried on a little Tahitian farming; that is to say, he owned several groves of the breadfruit and palm, and never hindered their growing." Melville was hardly thinking of comic wit when he wrote, in a later essay, of Shakespeare's "short, quick probings at the very axis of reality"; [2] but the ideal is one that neither he nor Shakespeare could have approached without the skeptical acumen of the comic spirit.

2

Nor could they have approached it without a stylistic ingenuity to match. Melville's, though hardly Shakespearean, is at its best when the probings are literally short and quick. Despite a lingering weakness for luxuriant verbiage which he shared with his age, Melville was capable of a pin-point accuracy of language that emerges with startling clarity from many of his humorous passages. There is a peculiar source of light in his brilliant selection and placement of *le mot juste*: in the account of Redburn's first climb into the rigging when, too green to recognize his risks, he "felt frightened enough in a promiscuous way"; in the picture of the surly Irishman M'Gee, in *Omoo*, whose eyes, with their "villainous cast. . . seemed suspicious of each other"; in the qualification of the abnormal ugliness of Beauty, carpenter of the *Julia* — "There was no absolute deformity about the man; he was symmetrically ugly." Altogether the best writing in these early books seems characteristically informed by the comic spirit. Nowhere in them can we find cleaner, more vital prose than in the quite incidental description of a ship briefly visited in the harbor of Imeeo: "Like all large, comfortable whalemen, she had a sort of motherly look: — broad in the beam, flush decks, and four chubby boats hanging at the breast." There is an easy charm about such efficient writing that one tends to take for granted until he bogs down in those strained and somber jungles of *Mardi* where Melville left his sense of humor behind.

The comic spirit was capable, however, of betraying him into less successful linguistic adventures. Sometimes, instead of aiming straight, he tried an oblique approach by either inflating or deflating his language. Deflated language — that is, slang — he had mercifully little to do with. On occasion it blended into an unimprovable picture: "A stray native once in a while got boozy, and staggered home, catching at the cocoanut trees as he went." [3] More often his ephemeral whimsicalities are the worse for their years of hard colloquial wear: "pins" for "legs," "cocoanut" for "head," and so on. The opposite tack, that of inflating his language, was more to Melville's taste and the taste of his age. The effect, when the author's intentions are clear, is the broadest kind of humor-by-incongruity. At bottom it is a sub-literary style, employing the ritual commonplaces of euphemism or circumlocution. Constructed with studied art, it can become very heavily literary indeed:

On one occasion I was so inconsiderate as to yawn while a number of [tropical flies] were hovering around me. I never repeated the act. Some half-dozen darted into the open apartment, and began walking about its ceiling; the sensation was dreadful. I involuntarily closed my mouth, and the poor creatures being enveloped in inner darkness, must in their consternation have stumbled over my palate, and been precipitated into the gulf beneath. At any rate, though I afterwards charitably held my mouth open for at least five minutes, with a view of affording egress to the stragglers, none of them ever availed themselves of the opportunity. [4]

But Melville did not stop with the mere dignified narration of undignified experiences. What he liked best to do was to puff up some slight or ridiculous thing in mock-heroic or mock-poetic terms, if possible with a bombastic apostrophe thrown in for good measure. It is a brand of humor whose air of quaint antiquity recommends it feebly to modern readers. Fortunately, its earliest appearances are relatively infrequent and unpretentious, blending easily with the mild mockery of the surrounding laughter. In *White-Jacket* it grows both thicker and higher, reaching its apogee in a mock-Homeric chapter entitled "The Great Mas-

sacre of the Beards," "a calamitous event, which filled the Neversink with long lamentations, that echo through all her decks and
tops."

As I now deviously hover and lingeringly skirmish about the fron-
tiers of this melancholy recital, a feeling of sadness comes over me that
I cannot withstand. Such a heartless massacre of hair! Such a Barthol-
omew's Day and Sicilian Vespers of assassinated beards! Ah! who
would believe it! . . . What! not thirty days' run from home, and
lose our magnificent homeward-bounders! . . . Lose them at one fell
swoop? Were the vile barbers of the gun-deck to reap our long,
nodding harvests, and expose our innocent chins to the chill air of
the Yankee coast! And our viny locks! were they also to be shorn?
. . . Captain Claret! in cutting our beards and our hair, you cut us
the unkindest cut of all! . . . Train your guns inboard, let the marines
fix their bayonets, let the officers draw their swords; we *will* *not* let
our beards be reaped — the last insult inflicted upon a vanquished
foe in the East!
Where are you, sheet-anchor men! Captains of the top! gunners
mates! mariners all! Muster round the capstan your venerable beards,
and while you braid them together in token of brotherhood, cross
hands and swear that we will enact over again the mutiny of the Nore,
and sooner perish than yield up a hair!

Occasionally this sort of stylistic mockery takes the form of
frank parody, as when a dead sailor's boots are auctioned off in
the manner of "Mark Antony over the body of Julius Caesar." [5]
Another instance, less neatly tagged but far more significant, is
the passage that closes Chapter 13 of *Redburn*:

Then was I first conscious of a wonderful thing in me, that responded
to all the wild commotion of the outer world; and went reeling on
and on with the planets in their orbits, and was lost in one delirious
throb at the center of the All. A wild bubbling and bursting was at
my heart, as if a hidden spring had just gushed out there; and my
blood ran tingling along my frame, like mountain brooks in spring
freshets.
Yes! yes! give me this glorious ocean life, this salt-sea life, this
briny, foamy life, when the sea neighs and snorts, and you breathe
the very breath that the great whales respire! Let me roll around the
globe, let me rock upon the sea; let me race and pant out my life,
with an eternal breeze astern, and an endless sea before!
But how soon these raptures abated, when after a brief idle interval,
we were again set to work, and I had a vile commission to clean out
the chicken-coops, and make up the beds of the pigs in the long-boat.

Miserable dog's life is this of the sea! . . . Yes, yes, blow on, ye breezes, and make a speedy end to this abominable voyage!

What Melville was mocking in this bathetic Transcendental rhapsody is clear enough in the light of one of his letters to Hawthorne in the summer of 1851, in which he made fun of Goethe's saying, "Live in the all."

What nonsense! Here is a fellow with a raging toothache. "My dear boy," Goethe says to him, "you are sorely afflicted with that tooth; but you must *live in the all*, and then you will be happy!" As with all great genius, there is an immense deal of flummery in Goethe, and in proportion to my own contact with him, a monstrous deal of it in me.[6]

The interesting thing about the *Redburn* passage is its ambiguity, the fact that it is comic only by virtue of the juxtaposition of two incongruous attitudes, each serious enough in its way. A postscript to the Hawthorne letter makes this clear too.

That "all" feeling, though, there is some truth in. You must have felt it, lying on the grass on a warm summer's day. Your legs seem to send out shoots into the earth. Your hair feels like leaves upon your head. This is the *all* feeling. But what plays the mischief with the truth is that men will insist upon the universal application of a temporary feeling or opinion.

It was only when Melville lost this sense of proportion that the "monstrous deal of flummery" that was assuredly in him worked irreparable damage to his art. In all of the books so far considered he had his comic guard up.

### 3

The controlling mode of irony that has appeared in so much of the comedy of *Redburn*, as well as in smaller patches elsewhere, reaches its theoretical culmination in outright satire. Yet there is relatively little sustained satire in the early books. The extent to which satire enters into the treatment of missionaries and missionary work in *Typee* and *Omoo* has already been noted. In the main these books deal with a people Melville liked better than his own, and he wove around them a friendlier, more sympathetic comedy. As he wrote in the Preface to *Omoo*, "Should a little jocoseness be shown upon some curious traits of the Tahitians, it proceeds from no intention to ridicule: things are merely de-

scribed as, from their entire novelty, they first struck an un-
biased observer." What might have been contempt in a smug
man was in Melville rather "a strain of self-protectiveness," as
though he were "too much aware of his own leanings toward a
Polynesian way of life not to adopt a defensive breeziness . . . in
speaking of the Polynesians." [7] His subjects on these occasions take
on a kind of Lilliputian air, but his laughter is never really critical
because it is disarmed by a tolerant affection that extends even
to Fayaway's most un-American trait — the eating of raw fish.
More often than not the comical mores of the savages are ingen-
iously converted into a backhanded commentary on the still more
comical mores of the civilized. There is thus a double-edged
quality in much of the comedy of *Typee* and *Omoo*, but it is
nearly always playful and lacking in satiric intention.

In *White-Jacket*, where there is less to be said for the local
order of life, the comedy is relatively one-sided and more nearly
satiric in tone. Much that Melville had seen aboard the *United
States* was nonsense too gross for laughter, but the more innocuous absurdities of naval convention provided him with a running
theme for critical comedy. An undercurrent of true social satire
is suggested by the italicized naval idiom "*the people*," used to
distinguish crew from officers, which recurs as an ironic leitmotif throughout the tale of "The World in a Man-of-War."
In effect, however, there is more of burlesque than satire in what
jesting Melville does at the expense of the *Neversink*'s self-impor-
tant hierarchy of command. The officers, except when conduct-
ing disciplinary floggings, are comic-opera figures, chiefly en-
gaged in sustaining dignity and protocol. The midshipmen, lacking both, are children Tarkington might have drawn.

Those boys are sent to sea, for the purpose of making commodores;
and in order to become commodores, many of them deem it indispensable forthwith to commence chewing tobacco, drinking brandy
and water, and swearing at the sailors. . . Some of them are terrible
little boys, cocking their caps at alarming angles, and looking fierce as
young roosters. They are generally great consumers of Macassar oil
and the Balm of Columbia; they thirst and rage after whiskers; and
sometimes, applying their ointments, lay themselves out in the sun, to
promote the fertility of their chins.[8]

Oddly enough, the only full-fledged satire in *White-Jacket* deals with a subject Melville was only cursorily concerned with elsewhere in his writings — the medical profession. But if the matter is atypical, the manner is an impressive bridge between the derivative exercises of *Mardi* and the controlled original satire of *Moby-Dick* and its successors. Notwithstanding such defects as a superficial debt to Smollett and an excessively archaic whimsy in the naming of the doctor and his colleagues, the episode of Surgeon Cadwallader Cuticle and his infamous operation is a minor masterpiece. Here, for the first time on a comparable scale, Melville gave his characters enough rope to carry out on their own terms the tragi-comedy of their ineptitude, and ultimately to hang themselves by. The portrait of Cuticle, the professional egotist, is a beautiful thing. If his outside is drawn with the grossness of a Smollett, his inside is explored with the sensitivity of a Hawthorne. Certainly the creator of Rappaccini and Chillingworth could have been proud of the moving description of the monstrous cast of a horned woman which the man of science kept on his stateroom wall; and he could have been proud — though perhaps he was incapable — of the dreadful levity of its symbolism: the doctor used it for a hat-rack.

The consultation scene is a perfect device for letting Cuticle display his dogmatism, hypocrisy, and inhumanity, and for letting his colleagues reveal their several weaknesses of pedantry, obsequiousness, and indecision. The operation itself, a theatrical and unnecessary amputation, is a fittingly climactic travesty. Cuticle lectures his juniors on the anatomy of the terrified patient; he lectures the doomed sailor himself, graphically enough to send him into shock, on his good fortune in losing his leg in an age when surgeons no longer use red-hot knives and boiling oil; he converts the surgery into an exhibition of professional virtuosity which an admiring audience observes with watches in hand. Finally, wiping his bloody hands on his handkerchief, he brings the scene and the episode to a close with a sense of timing that his author could scarcely have improved had he been a practicing satirist since Cuticle was an interne.

"I must leave you now, gentlemen" — bowing. "To-morrow, at ten, the limb will be upon the table, and I shall be happy to see you all upon the occasion. Who's there?" turning to the curtain, which then rustled.

"Please, sir," said the Steward, entering, "the patient is dead."
"The body also, gentlemen, at ten precisely," said Cuticle. . .[9]

"The satire is perfect," Lewis Mumford has written of these
chapters, "and it is perfect because, at the broadest extreme of
caricature, it does not lose sight of the pathetic reality under-
neath. Melville did not waste breath dissecting the obvious im-
posters and charlatans. . . It is the man in command, the man we
admire, respect, put all our confidence in, that Melville so skill-
fully opened up. No one has done a better job of it. . ." [10] In
this sense Surgeon Cuticle prefigures a type to which Melville
was one day to devote a whole volume of satire.

### 4

While Melville's art was thus growing in range and grip, it
was also growing in metaphoric power, a quality which was to
become a Melvillian trademark and which owed more of its
original impetus and singularity of character to the comic spirit
than has been generally recognized. In one of the earliest critical
reappraisals of Melville, Carl Van Vechten acknowledged that
*Typee*, *Omoo*, *Redburn*, and *White-Jacket* are "sparkling with a
sophisticated and cosmopolitan humor. There are, however," he
went on, "no metaphysical overtones, no 'ontological heroics,' in
these books." [11] He was right about the first two books but wrong
about the last two. The philosophical interests Melville had played
with in *Mardi* were subdued but not laid aside in the bread-and-
butter work that intervened before *Moby-Dick*. They account
for a departure from the jocular-hedonic strain of the South Sea
frolics which is at times quite distinct from the simple "sparkling"
effect Van Vechten noted. After *Mardi* Melville's humor oper-
ated increasingly in terms of tropes and puns. Few of them in
*Redburn* and *White-Jacket* are metaphysical in the strict ontological sense, but they point to the more elaborate ones of later
books which are, and they are at least metaphysical in the special
sense in which that word has been traditionally applied to literature. They are, in other words, conceits, and their comedy is philosophical to the extent to which it seeks its laughter in unexpected congruities rather than in unexpected incongruities.

Trope, or metaphysical wit, seems far too pretentious a term
for the kind of figurative joke we find in two or three places in
*Redburn*. Yet the fact remains that nothing in *Typee* or *Omoo*
quite corresponds in technique to the description of the professional tippler, Bob Still: "The more he drinks, the fatter and
rounder waxes Bob; and the songs pour out as the ale pours in,
on the well-known principle, that the air in a vessel is displaced
and expelled, as the liquid rises higher and higher in it." Even
more distinctive is the description of the one-man "salt-droghers"
in Liverpool harbor, whose "skippers" are justified in their comical self-importance by the high moral ability evinced in the gov-
ernance of their "crews." Figurative jesting we have seen before,
certainly; none better than the description of the "extinguished"
priests in *Omoo*. But always the figure has been a convenient tool
for exaggeration or some other projected comic or pictorial effect.
Now there is a tendency to explore correspondences for their
own sake or the sake of their philosophical implications.

If the tendency is merely suggested in *Redburn*, it appears as a
marked change of manner in *White-Jacket*, where both the title
and the subtitle are themselves indicative of underlying conceits
of a more or less philosophical cast. Here even fundamentally
jocular topics like food are occasionally turned to thoughtful
metaphoric account. The sliding carriage of a gun being "something like an extension dining-table," Melville is now moved to
observe "that the goose on it . . . is a tough one, and villainously
stuffed with most indigestible dumplings." Grapeshot ("a bunch
of iron grapes in the abdomen") is spoken of as a "sorry dessert."
Having conceived the character of Quoin, an old gunner whose
disposition matches that of his "ill-tempered cannon," Melville
was carried away by the implications of his conceit and expanded
it into an entire chapter bearing the entire title, "The Good or
Bad Temper of Men-of-War's Men, in a Great Degree, Attribu-
table to their Particular Stations and Duties Aboard Ship." Conceived in the sheerest whimsy, the notion is tossed about through
variation after variation until by the law of averages a few serious
changes have turned up along with the comic ones. The comic
predominate here — commencing with Quoin and ending with
the First Lieutenant, who is drop-shouldered because he wears
only one epaulet — but it was not always to be so in this sort of

play. Even the funniest conceit in *White-Jacket* has its figurative reverberations as well as its literal ones, and they range from thoughtful to downright bitter. The story is told of a sailor named Lemsford, an off-duty poet, who congratulates himself on having found the perfect repository for his precious manuscripts until one morning the *Neversink* fires an unexpected salute off Rio.

"O Lord!" cried Lemsford, "my *Songs of the Sirens!*" and he ran down the rigging to the batteries; but just as he reached the gun-deck, gun No. 20 — his literary strong-box — went off with a terrific report.

"Well, my after-guard Virgil," said Jack Chase to him, as he slowly returned up the rigging, "did you get it? You need not answer; I see you were too late. But never mind, my boy: no printer could do the business for you better. That's the way to publish, White-Jacket," turning to me — "fire it right into 'em; every canto a twenty-four-pound shot; *hull* the blockheads, whether they will or no. And mind you, Lemsford, when your shot does the most execution, you hear the least from the foe. A killed man cannot even lisp." [12]

## 5

Closely allied to this technique — really all of a piece with it in the trend toward ambiguity — is Melville's use of puns. His fondness for word-play is perfectly evident to even a casual reader and has been remarked in print by most of his commentators. The more indulgent ones compare it to Shakespeare's by way of putting him in good company without having to defend punning; but so far only one commentator seems to have sensed sufficient critical importance in the habit to suggest that it "has never been adequately explored." [13] The full flowering of Melville's enigmatical punning is part of his later work, but a trend toward it in the early books is indicated in two ways. The first indication is the increasing frequency with which puns appear in the four books under consideration: in *Typee* I count two; in *Omoo*, three; in *Redburn*, six; in *White-Jacket*, sixteen. The second indication is the character of the puns. Only three of the twenty-seven are of the garden variety that trade on accidental correspondence in the sound of words. Most of them involve a switch on the meanings of words. From the start, evidently, Melville was fascinated by words of potential ambiguity or hidden symbolic content, though in his early work we rarely find them harnessed to the serious organic plan of a book.

First and foremost, a pun was to Melville what it is to any native punster — a kind of joke, a way of having fun. Often he nudges the reader with italics to make sure the pun will not be missed. In *Typee* he is afraid of being cornered by an aggressive tribal tattooer and "disfigured in such a manner as never more to have the *face* to return to my countrymen." In *Redburn* he describes the glass captain of the glass ship model on his father's mantel as looking "very glassy out of the eyes." In *White-Jacket* the highly polished weapons in the *Neversink*'s armory "may truly be said to *reflect* credit on the Yeoman and his mates." Such puns are natural, relatively infrequent, and fairly inoffensive. Occasionally they are even inspired to the point of being a positive asset, as in the distinction drawn in *Omoo* between the church singing in Tahiti and that in the Sandwich Islands, "where the parochial flocks may be said rather to *bleat* than to *sing*."

But Melville was not content merely to take puns as they came to him. He was quite capable of altering or extending his material for the sole purpose of setting one up. The description of the "Unaccountable Cabin-Passenger" in *Redburn*, itself a digression, gains nothing but the dubious value of the pun from the following remark: "Perhaps he was a deputy from the Deaf and Dumb Institution in New York, going over to London to address the public in pantomime at Exeter Hall concerning the signs of the times." In one case we have documentary evidence of Melville's alteration of material for the sake of a pun. In a description of a certain churchyard in an old Liverpool guidebook which he used as a source for his own description in Chapter 36 of *Redburn*, a particular tombstone is cited as bearing the quaint name of one Timothy Horsefield, an early parish clerk of the town.[14] What Melville made of it was this:

Often, I saw men stretched out in a drunken sleep upon these slabs; and once, removing a fellow's arm, read the following inscription, which in a manner, was true to the life, if not to the death:–

HERE LYETH YE BODY OF
TOBIAS DRINKER.

The significance of punning for Melville's art is his exploitation of the possibilities in it for extending his meaning in more than one direction or on more than one level. The fact behind the striking increase in the incidence of puns in *White-Jacket* is almost certainly his discovery of the usefulness of the pun as a form of symbolism. At this early stage he usually goes to some lengths to point out such applications lest the reader miss the point. The gesture is of course a kind of artistic naïveté and as such may make us smile at the author more than at the pun, though many a bewildered reader of *Pierre* and *The Confidence-Man* has wished for a little of the youthful naïveté to light him through those jungles of unexplicated puns. In one instance we can all but see Melville's mind discovering a useful pun as his pen stumbles on it. Speaking of Captain Claret's indulgence in permitting the crew to play checkers on deck, he says:

> More than once have I known him, when going forward to the forecastle, pick his way carefully among scores of canvas checker-cloths spread upon the deck, so as not to tread upon the men — the checker-men and man-of-war's men included; but, in a certain sense, they were both one; for, as the sailors used their checker-men, so at quarters, their officers used these man-of-war's men.[15]

There is no false modesty in Melville about these puns; indeed, much of the expanded treatment he gives them seems due less to expository naïveté than to a desire to capitalize on a kind of contrapuntal effect they give to the development of his thought and the rhythm of his prose. An early apostrophe to the troublesome jacket is a case in point:

> "Jacket," cried I, "you must change your complexion! you must hie to the dyers and be dyed, that I may live. I have but one poor life, White-Jacket, and that life I cannot spare. I cannot consent to die for *you*, but be dyed you must for me. You can dye many times without injury; but I cannot die without irreparable loss, and running the eternal risk."[16]

Perhaps the most wonderful of the "loaded" puns Melville wrote into these early books is one of which Joyce, the greatest punster of them all, might have been proud — the word "snivelization." But it must be added that Melville was not yet able to leave even this satiric masterpiece unimproved. "And what's the

use of bein' *snivelized?*" the cynic of the *Highlander* says to
Redburn; "snivelized chaps only learns the way to take on 'bout
life, and snivel." As often as not, the technique of punning was
at this stage clumsy and groping, more distracting than helpful
to the artistic purpose of the books; but, polished, it was due to
make a distinct contribution to the art of *Moby-Dick* and to the
very meaning of some of the later works.

6

Broadly similar as Melville's autobiographical romances are in
the jocular-hedonic character of their comedy, the examination of
his comic techniques makes it increasingly clear that the differences are more significant than the similarities in explaining the
evolution of his creative impulse. The comic tone of the two
Polynesian tales is, as Constance Rourke has described it, "tem-
perate and sweet," giving them an idyllic temper" found nowhere
else in Melville.[17] *Typee* is firmly famous for its tonic humor; and
its picaresque sequel, full of astonishingly independent merit, is
certainly his most hilarious, possibly his most underrated, book.
*Omoo* alone among his books floats raft-like above the undercurrent of outer problem and inner drama that tugs even at parts of
*Typee*. It is his first and last unreflecting horselaugh at the sober
world of respectability, responsibility, and authority. After this
summer interlude Melville's experience with authority and respectability were less conducive to such response. He never
stopped laughing at them, but the laughter shifted steadily down
the scale toward those devilish notes that cause curling sensations
along the spine.

In the two books that follow *Mardi*, and of course in *Mardi*
itself, the symptoms of that shift become increasingly plain. These
books are essentially grave, and the gravity makes for a new
depth in a flow of narrative which is still, on the surface, lively,
full-bodied, and bracing. Beneath the "greenhorn" comedy of
*Redburn* lie hints of the bitter mockery of *Pierre* and *The Confidence-Man*. "We feel that this raillery is sad," writes Jean Simon,
"and our emotion at times is double." The same doubleness of
effect has been noted in *White-Jacket* by Carl Van Doren, who

cites Surgeon Cuticle's operation and the contention of the sail-
makers over "The Last Stitch" as instances in which "the comedy
and tragedy cannot be separated because they were both dreadfully inherent in the case." [18] The result of this mingling of values
is an ambiguity of tone that darkens comedy to the point where
we can see the native pain in it to which we are normally blinded
by the brightness of laughter.

The subtleties of perception to which the reader of Melville
must adjust himself in the resultant half-light are demonstrated in
the contrasting treatment given the Articles of War in three successive chapters (70–72) in *White-Jacket*. These chapters are all
polemical, their tone far removed from what we normally construe
as comic. Yet there is a difference among them. The first sentence
of Chapter 71 reads: "As the Articles of War form the ark and
constitution of the penal laws of the American Navy, in all sobriety and earnestness it may be well to glance at their origin." In
other words, the preceding chapter was *not* entirely sober and
earnest in its treatment of the subject; and the ways in which it
differs from the philippics that follow will give us some insight
into Melville at play with a serious idea and therefore being comic
without being merry.

The form of Chapter 70 is dramatic, beginning as literal narrative with a routine reading of the Articles of War to the crew
around the capstan; but the elements of drama undergo distortion
as the chapter progresses. The reading becomes stylized into a refrain ("shall suffer death"), alternated and embellished by hyper-
bolic apostrophe, first to Jack Ketch and the Spanish Inquisitors,
thereafter to the narrator himself. This dialogue is playful in conception but not in effect; comic in manner but not in matter. The
method can be seen in a single sampling:

> Have a care, then, have a care, lest you come to a sad end, even the
> end of a rope; lest, with a black-and-blue throat, you turn a dumb
> diver after pearl-shells; put to bed forever, and tucked in, in your own
> hammock, at the bottom of the sea. And there you will lie, White-
> Jacket, while hostile navies are playing cannon-ball billiards over
> your grave.

The familiar comic techniques are here in abundance: there is
the pun on "end"; there is the play on the bruised throat and
dumbness; there is the joke about the permanent "bed," a sailor's

shroud being a hammock-like strip of canvas into which he is "tucked" with needle and thread; there is the final grotesque metaphor with its polar incongruities of billiards and death. The result is unquestionably humor of a sort; but it is the humor of a *danse macabre*. The comic spirit was tuning up the mocking laugh of the hyena in preparation for the big concert in *Moby-Dick*.

*Part Two*

# TRIAL AND ERROR

# 3

# Point of Departure

In the Preface to *Omoo* Melville wrote: "In no respect does the author make pretensions to philosophic research. In a familiar way, he has merely described what he has seen; and if reflections are occasionally indulged in, they are spontaneous, and such as would very probably suggest themselves to the most casual observer." In diametric opposition to this approach, his third book, *Mardi*, makes every pretension to philosophic research. In it the author describes, not what he has seen, but what he has thought and felt. His reflections are not spontaneous, in precisely the sense that they would rarely suggest themselves to the casual observer. From its beginning *Mardi* was projected as a work of pure fiction. Yet its novelty does not result primarily from invention; reading had merely replaced experience, temporarily, as the source of material. What makes *Mardi* so radically different is its author's determination to air the inner man for a change — to be, as he put it, "frank with his readers." His mounting ambition looked down on the rattling adventures that wrote themselves and sold like newspapers. "Peedee, Hullabaloo & Pog-Dog," he called them.[1] Nothing would do now but to convert his Polynesian paradise into a microcosm, an allegorical frame for a "world of mind."

It is bound to be a somewhat altered comic spirit that inhabits such a world. But the change is gradual and the displacement never complete, except in the sense that all kinds of humor disappear together from the last twelve chapters of the book. In the beginning, at least, the old Melville is with us as jocular and hedonic as ever, nearly indistinguishable from the Melville of

*Typee* and *Omoo*. Here is the same native laughter, seasoned by
characteristic Melvillian twists: the rollicking, coarse-grained
comedy of hardship, still geared to the perils of the sea and
strange lands; the same earthy, well-loved themes of wine, women,
and food; the same salty view of human nature.


I

For the third and last time Melville began his tale with a de-
sertion from an undesirable whaling ship in mid-cruise. In the
case of the *Arcturion* it was in mid-ocean as well: the narrator
and his companion, Jarl, set out in a scantily provisioned whale-
boat in the dead of night a thousand miles from land. The hardships attendant upon this harebrained excursion are no doubt
less colorful in the telling than if Melville had actually experienced
them. Certainly he knew enough of the likely hazards of sixteen
days in an open boat to fabricate a reasonably terrifying account,
had he chosen to do the kind of thing Poe had done ten years
earlier in "The Narrative of A. Gordon Pym." Instead he elected
to continue the light comic vein he had so profitably opened in
*Typee* and *Omoo*. Once again his instinctive humor turned the
latent terror of his material into gross comedy. The desperate
adventure is undertaken in a purely sporting mood; the companion chosen to share it is an unconscious comedian of the dead-pan
variety; the inevitable shortage of water is less a thing of horror
than a comic vehicle for Jarl, who nurses the keg like an anxious
grandmother, uses one of his shoes for a ladle, hesitates to discard
a well-saturated insect dredged up in it, and ultimately sacrifices
a thirst-provoking quid of tobacco so enormous that the boat
could be trimmed by shifting it from one cheek to the other.

The frontier quality of the humor persists in the portrait of
Samoa, the one-armed islander whom the voyagers encounter
on the drifting brigantine *Parki*. Samoa is a specialist in primitive
surgery. He belongs to a race in which "every man is his own
barber and surgeon, cutting off his beard or arm as occasion de-
mands" — usually over a period of days with a serrated sea shell.
Samoa's own amputation, following a nearly fatal skirmish with
pirates, had been accomplished with more dispatch, aided by a
blunt axe and the detached aim of his domineering wife, Annatoo.

Later in the story, before the decreasing muscularity of its humor required his removal, Samoa tries his hand at nothing less than the trepan, picking bone fragments out of the battered brain of a native diver and patching the hole with cocoanut shell. The end of the joke is the old one (the operation was successful but the patient died), but the episode was useful in providing a trial sketch for the more important operation of Cadwallader Cuticle and in providing an occasion for one of the few genuine tall tales in *Mardi* — the story of a more successful "cobbling" operation involving the transplantation of pig brains.

The familiar jesting about food and drink becomes admirably naturalized to its new setting. In the early chapters there is one typically revolting joke about ship's food [2] and an entire comic chapter on the discovery and carefully rationalized disposal of a cask of wine in the hold of the *Parki*. But it is not until the philosophic phase of the voyage is under way that the book becomes "almost Rabelaisian with its prodigious feastings and drinkings and smokings." [3] After Taji (as Melville called himself in his Mardian incarnation) and his companions set forth on the mystical quest for the maiden Yillah, the three functions of eating, drinking, and smoking become the thematic handmaidens of social intercourse: "Now a mouthful of citron to season a repartee; now a swallow of wine to wash down a precept; now a fragrant whiff to puff away care."

The keynote is struck instantly upon Taji's arrival in the mythical kingdom of Odo, his base of operations for the great Mardian adventure.

Sublimate, as you will, the idea of our ethereality as intellectual beings, no sensible man can harbour a doubt but that there is a vast deal of satisfaction in dining. More, there is a savour of life and immortality in substantial fare. Like balloons, we are nothing till filled.

In Odo, he waggishly observes, "the matter of eating and drinking is held a matter of life and death," and he quotes a conquered king as saying, "Drag away my queen from my arms . . . but leave me my own cook." King Media, out of reverence for a matchless plantain pudding, deified his departed cook. Of all the kings whose courts are visited in the course of the voyage, the sociable ones are the big feeders. Most sociable of all is Borabolla, who is both a big and a continuous eater. He moves nowhere without a "battalion of butlers" in attendance, and the rafters of his palace are hung with "endless rows of brown calabashes and trenchers . . . readily accessible by means of cords; [and] gourds, containing arrack, suspended neck downward . . . within easy reach where they swung." [4]

Even as *Mardi* becomes more nebulously philosophical, an occasional touch of the old gastronomic humor clears the atmosphere and reminds us that Melville has not quite left this planet. One of the most entertaining of the digressions that threaten to overwhelm the story is Babbalanja's discourse on the "sandwich" theory of geology, in which he reconstructs the epochs of geologic history in terms of the courses of a banquet. According to this preposterous yet surprisingly operative analogy, "Nature's first condition was a soup . . . ere the substantials came."

And next, my lord, we have the fine old time of the Old Red Sandstone sandwich, clapped on the underlying layer, and among other dainties, imbedding the first course of fish — all quite in rule — sturgeon-forms, cephalaspis, glyptolepis, pterichthys; and other finny things of flavour rare, but hard to mouth for bones.

Other courses follow, age upon age, all detailed with Rabelaisian particularity: the "Ool, or Oily sandwich," consisting of "fat old joints, and hams, and rounds"; and the "Chalk, or Coral Sandwich . . . made up of rich side-courses," beginning with "wild game for the delicate," and ending with "barbecued mastodons and megatheriums, gallantly served up with fir-trees in their mouths, and tails cocked." "Thus," concludes Babbalanja, "fared the old diluvians; arrant gormandizers and beef-bolters. We Mardians famish on the superficial strata of deposits; cracking our jaws on walnuts, filberts, cocoanuts, and clams." [5]

The stomach often serves as a useful counterbalance to the head at moments of threatened intellectual submersion. When Babbalanja deserts the group at lunch time to "feed upon an author," he is told that he will "weigh more" with a banana or two in him and is advised to "drop [his] metaphysics and fall to on the solids." Both Media and Mohi have a mercifully limited appetite for the philosophical effusions of Babbalanja and the poetic effusions of Yoomy. Philosophy, Media complains, "ever impairs my digestion." As for the poetic spirit, Mohi attributes its most rap-

turous flight to indigestion and recommends a swallow of sea
water as an anodyne. Even Bábbalanja's idol, the ancient sage
Bardianna, is quoted as saying, "Did I not so often feel an appetite
for my yams, I should think everything a dream." [6]

Matching the comic enthusiasm for food in *Mardi* is a ritual
passion and Gargantuan capacity for wine. Its chief exponent and
apologist is Media, who thus describes his ideal world:

> Hark ye! were I to make a Mardi now, I'd have every continent a
> huge haunch of venison; every ocean a wine-vat! I'd stock every cav-
> ern with choice old spirits, and make three surplus suns to ripen the
> grapes all the year round. Let's drink to that! Brimmers! So: may the
> next Mardi that's made, be one entire grape; and mine the squeezing! [7]

Media's enthusiasm is lusty but by no means so indiscriminate as
that of his forerunners in *Omoo*. His taste runs to a choice vintage
which he calls "the circumnavigator" because his father had sent
a canoe-load of it three times around the world at a careful three
knots to give it a flavor. Most of Mardi's kings are Media's peers
as drinkers. Donjalolo, as host to a sybaritic congress of Mardian
royalty, amazes Taji with "the flexibility of the royal elbow and
the rigidity of the royal spine." Borabolla rarely stops drinking
except to eat or to sustain a periodic attack of gout; and as a
guest in his well-stocked palace, Jarl, we are told, "unmindful of
the unities of time and place, went freely about, from gourd to
gourd, concocting in him a punch." In a world of abandoned
tipplers only Babbalanja is a calculating sipper. Except to him
and the psychotic Donjalolo, the hangover is not a matter of
serious concern to Mardians. Most of them, like Taji, view the
"juice of the grape" as an unalloyed blessing which "loosens the
tongue, and opens the heart," and is a specific for "dissolving the
crystallization of the brain, leaving nothing but precious drops of
good humor, beading round the bowl of the cranium." [8]

An additional comic catalyst in *Mardi* is tobacco. If there was
little reference to the pleasures of smoking in *Typee* and *Omoo*,
it is because smoking was primarily a gloom-disperser for Melville, and in those books there was little gloom to disperse. In
*Mardi*, on the other hand, the moody little group in search of
Yillah are at times so bowed under the weight of their quest and
their philosophical discourse that their "gloomy canoe seemed a
hearse." To such an atmosphere the irrepressible Media has a

sovereign corrective in the outlandish pipes which he orders out from time to time. In the conventional pattern of contrasting scenes that develops in the latter half of the book these pipe-smoking interludes become a routine dramatic device for reviving the comic spirit. At lowest ebb an entire chapter (121) is given over to a whimsical panegyric on pipes and the joys of smoking. A good deal of fun is extracted from the burlesque rococo architecture of the royal pipes and from a ludicrous argument over the nature of meerschaum; and the episode ends in a fragrant cloud of preternatural amicability among the bickering voyagers.

In the product of Melville's first year of marriage it is not surprising to find the comedy of sex recurring, especially in its domestic phases. While he is not seriously critical of marriage, as he was sometimes to be in *Pierre*, he is clearly enjoying the time-honored comic myth of the husband as underdog. According to the rules of the jest, the husband is equally pitiable whether he is lone Tanee to a single Pomaree, as in *Omoo*; or shares his spouse with others, as in *Typee*; or is possessed of many wives, like Donjalolo, whose thirty queens were "the delight and torment of [his] days and nights." This kind of humor has been labeled and popularized in our own day by James Thurber in his "War Between Men and Women," but Melville made a substantial pre-Thurber contribution to it in the early chapters of *Mardi* exploiting the marital tribulations of Samoa and Annatoo. As Melville's vigorous humor painted it, "their married life was one long campaign, whereof the truces were only by night. . . Her voice was a park of artillery; her talons a charge of bayonets." "Upon this pair," Raymond Weaver noted, "Melville has lavished chapter after chapter of the most finished and competent comedy." [9] Had he continued in that vein he would unquestionably have made *Mardi* the popular success its predecessors had been instead of what it has been well called, "the brilliant notebook of a thinker." [10] But the wraith-like Yillah brought with her into the story a sympathetic sobriety about sex that is broken seldom and briefly; and the only genuine flash of the old bachelor humor thereafter comes in Yoomy's subtly torrid shell-maiden song in Chapter 156, and in the snatch of comic dialogue that follows it. Thus the departure from the purely jocular in Melville's comedy

was signaled. In his treatment of religion and other speculative matters he was to make it explicit.


2


The direction and extent of the shift Melville's comic art was to undergo in the course of *Mardi* are most clearly indicated in his characterizations. With Jarl, Samoa, and Annatoo we are in the familiar company of the sailors and islanders of the mid-nineteenth century South Pacific — the embroidered but realistic company of a humanity as vital as that of *Typee*, *Omoo*, *Redburn*, or *White-Jacket*. With Taji, Yillah, and the denizens of Mardi we are in the unfamiliar company of a quaintly stylized cast of fairies inhabiting Herman Melville's personal "world of mind." When the little band of adventurers lands with the mythical maiden Yillah upon the mythical island of Odo, Annatoo is already dead, and Jarl and Samoa have automatically ceased to be the sole and therefore central remaining figures in the story. That is the situation in Chapter 55. By the end of Chapter 102, slightly less than halfway through the book, Jarl and Samoa, now faded and out of place, serve their last literary function and are buried with honors. The new cast consists of Media, the demigod king of Odo, and three members of his court: Babbalanja, the philosopher; Mohi, the historian; and Yoomy, the poet. The author, assuming the shadowy guise of Taji, a reincarnated demigod, continues on in the role of narrator, in whose behalf is undertaken the search for the vanished Yillah which occupies the remainder of the book. All of these characters are primarily comic in their conception, though with differences — from each other and from their predecessors — which deserve examination.

Funniest and most important of the Mardians is Babbalanja, who occupies a position of prominence in the story comparable to that of Doctor Long Ghost in *Omoo*. In nearly all other respects, however, the two characters are so radically different as hardly to seem products of the same pen or, for that matter, of the same age. In a sense they are neither, for the Melville who wrote *Mardi* was in the excited and chaotic process of assimilating a liberal literary education and of experimenting in a vigorous if undisciplined manner with its half-digested products. For that reason, and for the more literal reason that he was most enchanted by such models as Burton, Browne, Rabelais, and Shakespeare, *Mardi* has a distinctively Renaissance frame of reference. It is this distinction that accounts for the striking disparity between the comic figures in question. Long Ghost was a folk-hero with strong contemporary American accents; Babbalanja is a Shakespearean fool. His role in *Mardi* is almost precisely defined in Viola's remarks on the clown in *Twelfth Night*, III, i, a passage which Melville marked in the margin of his copy with a double line:

> *This fellow is wise enough to play the fool;*
> *And to do that well craves a kind of wit:*
> *He must observe their mood on whom he jests,*
> *The quality of persons, and the time,*
> *And, like the haggard, check at every feather*
> *That comes before his eye. This is a practice*
> *As full of labor as a wise man's art:*
> *For folly that he wisely shows is fit;*
> *But wise men, folly-fall'n, quite taint their wit.*[11]

At the very outset of the voyage Babbalanja is granted the license of the royal jester. Thereafter, anything goes between him and his king, and he continually takes liberties that neither Mohi nor Yoomy would dream of taking. One of the many uses of "Azzageddi," the demon Babbalanja claims to be possessed of, is to stand, by unspoken mutual agreement, for the unassailability of his position as free-lance commentator. The role and the relationship are clearly outlined in an exchange between king and philosopher on the subject of life. Babbalanja poses the problem of what the sensation of living must be to a colony of mollusks.

"Answer your own question, Babbalanja."

"I will, but first tell me what sort of a sensation life is to you, yourself, my lord?"

"Pray, answer that along with the other, Azzageddi."

"Directly; but tell me, if you will, my lord, what sort of a sensation life is to a toad-stool?"

"Pray, Babbalanja, put all three questions together; and then, do what you have often done before — pronounce yourself a lunatic."

"My lord, I beseech you, remind me not of that fact so often. It is true, but annoying. Nor will any wise man call another a fool."

"Do you take me for a mere man, then, Babbalanja, that you talk to me thus?"

"My demi-divine lord and master, I was deeply concerned at your indisposition last night — may a loving subject inquire, whether his prince is completely recovered from the effects of those guavas?"

"Have a care, Azzageddi; you are far too courteous to be civil. But proceed."

"I obey. In kings, mollusca, and toad-stools, life is one thing and the same. . ." [12]

Even when Babbalanja clearly overplays his hand and rails intolerably at one of his master's royal hosts, Media himself commits a breach of decorum in defense of his retainer's sacred privilege.

At all times Babbalanja is, like the Shakespearean fool, the official wit of the court, usually self-activating, but always at the beck of his king if a special *mot* is required. "Come, philosopher," says Media as they leave the proud and ludicrous isle of Pimminee, "let us see in how few syllables you can put the brand on these Tapparians." And Babbalanja, after taking suitable thought, produces the desired epigram: "Full to the brim of themselves, for that reason, the Tapparians are the emptiest of mortals." Again, to charm away a silent and gloomy hour in the canoe, Media calls upon him to "start some paradox, that we may laugh." On the other hand, it sometimes becomes necessary for Media to turn him off: "Enough, enough, Babbalanja. . . You are a very wise Mardian; but the wisest Mardians make the most consummate fools." In view of the analogous versatility of Babbalanja's role as teller of moral tales, riddler of ambiguous riddles, talker of nonsense, and slightly syncopated voice of wisdom, it seems scarcely possible that Melville's repeated reference to him as a madman and a fool is entirely fortuitous. The clown was perhaps born in an eccentric fellow who seemed half prophet, half buffoon to the callous and superstitious court that patronized him. [13]

But Babbalanja is not all Shakespearean clown. He owes at least this much to the folk origin of Melville's other comic heroes, that he occasionally finds himself in the position of sucker or goat in the group. It is especially interesting that this indignity should befall him in his loftiest moments of intellectual gravity, when he sounds most like the author's undisguised mouthpiece. Through him we see Melville laughing at himself just as heartily as in his more externally oriented books. It is as though Melville had taken upon himself the role of the fool, whose stock-in-trade was the comic explosion of his own dignity. One case in point is particularly significant in suggesting, beneath the covering persiflage, the trend toward depth and ambiguity in comedy which was increasingly the direction of Melville's literary experimentation in *Mardi*. Mohi ("Braid-Beard") has told a story the point of which eludes Babbalanja.

"But has it any meaning you know of?"
"Thou art wise, find out," retorted Braid-Beard.
"But what comes of it?" persisted Babbalanja.
"Beshrew me, this senseless catechising of thine," replied Mohi; "naught else, it seems, save a grin or two."
"And pray, what may you be driving at, philosopher?" interrupted Media.
"I am intent upon the essence of things; the mystery that lieth beyond; the elements of the tear which much laughter provoketh; that which is beyond the seeming; the precious pearl within the shaggy oyster; I probe the circle's center; I seek to evolve the inscrutable."
"Seek on; and when aught is found, cry out, that we may run and see."
"My lord the king is merry upon me. To him my more subtle cogitations seem foolish. But believe me, my lord, there is more to be thought of than to be seen. There is a world of wonders insphered within the spontaneous consciousness; or, as old Bardianna hath it, a mystery within the obvious, yet an obviousness within the mystery."
"And did I ever deny that?" said Media.
"As plain as my hand in the dark," said Mohi.
"I dreamed a dream," said Yoomy.
"They banter me; but enough; I am to blame for discoursing upon the deep worlds wherein I live. I am wrong in seeking to invest sublunary sounds with celestial sense. Much that is within me is incommunicable by this ether we breathe. But I blame ye not." And wrapping around him his mantle, Babbalanja retired into its most private folds.[14]

This eloquent gesture of wounded dignity was useful on more than one occasion for Babbalanja, and Melville liked it well enough to use it in his own name when, in *White-Jacket*, he built himself into a similar situation. Blackballed by his messmates for his miserable "duff" and perpetually damp garment, White-Jacket receives their final, unequivocal insult with all the courtly aplomb of his Mardian philosopher: "I immediately rose, tucked my jacket about me, bowed, and departed."

Butt or hero, whatever his position at any given moment, Babbalanja is the indisputable star of the Mardian show, the rest being little more than foils to him. Of the remaining three, Media comes closest to having an independent existence, partly because his position of command gives him a natural force of character denied the others, and partly because, as his name implies, he serves in *Mardi*'s endless conversations as mediator and the voice of popular common sense. In both respects he is consistently comic: as a king and a demigod he is delightfully human in his insistence on being superhuman; as a hardheaded, practical thinker he supplies a much-needed breeze in the book's superheated metaphysical atmosphere. He is refreshingly unsentimental. When Yoomy sings an elegiac monody on the dead hero Adondo — a piece that sounds suspiciously like "Adonais" — everyone is dissolved but Media, who utters a sarcastic snort about "lacrymose rivulets, and inconsolable lagoons." He is also short with the interminable vaporings of Babbalanja, an attitude which makes him doubly attractive to the average reader. When his command to Yoomy for entertainment is interrupted by a lengthy discourse from Babbalanja on the inner springs of creative personality, he stands it just so long, then roars, "The song! the song! . . . Never mind the metaphysics of genius." As a foil to Babbalanja his role is epitomized in his periodic outbursts of exasperation with old Bardianna, the classic Mardian sage whose opinions are reverently quoted by the philosopher on all issues. In a purely nominal sense, Media is Melville's autocrat of the breakfast table. He does not monopolize the conversation, but he controls its flow, and he does so in as amusingly highhanded a way as Holmes ever thought of doing.

Mohi and Yoomy, too, have their independent functions in the story — Mohi as the convenient expositor of Mardian history and manners, Yoomy as the singer of the mediocre and possibly satiric verses [15] with which Melville chose to punctuate the book. As personalities, however, they are even more dependent than Media upon the comic interplay of the group for the breath of life.

They are little more than walking "humors," and such characters
tend to evaporate when they are not kept in comic conflict with
each other.[16] Melville did well to provide them with about a
dozen scenes, some of them of full chapter proportions, in which
to bait and rally each other over various kinds of sense and nonsense. He did well, too, in endowing them with contrasting and
roughly complementary "humors": Babbalanja is the melancholy
and acidulous jester, having some features in common with
Shakespeare's Jaques; Media is the merry extrovert; Yoomy is the
man of imagination, dreamy and naïve; Mohi is the unimaginative
man, cranky, dogmatic, humorless. Put them all together, equip
them with a sufficiently ludicrous subject, and something like the
following results. The scene is the canoe; the subject, the nature
of amber. Mohi has just cited, with an air of consequence, the
recondite theories of a number of ancient authorities.

"Why, old Braid-Beard," cried Media, placing his pipe in rest, "you
are almost as erudite as our philosopher here."
"Much more so, my lord," said Babbalanja; "for Mohi has somehow
picked up all my worthless forgettings, which are more than my
valuable rememberings."
"What say you, wise one?" cried Mohi, shaking his braids, like an
enraged elephant with many trunks.
Said Yoomy, "My lord, I have heard that amber is nothing less than
the congealed tears of broken-hearted mermaids."
"Absurd, minstrel," cried Mohi. "Hark ye; I know what it is. All
other authorities to the contrary, amber is nothing more than gold-
fishes' brains, made waxy, then firm, by the action of the sea."
"Nonsense!" cried Yoomy.
"My lord," said Braid-Beard, waving his pipe, "this thing is just as
I say. Imbedded in amber, do we not find little fishes' fins, porpoise-
teeth, seagulls' beaks and claws; nay, butterflies' wings, and sometimes
a topaz? And how could that be, unless the substance was first soft?
Amber is gold-fishes' brains, I say."
"For one," said Babbalanja, "I'll not believe that, till you prove to
me, Braid-Beard, that ideas themselves are found embedded therein."
"Another of your crazy conceits, philosopher," replied Mohi, dis-
dainfully. . ."[17]

*Mardi* is far too long, its dialogues too prolix, for the mainte-
nance of the comic intensity needed to give the book a consistent
tone. Yet these four central characterizations remain reasonably
intact until very near the end (Chapter 184, to be precise) and

might have served to bind the story together a good deal more effectively, at least to that point, had they not been burdened almost from the beginning of the voyage with a completely unrealized presence in the canoe — the character of Taji. It is in the figure of Taji that the characterization in *Mardi* differs most sharply from that of the autobiographical romances. In each of those stories Melville himself is the central figure, not just by virtue of his position as narrator, but by virtue of the active force of his personality. Even in *Omoo* one is never so dazzled by the presence of Long Ghost as to forget the controlling personality through whose eyes that droll vagabond world is being seen. The same sense of control is felt in *Mardi*, too, for a time. In the early chapters it is not Jarl or Samoa or Annatoo that gives the tale substance or coherence for us; it is the comic and dramatic vision of the narrator — his estimate of the characters, his sense of the scene, above all his very vivid participation in the action — that gives the story the dimensions of reality.

The feeling remains, is even heightened, when the author first takes the name of Taji. That act and the circumstances prompting it are precisely those on which Mark Twain constructed his own satiric fantasy in *A Connecticut Yankee*. For a chapter or two it even looks as though Melville were going to anticipate one of Twain's plots as well as some of his comic techniques. Just as Twain's Yankee contrives to be accepted for a magician among his sixth-century hosts, so Melville seizes an opportunity to pass himself off among the superstitious Polynesians as one of their own demigods dropped in from the sun for a visit, and he is confronted by the same sort of problems in maintaining the deception upon which his life may depend. His first shock is that the native chiefs do not fall down and worship, but instead ask some rather embarrassing questions about the unexpired period of his last incarnation, "furnishing," says Melville, "a curious example . . . of the reception given to strange demigods when they travel without their portmanteaus." "But nothing like carrying it bravely," he decides, and he turns the trick by delivering a stinging rebuke to the assembled kings for their inhospitable reception. After solving the pressing problem, "Did deities dine?" he discovers that his host is just as divine as he, and that neither Media nor his people are especially impressed either with his divinity or with his miraculous voyage from the sun. "Whether he [Media] had ever been there himself, that he regarded a solar trip with so much unconcern, almost became a question in my mind." The upshot of these observations is an expedient access of humility in the self-appointed demigod: "Be not a 'snob,' Taji," he tells himself.

The transplantation of the resourceful Yankee to his fantastic new setting is complete. The hard work is done: the reader is now prepared to accept the incredible as seen by an eye he has learned to know and trust. And then comes Chapter 62, prophetically entitled "Taji Retires from the World." From that moment on, Taji, completely absorbed in his metaphysical phantom-maiden, grows progressively more featureless until he becomes a disembodied spirit telling a disembodied story, and we are annoyed when occasional references to the faceless cipher in the canoe remind us that we have been deserted by the only character who could have made us believe in this windy nonsense. When, on the final page, our now mad and wraith-like narrator himself commits symbolic suicide and strikes out over an "endless sea," we are not surprised but only bored.

Melville was of course too keen an artist not to recognize the wilderness into which he had written himself. "Oh, reader, list! I've chartless voyaged," he confesses in Chapter 169. "And though essaying but a sportive sail, I was driven from my course, by a blast resistless." When a sensible man writes like that, something crucial has happened to his sense of humor.

# 4

# The Philosophic Voyage

For better or for worse, *Mardi* ceases to be a novel in the neighborhood of Chapter 40, where Melville abandoned himself to the philosophic-voyage formula of Lucian, Rabelais, Cyrano de Bergerac, and Swift. From that moment he was irrevocably committed to allegory. His voyagers, leaving flesh and the Pacific forever behind them, became symbols pursuing ideas across a metaphysical lagoon. Such a voyage is undertaken not for fun but for improvement — "to vex," as Swift put it, "not to divert, the world." Yet, for all their bitter preaching, books like *Gulliver's Travels* are entertaining too. Moral philosophers are not always without imagination and wit, and the fantastic voyage by nature involves the unexpected congruities and incongruities that are the basic fare of the comic spirit.

Melville's own model was not Swift (there is no evidence of his having read Swift) but Rabelais, whom he was reading even as he wrote *Mardi*. The whole structure of the voyage in search of Yillah is a close, sometimes an exact, parallel of the voyage of Pantagruel in search of the Holy Bottle. What principally attracted Melville to Rabelais, beyond the rowdiness of his humor, was a spirit which he profoundly shared with the Frenchman — "the spirit which has the wish and resolution at any cost to maintain itself inviolate, free, superior to chance and circumstance, immune to every debilitating contagion of the mass-mind and mass-temper." [1] In its purest form it is what Rabelais himself called "Pantagruelism" — "a certain jollity of mind, pickled in the scorn of fortune" — something Melville achieved only in *Omoo*. In *Mardi* the characters, particularly Taji, are not so much "superior to chance and circumstance" as at bay from them. That fact alone is sufficient to account for the losing struggle of the comic spirit to maintain throughout the book that "certain jollity of mind" with which it begins.

Still there is abundant humor in *Mardi* of one sort or another, growing out of the alien, nonconforming cast of mind which Rabelais encouraged but did not implant in Melville. In *Mardi* Melville merely reveals for the first time on a major scale the "critical and protestant" order of mind to which he naturally belonged and which, together with his experiences, was shaping a mature attitude toward his civilization that combined "skepticism, humorous contempt, and the anger of an outraged sense of right." [2] His unvarnished observations of life abroad had been in half-ludicrous, half-tragic contrast to the "Panglossian environment of complacent respectability and easy ideals" [3] in which he had been reared and to which he returned. *Mardi* is his first impetuous revolt against large-scale social and religious hypocrisy, against what Newton Arvin calls the "unmodulated affirmations" of Emerson and the Transcendentalists, against the "smugness of the American democratic philosophy, the conviction of its prophets that God and the constitution of the universe were on their side." [4] The artistic effect of that revolt turned out to be, like the contrasting impressions that stirred it, half-ludicrous and half-tragic; but the failure paid its way in what it showed Melville of the boundless possibilities of imaginative-critical comedy.

I

As a rebel, Melville used the philosophic voyage for the same primary purpose for which his predecessors had used it — as a framework for satire. By the nature of the voyage pattern this satire takes on a conveniently episodic structure, and by the nature of Melville's interests the satiric episodes resulting are of two kinds. They are either general or specific. That is, they deal with abstract principles, institutions, and characteristics, or else they deal with actual policies, places, and persons. In the first case Melville used comedy as a tool in the criticism of ideas; in the second, as a tool of caricature, in the manner of a political cartoonist.

The range of ideas which Melville criticized in *Mardi* is great and the range of his comic tones appropriately broad. The more inconsequential the idea, naturally, the more rollicking the laughter. At this extreme of the scale is a volatile little chapter (86) playing with the human tendency to seek a scapegoat, however irrational, for the consequences of stupidity, negligence, and the vicissitudes of circumstance. The standard scapegoats on the Island of Quelquo were a tribe of "invisible spirits, ycleped the Plujii, arrant little knaves as ever gulped moonshine." They are of common ancestry with the "gremlins" of World War II, defined in the current Webster as "impish foot-high gnomes whimsically blamed by airmen for interfering with motors, instruments, machine guns, etc." Conceived in the same light-hearted vein is the philosopher Doxodox, whose burlesque lucubrations are a broadly Rabelaisian dig at intellectual hocus-pocus.[5] Even more slavishly Rabelaisian is the account of the pedantic antiquarian Oh-Oh. Just as Rabelais had detailed the contents of the library of St. Victor in Book II, so Melville details in tabular form the contents of the museum and archives of Oh-Oh. In so doing he had a multitude of miniscule opportunities for secondary satire of which he availed himself with considerable energy and somewhat less success.

The tone is less playful when the subject takes on more substantial social significance. The laughter is tinged with malice now, and the smile shows more teeth than throat. One of the best pieces of this type is a short and skillful chapter (144) on lawyers in which Melville proves himself thoroughly at home in the company of his great satiric precursors. In fact, Mohi's story "Of the Sorcerers in the Isle of Minda" has a good deal more point and wit for the modern reader than Rabelais' chapters on the "Furred Law-Cats" (Book V), from which it obviously derives. The description of the mercenary magicians indefatigably casting spells on people "to the very last tooth in their employers' pouches" is worked out economically but in sufficient detail to emerge as a startlingly full portrait of the legal profession seen from the lowest point of view. Quite as malicious, though not as consistently comic, is the treatment of the self-appointed aristocracy, the social-climbers of the world. These characters are distinguished by the elegance of the robes they wear — their "tappa"

— and hence are called Tapparians, a conception which suggests the influence of Carlyle.[6] In their society it is dress rather than conduct which is legislated upon, and a man's position in the social register is determined, not by the respectability of his ancestry, but by the artistry of his tailor. Water is despised as a vulgar commodity, though the natives "occasionally employ it for medicinal purposes"; and the dandies of Pimminee wear curious little tasselled cords "to measure and graduate their movements; keeping their gestures, paces, and attitudes within the prescribed standards of Tapparian gentility." [7] The sharp, Swiftian touches are scattered, but there are enough of them to sustain the satiric tone at a fairly high level.

Among the objects of his social disapproval Melville held a particular brief against kings as symbols of the political despotism to which society has always owed so many of its ills. *Mardi* is by the very nature of its parable full of kings, none of whom comes off unscathed. Even Media, the best of the autocrats, gets a gentle Melvillian deflation early in his career, and the sybaritic Abrazza, the worst of them, comes in for a terrible roasting at the hands of Babbalanja in later chapters — chapters which, insofar as they represent social protest, are wrung dry of humor. In between is a nicely shaded gallery of monarchs deftly illustrating nearly every major evil of the species. Best of all are the twin portraits of Hello and Piko, kings of overpopulated Diranda, in whose dominion is satirized at once the blithe callousness of monarchs and the tragic absurdity of war. Cursed with political amity, a salubrious climate, and a low death rate, they devise their own Malthusian check in the form of periodic war-games, in which their silly armies are tricked into murdering each other for fun and glory, like college football teams, while the crowds roar and the "bards" stand by in chorus, like Aristophanic cheerleaders, to rally the faint of heart. The master touch is the picture of Hello and Piko themselves, discovered in their royal inn like a sinister Tweedledum and Tweedledee, merrily shaking coins in a skull. The scene is an almost preternatural anticipation of Lewis Carroll:

"What says your majesty?" said Piko; "heads or tails?"
"Oh, heads, your majesty," said Hello.
"And heads say I," said Piko.

And heads it was. But it was heads on both sides, so both were sure to win.

After their bloody war-games, at which the cry is all but literally "Off with their heads!" they are back at it in their inn, emptying gourds and yelling "Heads!" [8]

Not unexpectedly, the subject that interested Melville most in *Mardi* was religion. In its positive aspects it is responsible for the disappearance of all humor from the closing chapters of the book, in which all but Taji find the ultimate answer to their earthly problems on Alma's (Christ's) own island of Serenia. In its negative aspects it is responsible for the book's most extensive concentration of general satire, the thirteen-chapter episode on Maramma, the realm of the organized church.[9] Unfortunately, it is in this most sustained attack that Melville most plainly reveals his weakness as a satirist. One of the fundamental faults of *Mardi* as a whole is represented here in the unsatisfactory mixture of tones, ranging without much artistic control from solemn allegory reminiscent of Bunyan to toothsome ridicule in some ways comparable to Swift. In the former category are a number of sequences featuring the blind priest Pani and a representative assortment of pilgrims. Occasionally these scenes seem about to come alive in a zestful touch, only to collapse again into a very pedestrian allegorical equation. Alternating with these scenes are the stages in the pilgrimage of a highly symbolic young man, whose direct allegorical significance, as he searches alone for his mystic Eldorado, is in destructive contrast to the inverted allegory of the satirically conceived characters. What Swiftian capabilities Melville possessed erupt in purple patches such as Babbalanja's demonstration that Christianity, as promulgated by the church, is not only completely unbelievable but the worst thing that could have happened to the world; or the voyagers' visit to an idol factory — "a trade," Babbalanja decides, "more reliable than the baker's." [10]

The unevenness of the religious satire comes out most clearly in those passages in which *Mardi*, by accident or intent, most closely resembles its classic paradigms. The Mardian equivalent of the dispute between the Big-Endians and the Little-Endians in the "Voyage to Lilliput" is an unflattering instance of how far short of Swift Melville could fall as a satiric humorist. Melville's figure

— whether a bird-track represents "three toes" or "one foot" —
is, if anything, more pertinent than Swift's, but he handles it with
a heavy artificiality of which Swift was never guilty.[11] On the
other hand, the incident in the Maramma episode that is most
reminiscent of Rabelais is handled at least as effectively as its
earlier counterpart. In the fifth book of Rabelais ten chapters are
given over to elaborate preparation for the climactic interview
with the Holy Bottle, and when the oracle finally speaks, all it
says is "Trinc!" which leaves Panurge "just as wise as I was last
year." The anticlimax is theoretically stunning, especially since
that scene is the objective of the entire voyage extending over
Books IV and V; yet it comes with no particular dramatic force.
In *Mardi* an equal number of chapters prepare the reader for the
climax of the Maramma sojourn, which is an interview with the
Pontiff Hivohitee himself. En route to the inner sanctum somewhere at the heart of the island, the voyagers encounter an old
hermit living in a bamboo pagoda and wearing a necklace of jaw-
bones. The naïve Yoomy is ideally selected to call on the old man
in his windowless tower and joins him there in the darkness and
silence with mounting apprehension.

> At last the silence was broken.
> "What see you, mortal?"
> "Chiefly darkness," said Yoomy, wondering at the audacity of the
> question.
> "I dwell in it. But what else see you, mortal?"
> "The dim gleaming of thy gorget."
> "But that is not me. What else dost thou see?"
> "Nothing."
> "Then thou hast found me out, and seen all. Descend."[12]

The reader of course recognizes the hermit as the Pontiff himself
and relishes the neatness of his self-exposure before the unconscious Yoomy. The dramatic force of the anticlimax lies in its
extension through the comic vacuity of Yoomy, who has to have
it explained to him as the party returns to the beach that they are
no longer seeking Hivohitee because they have already seen him.

Such features of Maramma as the Pontiff Hivohitee arouse the
occasional suspicion that Melville is being uncomfortably specific
in his criticism. The context, however, is more broadly applicable,
and it seems reasonable to conclude, with William Braswell, that

the episode is intended to lampoon organized Christianity at large rather than any one church.[13] Where the entire satire does have a specific target, the issue is not in doubt. It becomes readily recognizable caricature in a series of chapters (145–168) dealing with world politics. Here Melville took little enough trouble with disguises. Great Britain he called Dominora, and her king, Bello; the United States became Vivenza; Europe, Porpheero; Africa, Hamora; all transparent enough. Other place names, like Franko and Kanneda, are little more than misspellings.

Of the eighteen chapters (omitting irrelevant links) devoted to this vast political parable, only four are predominantly comic, a fact which demonstrates the seriousness with which Melville viewed the state of the world and the political conditions of man. Yet the tiny core of comedy is vigorous enough to sustain life in the desert of allegorical preachment in which it is set. The thumbnail sketch of Porpheero and its kings, with which this section begins, demonstrates the potential felicity of the savage-Polynesian metaphor of *Mardi* in creating satiric distortion. The various kings are struck off in appropriate terms — Franko's, for example, as "a small-framed, poodle-haired, fine fiery gallant; finical in his tattooing; much given to the dance and glory" — and in the end they are lumped together as "their Serene Superfluities," among whom old Bello was vitally concerned to maintain an "Equipoise of Calabashes."

Principal among the nations anatomized are England and the United States. Deftly Melville prods the British in their most vulnerable spot:

It seems that his love of wide dominion sometimes led the otherwise sagacious Bello into the most extravagant actions. If the chance accumulation of soil and driftwood about any detached shelf of coral in the lagoon held forth the remotest possibility of the eventual existence of an islet there, with all haste he dispatched canoes to the spot, to take prospective possession of the as yet nearly submarine territory; and, if possible, eject the zoophytes.

With cool impartiality and unerring aim, Melville then deflates the upstart pride of his own nation, beginning with its backhanded success in the War of 1812.

Solely imputing these victories to their superior intrepidity and skill, the people of Vivenza were exceedingly boisterous in their triumph; raising such obstreperous peans, that they gave themselves hoarse throats; insomuch that, according to Mohi, some of the present generation are fain to speak through their noses.

The gaping flaw in American democracy is neatly hit as Media's party, approaching Vivenza in his canoe, spell out the inscription on a great arch: "In-this-re-publi-can-land-all-men-are-born-free-and-equal," and then discover the fine print in the corner: "Except-the-tribe-of-Hamo." The picture of Congress in session is still a potent one beneath its archaic idiom and demonstrates the genuinely Rabelaisian gift for imaginative-critical comedy that was burgeoning in *Mardi*:

> Some were sociably laughing, and chatting; others diligently making excavations between their teeth with slivers of bamboo; or turning their heads into mills, were grinding up leaves and ejecting their juices. Some were busily inserting the down of a thistle into their ears. Several stood erect, intent upon maintaining striking attitudes; their javelins tragically crossed upon their chests. They would have looked very imposing were it not, that in rear their vesture was sadly disordered. Others, with swelling fronts, seemed chiefly indebted to their dinners for their dignity. Many were nodding and napping. And, here and there, were sundry indefatigable worthies, making a great show of imperious and indispensable business; sedulously folding banana leaves into scrolls, and recklessly placing them into the hands of little boys, in gay turbans and trim little girdles; who thereupon fled as if with salvation for the dying.

Melville's political satire might have been great had it been maintained at such a level of comic vigor. But here as elsewhere in *Mardi* the heavy, for all its brave intellectual determination, is artistically intrusive and fundamentally inimical to the light. The sprightly commentary on England degenerates into a labored parable of the Chartist movement, and the brilliant congressional burlesque is followed by chapters of solemn preachment on democracy and slavery in which impassioned sermon and fantastic nomenclature are an acute mutual embarrassment. By the end of Chapter 162 Melville himself has fallen into a theatrical rhapsody almost as appalling in its bombast as that of his ludicrous senator from Hio-Hio. One critic has put it this way: that all that keeps *Mardi* from being the "*Gulliver's Travels* of the mid-nineteenth century" is Melville's lack of the true satirist's temper, which is to say an excess of "tolerance, humanity, wisdom, and faith." An-

other critic, a Frenchman, has written: "This harlequinade reminds us too much of our own Rabelais, so fruitful in appellations,
whose grotesque sound suffices to provoke the pantagruelian titil-
lation. Mr. Melville is not a magician of this kind. He has good
sense and sagacity, he would make out of them humor, which is
not the same thing." [14] The sad fact is that he *could* make out of
them humor and so often chose not to. He made up his mind to
sacrifice everything for truth in *Mardi*, and the extremity of his
sacrifice simply proves that truth is not, after all, necessarily
beauty.


2

The satire which looms thus large in the complex of *Mardi* certainly provides one compelling motive for Melville's choice of the
Rabelais plan as the vehicle for his story. His second motive was
in a sense even more compelling: as a thinker, whether in revolt or
not, he needed a medium in which to expatiate and explore — a
narrative structure so accommodating that he could start, stop,
and steer it at will, or at whim. *Mardi*, like the "Koztanza" of
Lombardo, which Melville invents as its apology, "lacks cohesion;
it is wild, unconnected, all episodes." It is exactly what its author
wanted it to be — a literary free-for-all, a grand philosophical
romp, in which the interest is never in what happens to people but
in what happens to ideas. Satire accounts for only a few of the
ideas Melville was teeming with when he wrote *Mardi*. The rest
erupted in a shower of digressions, by-blows, puns, tropes, and
paradoxes that make hash of the story yet stimulate and entertain
in their own right by virtue of their very energy and abundance
and diversity. Not more than half of these miscellaneous divaga-
tions are wholly or even partly comic, yet in view of the impassioned metaphysical solemnity of the search for Yillah, which is
the story's *raison d'être*, one is surprised to find as much candid
comedy as there is in its reflective embellishments.

The most disarming of these embellishments are the products
of pure fancy. One of the ways in which *Mardi* differs from Melville's more elementary books is in being a fairy story — not the
Grimm-Andersen type, but the Thurber type, in which an adult

point is deftly concealed beneath a childlike tale. Among Melville's books only *Mardi* and *The Confidence-Man* have this quality, and in both it is most evident when the author is telling a tale within a tale. In *The Confidence-Man* we feel it most strongly in "The Story of China Aster"; in *Mardi*, though the quality pervades the lagoon and all that happens there, it emerges most forcibly in the little legends the voyagers tell from time to time to illustrate a point in their endless commentary on life. All of these stories are part of a general pattern of digression which utilizes the passages from island to island as theatrical entr'actes for the discussion of a dizzying assortment of philosophical topics. Babbalanja's reduction to absurdity of religious authority, for example, is painlessly accomplished in a ludicrous "nursery tale" about nine blind men and a banian tree and how each of them, stumbling on one of its many rooted boughs, claimed to have found the one central and original trunk. Even the charming legend of the elves of Tupia (Chapter 93), with its nearly flawless blend of humor and poetic imagery, is told with an ulterior motive, Mohi's comic skepticism providing a perfect opportunity for Babbalanja to expound the nature of truth. Such scenes are at once the punctuation and the substance of a book whose central plot becomes more and more a literary vacuum.

In addition to the extracurricular sport which Melville surrendered to his Mardian puppets, there is a good deal that he kept for himself as author. Never a great respecter of the sacredness of movement in a story, in this book he scuttled it altogether, emerging from his fiction where it pleased him for a paragraph or a chapter, sometimes to rhapsodize in high earnest, more often to indulge in those small dallyings-by-the-way that were to become so distinctive a feature of *Moby-Dick*'s thoughtful comedy. Depending on one's taste in humor, these little digressions are either charmingly or irritatingly unpredictable. The point of departure can be anything or nothing, and the process by which Melville launches himself into them is often so plainly one of free association that the reader is likely to find himself fairly into one without the slightest recollection of how he got there. In the chapter on Samoa's self-amputation, for example, a series of playful references to the mangled warriors of history leads Melville off on the following blithe excursion into the so-called romance of chivalry:

At the battle of Brevieux, in Flanders, my glorious old gossiping ancestor, Froissart, informs me that ten good knights, being suddenly unhorsed, fell stiff and powerless to the plain, fatally encumbered by their armour. Whereupon, the rascally burglarious peasants, their foes, fell to picking their visors; as burglars, locks; or oystermen, oysters; to get at their lives. But all to no purpose. And at last they were fain to ask aid of a blacksmith, and not till then were the inmates of the armour despatched. . . Days of chivalry these, when gallant chevaliers died chivalric deaths!

And this was the epic age over whose departure my late eloquent and prophetic friend and correspondent, Edmund Burke, so movingly mourned! Yes, they were glorious times. But no sensible man, given to quiet domestic delights, would exchange his warm fireside and muffins for a heroic bivouac, in a wild beechen wood, of a raw gusty morning in Normandy: every knight blowing his steel-gloved fingers, and vainly striving to cook his cold coffee in his helmet.

It was this digression, presumably, that Carl Van Doren had in mind when he cited this chapter, among the "sumptuous inventions" of *Mardi*, as "one of the wittiest in English." [15]

From the standpoint of continuity in Melville's comic art, the most interesting of these digressions are those which reflect or foreshadow topics which he developed more fully in later works. The paragraphs on ship names in Chapter 28 are instantly recognizable as a little treatise on a type of irony in which Melville never ceased to take hearty delight, from the tireless whaler *Perseverance* in *Typee* to the *Rights of Man* and the *Indomitable* in *Billy Budd*. Equally recognizable, as forerunners of the playful cetology of *Moby-Dick*, are the mock-scientific chapters on the "Chondropterygii" (sharks) and the "Xiphius Platypterus" (swordfish). And within the former is a further digression brought on by Jarl's hatred of the Tiger shark, "a round portly gourmand, with distended mouth and collapsed conscience." The humorously admonitory paragraph on hate thus evoked points in two directions. Its ironic opening assumption ("Yet this is all wrong. As well hate a seraph as a shark. Both were made by the same hand.") was to receive explicit answer from Queequeg: "God what made shark must be one dam Ingin." The rest of the paragraph, on the moral principle of hate, brief and light as it is, is clearly the germ of the longer and subtler comic treatise on "the metaphysics of Indian-hating" in *The Confidence-Man*.

Finally, in a further exploration of the potentialities of fish and theology, Melville roughed out in *Mardi* what was to become one of *Moby-Dick*'s funniest scenes — the Christianizing of the sharks (Chapter 64). Writing of King Borabolla's pet fish, he described their keeper as calling them by name, stroking their scaly backs, and "carrying on some heathenish nursery-talk, like St. Anthony, in ancient Coptic, instilling virtuous principles into his finny flock on the seashore."

But alas for the hair-shirted old dominie's back-sliding disciples. For of all nature's animated kingdoms, fish are the most unchristian, inhospitable, heartless, and cold-blooded of creatures. At least so they seem to strangers; though at bottom, somehow, they must be all right.[16]

He continues the jest by assuming the likelihood of a fish-heaven, real enough to the mentality of the fish. Shark-heaven, for example, would be "one vast Pacific, ploughed by navies of mortals, whom an endless gale forever drops into their maws." "As for the possible hereafter of the whales," he concludes, " a creature eighty feet long without stockings, and thirty feet round the waist before dinner, is not inconsiderately to be consigned to oblivion."

Numerous and miscellaneous as these digressions are, they can only suggest the Rabelaisian abundance and variety that make *Mardi* the source book of Melvillian thought and the bewilderment and delight of Melville enthusiasts from Hawthorne on. The playing with ideas, the exploration of comic congruities and incongruities, always a distinguishing feature of Melville's writing, becomes in *Mardi* a ritual mode of expression. Scarcely a subject arises that does not suggest to him a multiplicity of correspondences or antitheses, which, if they do not distract him into a full-fledged digression, at least crop out in a decorative sentence or phrase. The book is flavored, as nothing he had written before had been, by its scores of little conceits, such as the conception of the whaler's swinging hammock as a pendulum telling the "hours and ages" of unrelieved boredom, or Babbalanja's remark on descending into Oh-Oh's subterranean archives: "My lords, this is like going down to posterity."

Often Melville condensed his trope to a single word, expressing the desired multiplicity of meanings in a simple pun. How much more important puns were to the purpose and method of *Mardi* than to those of the autobiographical romances is immediately suggested in the fact that there are twenty-nine of them in *Mardi* — more than in the other four books together. If some of *Mardi's* puns are no better than they should be, it is significant that most of them are useful as well as funny. The spear of the god Keevi is a "pointed" argument in defense of his cult; Babbalanja one black night discourses "in the dark" on a subject he knows little about; the congressmen of Vivenza are all "chiefs of immense capacity — how many gallons, there was no finding out."

The secret of Melville's fascination with puns lies in his understanding of a fundamental principle of semantics: "that words are but algebraic signs, conveying no meaning but what you please." [17] By this definition, those puns whose multiple meanings contribute to the complexity of the book's poetic and intellectual fabric are entitled to be called metaphysical. At their most interesting they are both intricate and problematical. There is an almost musical pattern of elaboration in the observation that Jarl was "nothing of an idealist, an aerial architect, a constructor of flying buttresses," and there is the true intricacy of the puzzle about some of Babbalanja's puns. When Media remarks that "No pastime is lost time," the philosopher, after a moment of reflection which the reader will at least duplicate, replies: "My lord, that maxim may be good as it stands; but had you made six words of it instead of six syllables, you had uttered a better and a deeper."

Such puns are in a sense problematical as well as intricate, but there is no question that a pun is intended and no question what it is intended to be. The true problem puns are those offered without warning or explanation, for the reader to make of what he will. The name of Babbalanja seems obvious enough in its intention, yet Matthiessen's suggestion that the name may as well mean "babbling angel" as "babbling on" points up the difficulty and inadvisability of attempting to define a Melvillian pun. [18] Again, Jarl is said to be from the Isle of Skye, and Melville admits that his being a Skyeman is very convenient in persuading the superstitious Mardians that "as his name imported, he came from above." Did he also intend, as Braswell thinks, that Jarl should therefore symbolize his "Northern Christian heritage"? [19] Did he intend the Joycean pun he achieved when he described the slave-laborers in Vivenza's southern fields as "collared men"? "As old Bardianna hath it, that question is more final than any answer."

Plentiful as puns and conceits are in *Mardi*, its antithetic ambiguities are even more abundant, though less consistently comic in
tone. Perhaps the best presumptive evidence of Melville's primarily comic intent is that he made paradox and ambiguity important
media of play for his Mardian voyagers — terribly intellectual
play, sometimes, to be sure, but none the less play. The failure of
*Mardi* as art is at least partly measured by the reader's failure to
appreciate much of the abstruse joking that goes on in Media's
canoe. It is nevertheless joking to those in the canoe. When Media
wants to dispel gloom during the voyage, he orders Babbalanja to
"start some paradox, that we may laugh." And on several occasions the whole party demonstrates a high regard for ambiguity as a source of entertainment. When Yoomy regales his companions with a little song of his own making, Mohi yawns and
offers him a regular job singing him to sleep nights.

"Mean you, old man, that my lines, setting forth the luxurious
repose to be enjoyed hereafter, are composed with such skill, that
the description begets the reality; or would you ironically suggest,
that the song is a sleepy thing itself?"
"An important discrimination," said Media. "Which mean you,
Mohi?"
"Now are you not a silly boy," said Babbalanja, "when from the
ambiguity of his speech, you could so easily have derived something
flattering, thus to seek to extract unpleasantness from it? Be wise,
Yoomy; and hereafter, whenever a remark like that seems equivocal,
be sure to wrest commendation from it, though you torture it to the
quick." [20]

Later, when Babbalanja delivers himself of one of his paradoxical
epigrams, Mohi congratulates him with another double-edged remark:

"In sooth, a most excellent saying; it should be carved upon his
tombstone. . ."
"What! would you have my epitaph read thus: — 'Here lies the
emptiest of mortals, who was full of himself!' At best, your words
are exceedingly ambiguous, Mohi."
"Now I have thee, philosopher," cried Yoomy with glee. "What
did someone say to me, not long since, Babbalanja, when in the matter
of that sleepy song of mine, Braid-Beard bestowed upon me an equivocal compliment? Was I not to wrest commendation from it, though
I tortured it to the quick?"
"Take thy own pills, philosopher," said Mohi.

Cornered, Babbalanja replies,

"since we philosophers bestow so much wisdom upon others, it is
not to be wondered at, if now and then we find what is left in us
too small for our necessities. It is from our very abundance that we
want."

"And from the fool's poverty," said Media, "that he is opulent; for
his very simplicity, is sometimes of more account than the wisdom
of the sage. . ."[21]

Paradox and ambiguity, then, whatever their other uses in *Mardi*,
must be considered part of the coin of its philosophic banter.
Together with the rest of the fantastic array of puns, tropes, and
digressions they help to give *Mardi* its uniquely Rabelaisian air of
Gothic plenitude, grotesquerie, and uninhibited experimentation.

## 3

The most telling effect of Melville's exposure to Rabelais and
other antique writers was their impact upon his style. Their example encouraged him in the quaint excesses to which he was
naturally prone, without materially correcting the fallibility of
his taste. Under the broad stimulus of his reading his own momentum carried him into more elaborately inflated language. *Mardi*
still reveals, at intervals, his talent for the dazzlingly correct word,
as in the observation that a calm at sea "revolutionises" a landsman's abdomen; and the low-comic effect of deflated language is
still sought in the occasional use of a slang phrase; but the stylistic
metamorphosis of *Mardi* results from a new and largely undisciplined magniloquence.

The extensive use of apostrophe is symptomatic. Whereas apostrophe was used on the rarest occasions in *Typee* and *Omoo*, and
then for strictly comic reasons, in *Mardi* its occurrences are num-
berless and its uses far more general. It ranges from the patently
comic ("Ay, ay, Arcturion! I say it in no malice, but thou wast
exceedingly dull") to the patently tragic ("Am I a murderer,
stars?"); and in between are a score of instances marked by irony
or good humor and at the same time by a serious striving after
poetic idiom ("Oh, Ocean, when thou choosest to smile, more
beautiful thou art than flowery mead or plain!"). The precise
point at which the intent ceases to be comic is impossible to de-

tect. We can be sure that Babbalanja's agonizing search for peace of soul, which reaches a purgatorial frenzy in Chapter 184, is a very serious matter indeed, yet what are we to make of a soliloquy culminating in an impassioned apostrophe to a moose that happens to be swimming by? Is this Babbalanja's demonic equivalent of Jaques' "weeping and commenting upon the sobbing deer"? Or is it, as seems more likely, merely an instance of the "vast deal of flummery" that Melville admitted was in him? The truth probably is that Melville was only imperfectly aware of the comic effect of inflated rhetoric, or that his concept of comedy led him to assume too close an identity between comedy and tragedy. All we can say with assurance is that he recognized the silliness of artificiality whenever he himself felt playful about the subject at hand. When Babbalanja quotes a particularly turgid passage from Bardianna on "cracked skulls," the ridicule is as prompt as it is deserved:

> "Seems to me our old friend must have been on his stilts that time," interrupted Mohi.
> "No, Braid-Beard. But by way of apologizing for the unusual rigidity of his style in that chapter, he says in a note, that it was written upon a straight-backed settle, when he was ill of lumbago, and a crick in the neck." [22]

It is a new consciousness of style — really, a self-consciousness about style — that prompts Melville to finish a comic passage on the Berkeleyan philosophy like this: "Besides being pervious to the points of pins, and possessing a palate capable of appreciating plum-puddings — which sentence reads off like a pattering of hailstones." Sentences are now engineered to include combinations like "goblins and goblets," "continence and calicoes," and "portly peltry"; and the titles in Oh-Oh's library are nearly all pointedly alliterative. Comic allusion, too, suddenly burgeons in *Mardi* — not just here and there, but in forests. Half a dozen chapters are wholly or partly given over to catalogs of historic or pseudo-historic precedent on one subject or another, from the brotherhood of man to the giving of suppers.[23] *Typee* and *Omoo* contain nothing of this sort, but from *Mardi* on it is a standard feature of Melville's comic style. Even *Redburn* and *White-Jacket* show traces of it, subdued but recognizable.[24]

Outstanding among these stylistic extravagances are certain

quirks bearing the patent earmarks of Melville's Shakespearean
and Rabelaisian models. The scene that introduces Azzageddi,
Babbalanja's personal demon, makes use of the old conversational
refrain-with-variation, a commonplace in Elizabethan comic dialogues:

". . . Whence come you, Azzageddi?"

"Whither my catechist must go — a torrid clime, cut by a hot
equator."

"A very keen and witty devil this. Azzageddi, whom have you
there?"

"A right down merry, jolly set, that at a roaring furnace sit and
toast their hoofs for ay; so used to flames, they poke the fire with
their horns, and light their tails for torches."

"A very funny devil this. Azzageddi, is not Mardi a place far
pleasanter than that from whence you came?"

"Ah, home! sweet, sweet home! would, would that I were home
again!"

"A very sentimental devil this. . ." [25]

Many familiar Shakespearean scenes could have taught Melville
the swing of this elementary patter. In *The Merchant of Venice*
alone are at least three scenes that owe their humor to such antiphonal dialogue: the meeting of Shylock and Tubal in Act III, the
by-play of Shylock and Gratiano in the court scene in Act IV,
and the whimsical romancing of Lorenzo and Jessica ("In such a
night. . .") in Act V. Very similar to this device is a slightly
more concentrated form of patter which was a stock-in-trade of
Shakespeare's clowns; for example, Launcelot Gobbo's struggle
with his conscience and Touchstone's analysis of country life in
Act III of *As You Like It*, a passage which Melville marked in his
copy:

Truly, shepherd, in respect of itself, it is a good life; but in respect
that it is a shepherd's life, it is naught. In respect that it is solitary,
I like it very well; but in respect that it is private, it is a very vile
life. Now in respect it is in the fields, it pleaseth me well; but in
respect it is not in the court, it is tedious. . .

In *Mardi* the method comes out in such passages as Babbalanja's
quotation from Bardianna on devils:

Devils are divers — strong devils, and weak devils; knowing devils,
and silly devils, mad devils, and mild devils; devils, merely devils;
devils, themselves bedevilled; devils, doubly bedevilled. [26]

The Rabelaisian quality of *Mardi's* style is even more pervasive. In its extremest form it is simply redundancy raised to the ultimate power, as in the many catalogs of allusions just referred to, or the many sentences which refuse to end until every conceivable synonym is accounted for. The following item from Bardianna's will, as quoted by Babbalanja, is pure Rabelais in all respects:

Item. My esteemed neighbor Lakreemo having since the last lunar eclipse called daily to inquire after the state of my health: and having nightly made tearful inquiries of my herb-doctor, concerning the state of my viscera; — I do hereby give and bequeath to the aforesaid Lakreemo all and sundry those vegetable pills, potions, powders, aperients, purgatives, expellatives, evacuatives, tonics, emetics, cathartics, clysters, injections, scarifiers, cataplasms, lenitives, lotions, decoctions, washes, gargles, and phlegmagogues; together with all the jars, calabashes, gourds and galipots, thereunto pertaining; situate, lying, and being, in the west-by-north corner of my east-south-east crypt, in my aforesaid tenement known as "The Lair." [27]

The trick lies in a burlesque exactitude which exhausts the resources of language and falls of its own breathless momentum into grotesque nonsense.

But Melville is not to be set down as a slavish imitator of Rabelais or anyone else, however fascinated he may have been by their peculiarities of style. Though he frankly experimented with a multitude of comic media in *Mardi*, he also achieved a sufficient synthesis of them to bring his own comic style very close to maturity. Synthesis and elements are both discernible in a good passage like this:

Indeed, in some quarters of Mardi, certain pagans maintain, that no fat man can be . . . immortal. A dogma! truly, which should be thrown to the dogs. For fat men are the salt and savour of the earth; full of good humour, high spirits, fun, and all manner of jollity. Their breath clears the atmosphere; their exhalations air the world. Of men, they are the good measures; brimmed, heaped, pressed down, piled up, and running over. They are as ships from Teneriffe; swimming deep, full of old wine, and twenty steps down into their holds. Soft and susceptible all round, they are easy of entreaty. Wherefore, for all their rotundity, they are too often circumnavigated by hatchet-faced knaves. Ah! a fat uncle, with a fat paunch, and a fat purse, is a joy and a delight to all nephews; to philosophers, a subject of endless speculation, as to how many droves of oxen and Lake Eries of wine might have run through his great mill during the full term of his mortal career. Fat men not immortal! This very instant, old Lambert is rubbing his jolly abdomen in Paradise.[28]

There is a sense of careless play with a subject casually stumbled on, yet at the same time a sense of powerful intellect reacting against an accepted commonplace. There is a gross pun. There is an earthy exuberance of manner, a redundant enthusiasm of phrase. There is a magnificent metaphoric audacity and a new richness of allusion. There is a Gothic rudeness and abundance, softened by a baroque musicality of prose. It is a style, Melville would be amused to hear, at once enormously complex and enormously simple. If *Mardi* fails, in its furious experimentation, to display it always at its best, it nevertheless taught him the potential orchestration necessary for a genuine masterpiece of imaginative-critical comedy.

# 5

# Devils

Of all the literary departures in *Mardi* none is so curious or so far-reaching in its effects on that book and those to follow as that of demonism. "Diabolism raised its head in the midst of the idyll with comic gusto," Constance Rourke has written in relating *Mardi* to Western comic tradition; "the narrative is a fairy tale plumbed by the opposing spirits of comedy and terror." [1]

In introducing devils into his book Melville was of course extending a much older tradition than the native American. The spirit of evil, of mischief and unrest, has always gripped the imaginations of men in one way or another. Maximilian Rudwin offers two explanations of that fascination which are particularly applicable to writers of Melville's time. [2] The first, a psychological view, sees in it a retreat to primitive or childish fears and beliefs in the face of profound dread, danger, and calamity. On the intellectual level there was an affinity with Satan, as the opposer of what Milton called "the tyranny of Heaven," on the part of men in revolt against a society of respectability — rebels such as Byron and Hugo, or frontiersmen and sailors. These were the inner motives which were to operate with increasing force in the art of Melville, sometimes with comic effect, sometimes with tragic, sometimes with both. The second view, a historical one, sees in Satan the "inspiration," the "patron saint," the "fount and foundation" of Romanticism, whose "shadow was cast over all the works of the Romantic period." At its most specific, "in modern literature the Devil's chief function is that of a satirist" — a detector of weak spots in human society and institutions. Thus understood,

diabolism was in the air, it was in Melville, and it was called forth
at both the Coleridgean and the Swiftian extremes of the book he
was writing.

Melville's Devil is not Milton's, or even Mark Twain's. It is
something older and more in keeping with the pagan culture in
which his tale is nominally set. Instead of a single figure of rather
awesome and well-defined character, *Mardi*'s Devil is legion, a
heterogeneous band of rebellious spirits, ranging from imps to
avenging furies. Purely comic are the devil that sired the Cholo
race, the devils that possessed Annatoo, and "those scamps the
Plujii" that tormented the inhabitants of Quelquo. On the other
hand, much of the book is haunted by the somber devils symbolized in Hautia and the specter sons of Aleema, who drive humor
before them as they drive Taji. The devils that interest us most
are the ambiguous devils that operate somewhere between those
extremes and whose function is to destroy the reader's com-
placency as they had destroyed the author's. These are the devils
that give *Mardi* its nervous tension and make it a stimulating experience despite its many artistic failings.

Two such devils dominate the story. We encounter the first at
the outset of the fantastic voyage through Mardi and, though he is
never mentioned again, he is in fact (to use Rudwin's term) the
"patron saint" of the voyage, destined by his very nature to lead
the travelers into all their adventures and to preside over all their
conversations. He is part of the totemic figurehead on Media's
canoe.

> But what is this in the head of the canoe just under the shark's
> mouth? A grinning little imp of an image, a ring in its nose, cowrie
> shells jingling at its ears, with an abominable leer like that of Silenus
> reeling on his ass. It was taking its ease; cosily smoking a pipe, its bowl
> a duodecimo edition of the face of the smoker. This image looked
> sternwards, everlastingly mocking us.[3]

The description is deceptively genial. The imp's leer is more
abominable than Silenus's if he owes what he appears to owe to
Melville's recollection of another figurehead — the one on the
funeral canoe in which a dead chieftain of Typee sat paddling in
effigy:

> Glaring at him forever, and face to face, was a polished human skull,

which crowned the prow of the canoe. The spectral figurehead, reversed in its position, glancing backwards, seemed to mock the im-
patient attitude of the warrior.[4]

Recast in comic form, this is the demon that establishes the
thematic mockery of *Mardi* and that makes of its author almost
literally what Lewis Mumford has called him at this juncture: "a
skeleton facing the world with its ultimate grin." [5]

But another sort of demon was needed to make that mockery dy-
namic, to give it active voice in the philosophical congress assembled in Media's canoe. That need was supplied by Babbalanja's
"demonic inner man," Azzageddi.[6] Azzageddi is a rather late en-
trant in the story, being introduced, like the chorus in Beethoven's
Ninth Symphony, only after the conventional orchestration has
become inadequate to the theme. He is uppermost when "the
moon's at full" — another point of resemblance between Babbalanja and such clowns as Touchstone and Lear's fool. The professional fool was traditionally conceived as "the mouthpiece of a
spirit," either demonic or divine, "a truth-teller whose real insight was thinly disguised as a form of insanity." [7] A certain proportion of Azzageddi's utterances are merely intellectual horse-
play; sometimes, in passages of double-talk, he indulges in the
sheerest nonsense. But always, lurking just beneath the grotesque
comic exterior, one senses his creator's conviction that much madness is divinest sense.[8] "From Azzageddi's mouth," Mumford has
written, "the deepest perceptions of Melville's spirit came forth
first, in the form of jests and demonic laughter." [9] The theme of
madness is prominent in *Mardi*, usually with a disarmingly jocular
effect. But the madness has a point. In Babbalanja's words, "We
madmen are all poets." Vavona was so great a poet that he was
generally considered "but a crack-pated god, not a mortal of
sound mind." And the irrepressible Bardianna, according to his
disciple, confessed that it was to the cracks in his head that he felt
himself "indebted for what little light he had in his brain." [10]

It is at the peak of his madness ("at the full of the moon") that
Babbalanja becomes the mouthpiece for Azzageddi's climactic
utterance, a paradoxical and blood-curdling theory of humor,
which gives us at last some first-hand explanation of the ambiguous comic temper of *Mardi* and its successors. Shorn of its incidental rhetoric, the theory emerges in these terms:

Life is an April day, that both laughs and weeps in a breath. But whoso is wise, laughs when he can. Men fly from a groan, but run to a laugh. . . . Weeds are put off at a fair; no heart bursts but in secret; it is good to laugh, though the laugh be hollow; and wise to make merry, now and for aye. Laugh, and you make friends; weep, and they go. Women sob, and are rid of their grief; men laugh, and retain it. There is laughter in heaven, and laughter in hell. And a deep thought whose language is laughter. Though wisdom be wedded to woe, though the way thereto is by tears, yet all ends in a shout. But wisdom wears no weeds; woe is more merry than mirth; 'tis a shallow grief that is sad. Ha! ha! how demoniacs shout; how all skeletons grin; we all die with a rattle. Laugh! laugh! Are the cherubim grave? Humour, thy laugh is divine; whence, mirth-making idiots have been revered; and therefore may I. Ho! let us be gay, if it be only for an hour, and Death hand us the goblet. . . All sages have laughed — let us; . . . the hyenas grin, the jackals yell — let us.[11]

When Media declines ("No, thank you, Azzageddi, not after that infernal fashion; better weep"), Babbalanja responds with the psychological heart of the concept: "Will you weep? then laugh while you weep. For mirth and sorrow are kin; are published by identical nerves." For Melville, mirth and sorrow were evidently twin products of a heightened sensibility. It is significant that the story's nonintellectual characters, Jarl and Samoa, are portrayed as lacking a sense of humor. Long afterwards, in the last years of his life, when Melville was wading through the works of Schopenhauer, he marked no less than three passages stressing the animalism of gravity.[12] But gravity fused with mirth was quite another thing: it was the most fascinating of the ambiguities he explored in *Mardi*. Early in the book he made specific reference to "the tragico-comico moods which at times overtook" him and which were to become increasingly characteristic of both his lightest and his darkest moments. When, later, he constructed a capsule portrait of his own project in that of the Mardian poet Vavona, he included this very ambiguity as one of its essential qualities: "I will build another world. Therein, let there be kings and slaves, philosophers and wits; whose chequered actions — strange, grotesque, and merry-sad, will entertain my idle moods." [13]

The most extended of *Mardi*'s literary self-portraits is that of Lombardo, author of that problematical epic the "Koztanza," subject of the longest chapter in the book (180) and the only one cast in dramatic form. As the discussion draws to a close, Babba-

lanja depicts the melancholy amusement of the great but neg-
lected poet as he reflects on the uncertainty and futility of the
fame that might come to him a millennium hence.

> *Abrazza* — He was very funny, then, at times?
> *Babbalanja* — Very funny, your highness: amazing jolly! And from
> my nethermost soul, would to Oro, thou couldst but feel one touch of
> that jolly woe! It would appal thee, my Right Worshipful Lord
> Abrazza!
> *Abrazza* (*to Media*) — My dear lord, his teeth are marvellously
> white and sharp; some she-shark must have been his dam: does he often
> grin thus? It was infernal!
> *Media* — Ah! that's Azzageddi.

The emergence of Azzageddi to drive the point home follows a
less diabolical discussion of Lombardo's "abounding humor,"
which is worth citing for an additional factor it suggests in Melville's comic rationale:

> *Mohi* — Doubtless, then, he always wrote with a grin; and none
> laughed louder at his quips, than Lombardo himself.
> *Babbalanja* — . . . Lombardo was a hermit to behold.
> *Media* — What! Did Lombardo laugh with a long face?
> *Babbalanja* — His merriment was not always merriment to him,
> your highness. For the most part his meaning kept him serious. Then
> he was so intensely rivetted to his work, that he could not pause to
> laugh.
> *Mohi* — My word for it, but he had a sly one, now and then.
> *Babbalanja* — For the nonce, he was not his own master; a mere
> amanuensis writing by dictation.

Not only are merriment and melancholy hopelessly mingled, Melville seems to say, but instinctive as well. The notion is clearly
if whimsically defended by Babbalanja when Media rebukes a
paddler who has offended decorum by laughing at one of the
philosopher's tales:

> My lord, he is not to blame. Mark how earnestly he struggles to
> suppress his mirth; but he cannot. It has often been the same with my-
> self. And many a time have I not only vainly sought to check my
> laughter, but at some recitals I have both laughed and cried. But can
> opposite emotions be simultaneous in one being? No, I wanted to
> weep; but my body wanted to smile; and between us we almost
> choked. My lord Media, this man's body laughs; not the man himself.[14]

This is what Babbalanja had meant by his cryptic remark on

Borabolla earlier in the voyage: "Ay, his lungs laugh loud; but is laughing, rejoicing?" And it is certainly what Melville meant in speaking of his own "infirmity of jocularity." Laughter was something not always to be controlled, nor did it have any necessary relation to joy. "We must laugh before we are happy," wrote La Bruyère, "or else we may die before we ever laugh at all"; and Melville checked the remark when he read it nearly fifteen years after undertaking *Mardi*. Through the devils in his book, explicit and implicit, he relieved himself of the sardonic laughter that was pitched beyond the range of conventional titters and guffaws, and found access of sorts to "the essence of things; the mystery that lieth beyond; the elements of the tear which much laughter provoketh." He was discovering the philosophical-psychological range of comedy that was to carry him to the ambiguous core of *Moby-Dick*'s human meaning.

*Part Three*

# CONSUMMATION

# 6

# The Face of Comedy

Like any chartless voyage, *Mardi* shows only a confused understanding of where it has been and where it is going. It was the thankless job of *Redburn* and *White-Jacket* to teach Melville, even as he railed at them,[1] the disciplines he needed to control his expanding conceptions. When he set to work on *Moby-Dick*, he had a chart, a plan that was both ambitious and practical: "To grope down into the bottom of the sea . . . ; to have one's hands among the unspeakable foundations, ribs, and very pelvis of the world; this is a fearful thing. . . But I have swam through libraries and sailed through oceans; I have had to do with whales with these visible hands; I am in earnest; and I will try." [2] Here at last the disparate motions of Melville's unique creative machine were brought into phase: the swimming through libraries and the sailing through oceans. The "groping" is here, as in *Mardi*, but this time it is done with "visible hands." The important change in the artist was not that the poet and metaphysician in him had grown, but that the humorist in him had grown proportionally. If he turned giant in *Moby-Dick*, it was because he had learned how to keep his feet on the ground while his head was in the clouds. He could scarcely have accomplished this without the technical trick of pacing his tragedy with comedy, of making his comedy operable on every level of his complex tale, from its placid, sunny surfaces down to its "very pelvis."

The face of *Moby-Dick*'s comedy is of course its jocular-hedonic aspect. It is the lightest of the book's ingredients and by virtue of that fact provides the buoyancy it needs to keep its ponderous cargo afloat. On the surface *Moby-Dick* sparkles with the rakish laughter of *Omoo*.

I

In the person of Ishmael, Melville once again portrayed himself "in flight from the deadly virtues."[3] Like Long Ghost, Ishmael is frank to "abominate all honourable respectable toils," and is troubled with an impish itch to tweak the nose of authority. He is a sociable sort of fellow whose sense of humor is admirably unimpaired when the joke turns out to be on him.

However, a good laugh is a mighty good thing, and rather too scarce a good thing; the more's the pity. So, if any one man, in his own proper person, afford stuff for a good joke to anybody, let him not be backward, but let him cheerfully allow himself to spend and be spent in that way. And the man that has anything bountifully laughable about him, be sure there is more in that man than you perhaps think for.[4]

By no means all that is in Ishmael is brought out by the simple laughter he provokes; yet from the beginning he spends himself freely for pure amusement and thus firmly establishes himself as a vital and sympathetic character.

He introduces himself with typical Yankee self-ridicule, setting his erstwhile dignity as schoolmaster and aristocrat in ludicrous contrast to his current forecastle status. In the opening action of the story he blossoms into a full-fledged Yankee sucker, not so callow as Redburn, but as comically green in the face of perilous contingencies. The laconic trickster to whom Ishmael plays goat is Peter Coffin, landlord of the Spouter-Inn at New Bedford. As much a stranger to whaling as young Redburn was to the sea at large, Ishmael is easily sold on the idea of sharing a bed with a "dark complexioned" harpooneer and only gradually succumbs to certain vague apprehensions, to the mounting amusement of the landlord — and the reader. The scene in which Peter Coffin hoodwinks him about the peddling of Queequeg's "head" is not a subtle one, but it is constructed with a sure professional touch. The compounded misunderstanding and the exaggerated alternation of furious and icily restrained reactions are devices as old and as new as farce itself. For the landlord the fun does not end until far into the night, when, still grinning happily, he is called by a frantic Ishmael to intercede with the tomahawk-wielding savage who has just leaped into bed with him. The reader, remaining with poor Ishmael in the interim, is in addition privy to all the comic alarms that Peter Coffin can only imagine — alarms that rapidly progress from mere nervous imaginings to a succession of hair-raising realities as Queequeg reveals his barbaric person and his more barbaric religious rites to the stunned Presbyterian in the bed. Such scenes, Weaver has written, "are, for finished humour, among the most competent in the language." [5]

Once Queequeg has revealed the gentleness beneath his horrific exterior, Ishmael ceases to be Peter Coffin's goat and turns to a bit of "skylarking" of his own. In the Try-Pots Inn at Nantucket he rallies the distracted Mrs. Hussey about her menu, promotes a second helping by uttering "the word 'cod' with great emphasis" through the kitchen door, and gulls his savage companion about the presence of a live eel in his soup. When, later, the devout owners of the *Pequod* refuse to sign on Queequeg unless he has been converted, Ishmael presents his tattooed friend as a deacon in the "First Congregational Church" and outfaces their indignant skepticism with a pious lecture on the brotherhood of man.

As parties to Ishmael's sportiveness, all of these lesser characters have, like Peter Coffin, comic qualities to match. Mrs. Hussey emerges from her negligible role with startling memorability. She runs her establishment with forthright masculinity, simplifying her bill of fare for all three meals to two kinds of chowder ("Clam or cod?") and depriving Queequeg of his inseparable harpoon as a precaution against suicide on her premises. When she discovers the harpoon missing in the course of Queequeg's day-long fast and meditation behind locked doors, her practical and humanitarian concerns war in her with a ludicrous alternation ("there goes another counterpane — God pity his poor mother! — it will be the ruin of my house"), and she crisply orders a sign made to eliminate the two principal banes of her professional existence: "No suicides permitted here, and no smoking in the parlor."

Bildad and Peleg, the first of *Moby-Dick*'s several comedy teams, draw laughter from the contrast and interplay of their idiosyncrasies. Both are of the anomalous Nantucket brand of "fighting Quakers," on the one hand given to religious exactitude and the faithful retention of their thee's and thou's, on the

other hand filled with intense commercial practicality and a
rock-hard seamanship. The comic difference between them is
largely one of proportion and emphasis in the distribution of these
qualities. Captain Peleg, a mere grammatical Quaker, is all sailor,
mercurial, profane, and full of whaling; Captain Bildad, "an in-
corrigible old hunks," is a fire-and-brimstone fundamentalist, an
enemy alike to joy and irreverence, an inexorable squeezer of the
last bead of sweat from his men and the last penny of profit from
his enterprises. Bildad, the sort of man who always sits "bolt-up-
right . . . to save his coat tails," dourly suffers his partner's irreverence and even his extravagant tendency to offer sailors a fair
"lay" or share of the profits. Ishmael's inquiry about a berth for
Queequeg fetches a fiscal groan from him ("What lay does he
want?"), yet in his distraction over the savage's evident paganism he ignores Peleg's unprecedented offer of a ninetieth lay and
solemnly commends to the illiterate harpooneer a tract entitled
"The Latter Day Coming; or No Time to Lose." Old Bildad's
characteristic parting sermon to the company of the *Pequod* has
become as well known as anything in the book: ". . . Don't whale
it too much a' Lord's days, men; but don't miss a fair chance,
either, that's rejecting Heaven's good gifts. . ."

Even Queequeg, however sober our respect for him in later
chapters, is at first no more to us than a "head-peddling purple
rascal" with quaint manners. Being still an "undergraduate" in his
Western education, his concept of propriety is nebulous and confused. He begins dressing with his hat (a tall beaver), skips next
to his boots, which modesty constrains him to put on under the
bed, and finally, after much innocent parading before an uncur-
tained window, is persuaded to put on the articles between. His
table manners are just as outrageous, though here, as so often in
*Typee*, Melville contrives by a brilliant twist to turn the laughter
back upon ourselves.

His greatest admirer could not have cordially justified his bringing
his harpoon in to breakfast with him, and using it there without ceremony; reaching over the table with it, to the imminent jeopardy of
many heads, and grappling the beefsteaks towards him. But that was
very coolly done by him, and every one knows that in most people's
estimation, to do anything coolly is to do it genteelly.[6]

Other features of Queequeg's behavior are similar food for light comedy, but the most ridiculous of his antics — the shouldering of his first wheelbarrow, load and all, which he laughingly recounts to Ishmael — touches off a trenchant chapter on the meaning of civilization and is an early indication of Queequeg's penetration to more sober depths in the novel.

After the sailing of the *Pequod* on its subtly modulated version of the "philosophic voyage," the dominant note of farce disappears, though less abruptly than in *Mardi*, and the jocular element tends to focus in a single Falstaffian characterization. The second mate, Stubb, becomes Melville's appointed clown aboard the *Pequod*, providing most of the comic ballast to the tragic intensity of Ahab. As such he has many roles. One of these is to serve as a convenient outlet for some of Melville's incidental whimsies, such as the grisly conjecture that the little round squid bones in the bowels of the whale might be "sailors' trowsers buttons," or the notion that, because of the web-like articulation of his four-fingered fins, the whale "can never be truly said to handle us without mittens." In a more independent vein Stubb resembles nothing so much as the tough, wise-cracking army sergeant of contemporary magazine and screen fiction, big-hearted but full of coarse sport, and insensitive alike to danger, propriety, and the nuances of other people's feelings. This brand of comic realism, so important yet so casually achieved, gives the narrative some of its most relaxed moments of pure and almost extraneous fun.

Typical of these moments and of Stubb's part in the proceedings is the *Pequod*'s pursuit of an unusually aged and decrepit whale in competition with the boats of the German whaler *Jungfrau*. Stubb is quick to note the "strange subterranean commotions" in their hobbled quarry, "causing the waters behind him to upbubble," and calls out, "Who's got some paragoric? . . . He has the stomach-ache, I'm afraid. Lord, think of having half an acre of stomach-ache! Adverse winds are holding mad Christmas in him, boys. It's the first foul wind I ever knew to blow from astern. . ." Racing to beat the Germans to the game, he urges his men on with his customary line of humorous patter: "Come, why don't some of ye burst a blood-vessel? Who's that been dropping an anchor overboard — we don't budge an inch — we're becalmed. Halloo, here's grass growing in the boat's bottom — and by the Lord, the mast there's budding. This won't do, boys. . ."

When finally his harpoon is fast and the Germans are dumped into the sea in the melee, he calls back at them — in the G.I. spirit, despite his antique idiom — "Don't be afraid, my butter-boxes . . . ye'll be picked up presently — all right — I saw some sharks astern — St. Bernard's dogs, you know — relieve distressed travellers. . . Hurrah! Here we go like three tin kettles at the tail of a mad cougar!" [7]

With his subordinates Stubb is all top-sergeant, and woe to the foolish, the cowardly, and the incompetent. Dough-Boy, the timorous steward, earns a blow and a truly stimulating tirade when he serves up ginger instead of grog, and when the hapless cabin boy causes his crew to miss a whale, it is Stubb who "cursed Pip officially." To complete Stubb's resemblance to the familiar barracks hero, he is what would now be called a "big operator," a slick promoter of the faintly illegitimate advantage. His most spectacular achievement is the cozening of a rival ship, the *Bouton de Rose*, in possession of a blasted whale, worthless for oil but almost certain to contain a goodly deposit of ambergris impacted in its bowels. Stubb adroitly "diddles" the French captain and his English mate and "benevolently" makes off with the rich, if pestilential, carcass. The deception is carried off, it has been well observed, "with the mind and tongue of Autolycus himself." [8]

2

An inevitable comic feature of both Stubb and Ishmael is their elaborate interest in food. Stubb's great hour upon the stage is the occasion of the midnight supper in Chapter 64, when he mercilessly baits the cook about his whale-steak and proposes a classic formula for its preparation: "Hold the steak in one hand and show a live coal to it with the other; that done, dish it." Stubb is what Ishmael calls an "unprejudiced" eater. As for himself, Ishmael speaks "reverentially" of broiled fowl, is rhapsodic about chowders, and nearly succumbs to the "plum-pudding" cut of whale; but on the whole he feels that "to sit down before a meat-pie nearly one hundred feet long . . . takes away your appetite." It is mostly through Ishmael, in his moments of earthy jocularity, that philosophy, theology, and sentiment are all, at one time or another, condemned as bad for the digestion. He is indistinguishable from the wry jester of *Typee* and *Omoo* when he describes the fare aboard the *Samuel Enderby*:

> The beef was fine — tough, but with body in it. They said it was bull-beef; others, that it was dromedary beef; but I do not know, for certain, how that was. They had dumplings, too; small, but substantial, symmetrically globular, and indestructible dumplings. I fancied that you could feel them, and roll them about in you after they were swallowed. If you stooped over too far forward, you risked their pitching out of you like billiard-balls. The bread — but that couldn't be helped; besides, it was an anti-scorbutic; in short, the bread contained the only fresh fare they had. But the forecastle was not very light, and it was very easy to step over into a dark corner when you ate it.

This account is followed by a burlesque treatise on the logistics of the Dutch whaling industry, making the most of the 400,000 pounds of beef and the 10,800 barrels of beer and so on that reportedly sustained and lubricated the whaling fleet of Holland.[9]

Here, as always, the subject of drinking goes hand-in-hand with that of eating, though there is not much of either spoken of aboard the *Pequod* itself. Large reserves of joy were not indigenous to her hold. True, there was grog in her, with which Stubb replaced the invidious "ginger-jub" sent aboard by Captain Bildad's teetotaling Aunt Charity. But the flask is a source of comedy largely and perhaps significantly divorced from Ahab's doomed ship. Stubb merely dreams wistfully of "old Orleans whiskey, or old Ohio, or unspeakable old Monongahela!" and Ishmael bemoans the *Pequod*'s lack of a crow's nest with its "faithful friend and comforter . . . that well replenished little case-bottle." There is plenty of alcoholic merriment on other ships, however, as Ishmael recalls with relish from an earlier visit to the *Samuel Enderby*.

> Flip? Did I say we had flip? Yes, and we flipped it at the rate of ten gallons the hour; and when the squall came (for it's squally off there by Patagonia), and all hands — visitors and all — were called to reef topsails, we were so top-heavy that we had to swing each other aloft in bowlines; and we ignorantly furled the skirts of our jackets into the sails, so that we hung there, reefed fast in the howling gale, a warning example to all drunken tars. However, the masts did not go overboard; and by and by we scrambled down, so sober, that we had to pass the flip again, though the savage salt spray bursting down the forecastle scuttle, rather too much diluted and pickled it to my taste.[10]

The companion theme of sex also figures prominently in *Moby-Dick*'s comedy, but elevated to a poetic utility that removes it from the merely jocular. It is worth noting, however, that Melville's masculine bias reveals itself here in an occasional scatalogical joke. In the main, this type of joke is accounted for by the nature of his subject. No fact about the whale is overlooked in this book, not even his most inglorious function, occasionally observable in the heat of the chase. Then, too, there is the phenomenon of ambergris, resulting from a disorder in the whale which Melville terms, with a delicate inaccuracy, "dyspepsia." His observation on that condition is in no worse taste (and a great deal funnier) than the story of Dr. Cuticle's "pudding" in *White-Jacket*: "How to cure such a dyspepsia were hard to say, unless by administering three or four boat loads of Brandreth's pills, and then running out of harm's way, as laborers do in blasting rocks." On the other hand, the first instance of this kind of humor in the book is called forth by no more compelling circumstances than his own Rabelaisian nature and a paradoxical concept of "winds" that must always have been fair comic game in the forecastles of windjammers. Recalling to mind the ancient injunction of Pythagoras "to abstain from beans because they are flatulent," Melville remarks that "in this world, head winds are far more prevalent than winds from astern (that is, if you never violate the Pythagorean maxim) . . ." [11] This is the civilized version of the "uncivilized laughter" of whalemen.

### 3

Such laughter is only another aspect of the pervasive Yankeeism of Melville's humor, which through *Redburn* and *White-Jacket* had come to reassert itself firmly over the alien intrusions of *Mardi*. Not infrequently, of course, the comic idiom betrays its Mardian adolescence. The "Etymology" and "Extracts" preceding the novel are distinctly Rabelaisian. In the story itself the Rabelaisian mannerisms with which Melville had been so infatuated in *Mardi* are barely discernible, so well are they controlled and so wisely used. Such redundant grotesqueries as the listing of races encountered in a whaling port or the catalog of obscure species of whales are carried just to, but not beyond, the point of diminishing returns. From his reading of Laurence Sterne, an intermediate disciple of Rabelais, just prior to the writing of *Moby-Dick*,[12] Melville was probably led to the extensive use of such characteristic Shandian tricks as carrying on ventriloquistic conversations with the reader and indulging in certain typographical whimsicalities. Already widely recognized is *Moby-Dick*'s indebtedness to *Sartor Resartus*, particularly in the "exaggerated facetiousness of quoting from imaginary authors." [13] Depending on the subject at hand, William Scoresby, Jr., whose *Account of the Arctic Regions* (1820) was one of Melville's source books, is parodied in a number of grotesque guises, all bearing a lineal relationship to Professor Diogenes Teufelsdröckh of Weissnichtwo.

In the main, however, *Moby-Dick* is a folk-epic, a kind of national prose-symphony, and the humorous idiom of the American frontier is one of the major keys in which it is composed.[14] It crops out everywhere in the talk of the seamen. Steelkilt, the Lakeman in the interpolated story of the *Town-Ho*, is a textbook example of the folk-hero.[15] Witness his "gay banterings" of Radney, the ugly and spiteful mate, whose uncommon concern about a leak in the hull has led to a belief that he has money tied up in her:

> Aye, aye, my merry lads, it's a lively leak this; hold a cannikin, one of ye, and let's have a taste. By the Lord, it's worth bottling! I tell ye what, men, old Rad's investment must go for it! He had best cut away his part of the hull and tow it home. The fact is, boys, that swordfish only began the job; he's come back again with a gang of ship-carpenters, saw-fish, and file-fish, and what not; and the whole posse of 'em are now hard at work cutting and slashing at the bottom; making improvements, I suppose. If old Rad were here now [he is and Steelkilt knows it], I'd tell him to jump overboard and scatter 'em. They're playing the devil with his estate, I can tell him. But he's a simple old soul, — Rad, and a beauty too. Boys, they say the rest of his property is invested in looking-glasses. I wonder if he'd give a poor devil like me the model of his nose.[16]

Stubb's running banter with his crew is full of frontier brashness and hyperbole; his "diddling" of the *Bouton de Rose* reveals at least as much Yankee peddler as Autolycus in him; and his tall-talk concerning Fedallah, whom he suspects of being the devil, is redolent of Western boastfulness and fantasy:

". . . I'll just take him by the nape of his neck, and say — Look here, Beelzebub, you don't do it; and if he makes any fuss, by the Lord I'll make a grab into his pocket for his tail, take it to the capstan, and give him such a wrenching and heaving, that his tail will come short off at the stump — do you see; and then, I rather guess when he finds himself docked in that queer fashion, he'll sneak off without the poor satisfaction of feeling his tail between his legs."

"And what will you do with the tail, Stubb?"

"Do with it? Sell it for an ox whip when we get home; — what else?" [17]

Oddy enough, the tall-tale crown in *Moby-Dick* goes to the English surgeon of the *Samuel Enderby*, but the story he tells of a patient who swallowed a jack-knife and later "heaved it up in small tacks" is just as paralyzing in its Yankee audacity as Dr. Cuticle's yarn about the bullet that went completely around a man's neck and shot the next man in line.

But the native humor in *Moby-Dick* is not merely quaint. It has a hard head, a quick eye, and a sharp tooth for pretense. In its quiet way it is typically at work in this picture of a visiting whaling captain in his small-boat, where, "having no place to sit in, [he] is pulled off to his visit all standing like a pine tree."

And often you will notice that being conscious of the eyes of the whole visible world resting on him from the sides of the two ships, this standing captain is all alive to the importance of sustaining his dignity by maintaining his legs. Nor is this any very easy matter; for in his rear is the immense projecting steering oar hitting him now and then in the small of his back, the after-oar reciprocating by rapping his knees in front. He is thus completely wedged before and behind, and can only expand himself sideways by settling down on his stretched legs; but a sudden, violent pitch of the boat will often go far to topple him, because length of foundation is nothing without corresponding breadth. Merely make a spread angle of two poles, and you cannot stand them up. Then, again, it would never do in plain sight of the world's riveted eyes, it would never do, I say, for this straddling captain to be seen steadying himself the slightest particle by catching hold of anything with his hands; indeed, as token of his entire, buoyant self-command, he generally carries his hands in his trowsers' pockets; but perhaps being generally very large, heavy hands, he carries them there for ballast. Nevertheless there have occurred instances, well authenticated ones too, where the captain has been known for an uncommonly critical moment or two, in a sudden squall say — to seize hold of the nearest oarsman's hair, and hold on there like grim death. [18]

At its best, it is a homely, low-keyed humor that gains force as well as charm from the rare ability to laugh at itself. The very New England reserve that gave it its dryness is repeatedly victimized by it. When Ishmael descends to his first breakfast among whalemen at New Bedford, expecting much talk of high adventure, he is met instead with a deep and "embarrassed" silence, though "here were a set of sea-dogs, many of whom without the slightest bashfulness had boarded great whales on the high seas — entire strangers to them — and duelled them dead without winking." It is the same "shyness" that, he tells us later, is apt to come between English and American crews when they meet on the sea: "for your Englishman is rather reserved, and your Yankee, he does not fancy that sort of thing in anybody but himself." Even Melville's pride in being a Yankee whaleman was sufficiently secure not to be solemn about itself. The chapters (24, 25, 82) on what one of them calls "The Honor and Glory of Whaling" are three of the funniest chapters in the book.

Thus the Yankee spirit materially helped Melville to maintain the sense of proportion which he had too often lost in his first published encounter with the difficult problems of metaphysical allegory. Native American humor is sly, crotchety, disenchanted, and essentially inimical to "flummery" of the sort that fatally blemished *Mardi*. In *Moby-Dick* its realistic touch — more precisely, its anti-romantic touch — is not only instantly observable in Ishmael as in the narrator of the earlier story, but maintained throughout the voyage of the *Pequod* to a degree unknown to Media's war canoe. It is perhaps impossible to determine whether or to what extent this sustained use of the comic corrective was intentional or reflexive. We know that *Moby-Dick* was a result of the most productive tension in Melville's artistic career — the tension between the subjective orientation of *Mardi* and the objective orientation of his other four books.[19] What we do not know is whether the experience of *Mardi* had taught Melville the conscious lesson that Meredith teaches in *The Ordeal of Richard Feverel*: "Mournful you call it? Well! all Wisdom is mournful. 'Tis therefore, coz, that the Wise do love the Comic Muse. Their own high food would kill them." [20] We can guess, though, that the lesson was at least in the back of his mind, for Meredith's words seem only a less figurative statement of the revelation that

came to Ishmael out of his nightmare experience at the tiller
behind the *Pequod*'s lurid try-works: "Give not thyself up, then,
to fire, lest it invert thee, deaden thee; as for the time it did me.
There is a wisdom that is woe; but there is a woe that is madness." [21]

Elsewhere Ishmael elaborates on this Meredithian psychology
in more apposite terms, even to the "food" metaphor, though he
ostensibly applies it to Ahab's willingness to dally with the pursuit of lesser whales than the object of his consuming passion:

> In times of strong emotion mankind disdain all base considerations;
> but such times are evanescent. The permanent constitutional condition
> of the manufactured man, thought Ahab, is sordidness. Granting that
> the White Whale fully incites the hearts of this my savage crew, and
> playing round their savageness even breeds a certain generous knight-
> errantness in them, still, while for the love of it they give chase to
> Moby-Dick, they must also have food for their more common, daily
> appetites. For even the high lifted and chivalric Crusaders of old times
> were not content to traverse two thousand miles of land to fight for
> their holy sepulchre, without committing burglaries, picking pockets,
> and gaining other pious perquisites by the way. Had they been strictly
> held to their one final and romantic object — that final and romantic
> object, too many would have turned from in disgust.[22]

It may be a dubious business to claim an allegory of the artist in
addition to the multifarious allegories already claimed for *Moby-
Dick*. But the passage in question appears suggestively in a chapter entitled "Surmises," and we may at least surmise that Melville,
like Ahab, had schooled himself to compromise his "mighty theme"
to the extent of granting his followers a salutary allowance of
"pious perquisites by the way." [23]

# 7

# Linked Analogies

To scratch the surface of *Moby-Dick* is to find beneath its decorative layer of comic "perquisites" a teeming substratum of metaphysical humor. What Melville had attempted in *Mardi* he accomplished here with a surer artistry — the vertical multiplication of meaning by a poetic principle which Ahab himself perfectly defines: "O Nature, and O soul of man! how far beyond all utterance are your linked analogies! not the smallest atom stirs or lives on matter, but has its cunning duplicate in mind." [1] The role of the comic spirit in this pattern of "linked analogies" may be understood in terms of one of the novel's profoundest symbols, the weaving of the sword-mat in Chapter 47. Though intended explicitly to illuminate the interaction of "chance, free-will, and necessity," this passage, like the chapter on "Surmises," is also a parable of the creative process. Humor was, by both choice and necessity, woven into the fabric of *Moby-Dick*; and the comic threads are as vital as the tragic ones to the rich suggestiveness of the story, to the multiplication of its pleasures and meanings — in short, to the poetic and ideological embellishment of the book. This is the imaginative-critical phase of its comedy.

I

Melville's comic conceits in *Moby-Dick* come in all sizes and shapes, in little spots of color as well as in larger patterns. Occasionally Melville throws in a conceit as a simple joke, in the same manner and spirit that accounts for a good deal of his punning: "At some old gable-roofed country houses you will see brass whales hung by the tail for knockers to the road-side door. When the porter is sleepy, the anvil-headed whale would be best." Sometimes he uses them for sheer pictorial effect, like an imagist poet: "His jets are erect, full, and black like soot; so that from so abounding a smoke in the chimney, you would think there must be a brave supper cooking in the great bowels below." Frequently they are ironical. He was fascinated by the whale's unwitting contributions to his own destruction and delighted in quips about eating him "by his own light," burning him "by his own body," and so on. At their best Melville's conceits brilliantly illuminate both objects of comparison. Not only the behavior of ships, but the behavior of the human types to which they are compared, is sharply caught in the passage contrasting the habits of other branches of the maritime family with those of the "godly, honest, unostentatious, hospitable, sociable, free-and-easy whaler":

Merchant ships . . . crossing each other's wake in the mid-Atlantic, will oftentimes pass on without so much as a single word of recognition, mutually cutting each other on the high seas, like a brace of dandies in Broadway: and all the time indulging, perhaps, in finical criticism upon each other's rig. As for Men-of-War, when they chance to meet at sea, they first go through such a string of silly bowings and scrapings, such a ducking of ensigns, that there does not seem to be much right-down hearty good-will and brotherly love about it at all.[2]

From the standpoint of imaginative technique nothing is so remarkable about Melville's conceits as their characteristic way of bridging the gap between the real and the ideal. He may work from abstract to concrete, as in telling the reader of a passage on the whale's skull to "carry it in your mind, or under your arm, as we proceed. . ." Or the direction may be from concrete to abstract, as in the description of the *Pequod* when the contents of her hold are piled high on deck: "Top-heavy . . . as a dinnerless student with all Aristotle in his head." Sometimes Melville strikes a perfect balance and we suddenly know all that mortal man can hope to learn, for example, about the smoke from a whale ship's try-works: "It smells like the left wing of the day of judgment." Such conceits are certainly metaphysical, in the sense that we apply the term to Donne's wit, but as Matthiessen has remarked, they "may well be nearer the fantasies of frontier humor."[3] The homelier the comparison, the nearer they are. In another place

Melville describes the smell of stored blubber — "somewhat similar to that arising from excavating an old city graveyard, for the foundations of a Lying-in Hospital."

The tang of frontier fantasy is distinct in *Moby-Dick*'s most spectacular conceit. Under the sober title of "The Cassock," Chapter 95 deals with the great phallus or "grandissimus" of the bull whale, "longer than a Kentuckian is tall, nigh a foot in diameter at the base, and jet-black as Yojo, the ebony idol of Queequeg." Its cylindrical pelt is dried and stretched by the "mincer" into a kind of tubular smock to protect him as he goes about his work of mincing the blubber into thin slices or "bible leaves" for the try-pots. As the short chapter comes to its end and "the mincer now stands before you invested in the full canonicals of his calling," the reader is suddenly staggered with the full-blown analogy that Melville has been so slyly constructing : "Arrayed in decent black; occupying a conspicuous pulpit; intent on bible leaves; what a candidate for an archbishoprick, what a lad for Pope were this mincer!"

2

A larger pattern of comic analogy appears in Melville's treatment of the whale in general, which is primarily humorous and richly figurative. What Howard P. Vincent has called the "cetological center" of the book is a gigantic zoological lark in which information, poetry, and jest are almost indistinguishably mixed. Cetology being the murky science it was in Melville's day, it no doubt "pleased his sense of humor" to play "the amateur mockingly attempting what the experts had bungled. . ."[4] In this light, the comedy of his initial whale chapter (32), with its division of species into "books," "folios," and "chapters," is largely that of parody. But what translates his treatment of the whale — and with it a substantial portion of the book — into comic mythology is the basic animal–man metaphor, which is one of the oldest figures in the world's folklore.

The mock-scientific tone of the "Cetology" chapter is set by such devices as enthroning the sperm whale as "monarch of the seas" in place of the "deposed" Greenland whale, and deporting from the "Kingdom of Cetology" the Lamatins and Dugongs, "a noisy, contemptible set, mostly lurking in the mouths of rivers, and feeding on wet hay. . ." The formal description of species proceeds with what Mumford has well called "Olympian levity," [5] resulting less in a collection of biological types than in a gallery of personalities: now one with "an everlasting Mephistophelean grin" and a fin "like a Roman nose," now one with "a neat and gentleman-like figure, . . . a lovely tail, and sentimental Indian eyes of a hazel hue." Observable facts are consistently reported in this figurative idiom. The thrasher whale, for instance, mounts a larger whale's back and "works his passage by flogging him; as some schoolmasters get along in the world by a similar process." And the many occult phenomena, far from giving Melville pause, merely move him to more outrageous burlesque, as in the suggestion that the eccentric tusk of the Narwhale, which gives him "the aspect of a clumsy left-handed man . . . would certainly be convenient to him for a folder in reading pamphlets."

Thus established, the whale–man metaphor recurs throughout the book as a comic leitmotif, except in the case of Moby-Dick himself, where it becomes whale–supraman and ceases to be comic. Representative, from its punning title on, is Chapter 88, "Schools and Schoolmasters," which plays with the social and domestic mores of the whale. Two types of school are distinguished in these terms: one "like a mob of young collegians . . . full of fight, fun, and wickedness, tumbling round the world at such a reckless, rollicking rate, that no prudent underwriter would insure them"; the other a "harem," presided over by one "luxurious Ottoman." The "ladies" are pictured as "comparatively delicate . . . not to exceed half a dozen yards around the waist," and the seasonal movements of these families are likened to those of "fashionables . . . for ever on the move in leisurely search of variety." It is in these domestic descriptions of whales that Melville uses the sexual comedy formerly reserved for his human characters. What he found in his sources as flat fact — that whales "couple *more hominum*" — the comic artist converted into a biological jape: "When overflowing with mutual esteem, the whales salute *more hominum*." [6] One such passage is especially notable for its subtle parody of Jaques' "seven ages" speech in *As You Like It* and for its almost verbatim anticipation, at the last, of the behavior of Kipling's Moti-Guj at the pickets:

Like certain other omnivorous roving lovers that might be named, my Lord Whale has no taste for the nursery, however much for the bower; and so, being a great traveller, he leaves his anonymous babies all over the world; every baby an exotic. In good time, nevertheless, as the ardor of youth declines; as years and dumps increase; as reflection lends her solemn pauses; in short, as a general lassitude overtakes the sated Turk; then a love of ease and virtue supplants the love for maidens; our Ottoman enters upon the impotent, repentant, admonitory stage of life, forswears, disbands the harem, and grown to an exemplary, sulky old soul, goes about all alone among the meridians and parallels saying his prayers, and warning each young Leviathan from his amorous errors.[7]

Even the somber plot of *Moby-Dick* itself is parodied in this pervasive comic metaphor. A kind of Gilbert and Sullivan commodore boasts the defiance of Ahab and is promptly stove "by a portly sperm whale, that begged a few moments' confidential business with him. . . I tell you, the sperm whale will stand no nonsense." [8]

### 3

Melville made good use of this figurative comedy for satire, too. *Moby-Dick*'s targets, like *Mardi*'s, are chiefly social, political, and religious; but even the few miscellaneous subjects attacked cannot seem entirely unfamiliar to those who have read the earlier book.

Melville's running quarrel with "civilization" dates back to the opening pages of *Typee*, and *Moby-Dick* bears witness to his unabated Rousseauism. Fine artistry is pronounced "full of barbaric spirit" and attributed with whimsical impartiality to the "sailor-savage," the "Greek savage," and the "Dutch savage." [9] Fine ethics are attributed with less impartiality to the cannibal, who stands in repeated contrast to the man-of-the-world. A "provident Feegee" is given a better chance at heaven for having "salted down a lean missionary in his cellar against a coming famine" than the gourmand who must have goose livers for his *pâté de foie gras* or the humanitarian who uses quills to publicize the "Society for the Suppression of Cruelty to Ganders." [10] Queequeg ("George Washington cannibalistically developed") is a standing satire on civilization. In the chapter called "Wheelbarrow" his function becomes explicit in the comparison he draws between his own trifling *faux pas* in Sag Harbor and a white captain's ghastlier *faux pas* at a native banquet, and in the revealing action that follows on the river boat between him and the complacent booby who mocks him and then is rescued by him. It was the underdog who interested Melville, and much of the incidental satire in *Moby-Dick* is a coalition of humor and poetry in his defense. Melville's comic villain is likely to be a "Dives, in his red silken wrapper — (he had a redder one afterwards)," and his comic hero a "Lazarus . . . chattering his teeth against the curbstone for a pillow," helpless before the winds of winter though he "plug up both ears with rags, and put a corn-cob into his mouth." [11]

The political satire is simply an extension of this basic social atttitude. The philosophy of law and the entire course of human events are brilliantly stripped to the black-and-white issue of Fast-Fish versus Loose-Fish, "a system which for terse comprehensiveness surpasses Justinian's Pandects and the By-laws of the Chinese Society for the Suppression of Meddling with other People's Business." Once fired off, the figure has the self-sustaining vitality of a chain reaction and demolishes a score of targets from the pauper's mortgage to the annexation of Texas before burning itself out in the puckish query, "And what are you, reader, but a Loose-Fish and a Fast-Fish, too?" [12] Crowned heads continue their susceptibility to Melville's satiric conceits. Reflecting that "a king's head is solemnly oiled at his coronation, even as a head of salad," he wonders further whether "they anoint it with a view of making its interior run well, as they anoint machinery?" And the ancient English law preëmpting for the king the heads of all whales taken in his territorial waters suggests to him a similar division of the royal sturgeon, "the King receiving the highly dense and elastic head peculiar to that fish, which, symbolically regarded, may possibly be humorously grounded upon some presumed congeniality." [13]

Religion, however, is the dominant subject of satire in *Moby-Dick*, as in *Mardi*, and one closely related to the central theme of the novel. The attack ranges widely through religious practice and ideology and is frequently infused with Melville's peculiar brand of comic diabolism.[14] But it is preserved from nihilism by the positive sublimity of Father Mapple's sermon (Chapter 9),[15] and surely

> *. . . points at no defect*
> *But what all mortals may correct.*

Chapter 83, "Jonah Historically Regarded," pokes fun at literal exegesis of the Biblical myth upon which Father Mapple had based his moving spiritual lesson. Melville's comic method is clear, sure-footed, and very funny: a Twainish inversion by which the palpable common sense of a Sag Harbor whaleman is defeated at every turn by the specious rationalizations of the theologians. Another attack upon the "reverend clergy," a description of the whale skeleton used as a chapel in the "Arsacides," is more typical of Melville's lushly figurative method.

Now, when with royal Tranquo I visited this wondrous whale, and saw the skull an altar, and the artificial smoke ascending from where the real jet had issued, I marvelled . . . that the priests should swear that smoky jet of his was genuine. . . . I saw no living thing within; naught was there but bones.

Cutting me a green measuring rod, I once more dived within the skeleton. From their arrow-slit in the skull, the priests perceived me taking the altitude of the final rib. "How now!" they shouted; "Dar'st thou measure this our god! That's for us." "Aye, priests — well, how long do ye make him, then?" But hereupon a fierce contest rose among them, concerning feet and inches; they cracked each other's sconces with their yard-sticks — the great skull echoed — and seizing that lucky chance, I quickly concluded my own admeasurements.[16]

More broadly philosophical and more richly humorous are the chapters detailing the attempted conversions of Queequeg and the sharks. Nowhere does Melville so strikingly anticipate Twain as in the account of Ishmael's adjustment to the benighted tenets of his savage friend. Though "born and bred in the bosom of the infallible Presbyterian church," Ishmael outgrows his comic ortho- doxy in the expanding belief that "Presbyterians and Pagans alike . . . are all somehow dreadfully cracked about the head, and sadly need mending." [17] What indignation remains in him concerning Queequeg's practices is purely secular and condemns together "all these Lents, Ramadans, and prolonged ham-squat- tings in cold, cheerless rooms." *Moby-Dick* is rich in comic epi- grams, and one of the choicest is Ishmael's conclusion that "hell

is an idea first born on an undigested apple-dumpling." In the
end, it is the ultimate refinement of Melville's early castigation of
the missionaries that emerges in Queequeg's unregenerate "pity
that such a sensible young man should be so hopelessly lost to
evangelical pagan piety." But beyond that, as Mattheissen has seen,
Melville's sense of the ironic disparity between fact and appearance matured in Ishmael's discovery of the meaning of Christian
brotherhood through his friendship with a tattooed pagan.[18]

On the other hand, a more negative indictment of the Christian
ministry is achieved in the cook's famous sermon to the sharks in
Chapter 64. Beneath the raw frontier jocularity of its idiom is the
full flower of *Mardi*'s involuted demonic comedy. The metaphor
of the shark-congregation, unheeding in its beastly midnight orgy
before its ineffectual priest and his cynical bishop, is only one
figure in a remarkable literary arabesque. Even more ironic is the
commentary expressed in the relationships between Stubb, the
whale he has killed and is now devouring with such shark-like
voracity, and the truculent black cook whom he bedevils to the
point of recognizing that Stubb is "more of shark den Massa
Shark hisself."

Of the lesser satiric sallies in *Moby-Dick*,[19] a brief fling at the
dreamy optimism of transcendental thought is most brilliantly revealing of Melville's growth in metaphoric power. Without ulterior motive, he had written in *Omoo* of a ship-rat that had died
a "luscious death" in a can of molasses, and later, in *Mardi*, of a
"deceased insect" fished out of a last, precious keg of fresh water
in mid-Pacific. In *Moby-Dick* he constructed a similar comic incident on a much larger scale. While "baling the case" — dipping
the prime oil out of the great well in the whale's head — Tashtego
falls in and is rescued by Queequeg, who dives into the sea with
his sword, makes an incision under water at the right spot, and
draws the Indian forth by his "great skill in obstetrics." "As for
the great head itself," Melville facetiously adds, "that was doing
as well as could be expected." The satiric overtones are implicit in
his final reflection:

Now, had Tashtego perished in that head, it had been a very precious
perishing; smothered in the very whitest and daintiest of fragrant
spermaceti; coffined, hearsed, and tombed in the secret inner chamber
and sanctum sanctorum of the whale. Only one sweeter end can readily

be recalled — the delicious death of an Ohio honey-hunter, who seeking honey in the crotch of a hollow tree, found such exceeding store of it, that leaning too far over, it sucked him in, so that he died embalmed. How many, think ye, have likewise fallen into Plato's honey head, and sweetly perished there?[20]

By the time he has finished with the episode Melville has no less than five themes going in perfect counterpoint: the circumstantial adventure, the exposition of the process of "baling," the humorous obstetrical conceit, the symbolic concept of rebirth (a recurrent theme in *Moby-Dick*), and the satire on transcendentalism. A single comic idea had come a long way from the rat in the molasses in *Omoo* and the bug in the water in *Mardi*.

4

Of all the contributions of humor to the poetic suggestiveness of *Moby-Dick*, the most significant is the complex network of puns which is woven into the story. In this greatest of Melville's books the curious correlation already noted between artistic reach and the incidence of puns is strikingly reaffirmed. Just as *Mardi* contained more puns than all four of the less ambitious works surrounding it, so *Moby-Dick* contains more of them than all five of its predecessors.[21] Thus, by an almost geometric progression, Melville applied the least honored of comic devices in expanding the metaphoric range of his art. Even in their baldest form of low-Shakespearean word-juggling, *Moby-Dick*'s puns reveal the climactic creative exuberance of their maker. The "visions," as he called them in one of his punning letters to Duyckinck in the summer of 1850, often came so "thick" that they burst out of him in volleys, and we get clumps of two, three, and as many as five verbal changes on a single idea.[22] At their most interesting, of course, these puns are of the metaphysical type with which he had begun to experiment in *Mardi*. As such, they tend to be implicit, defying any objective demonstration that Melville was punning at all; and they tend to lose their native comedy in the darkness of profound contexts.

Eight of the most somber and intriguing metaphysical puns in *Moby-Dick* pertain directly to Ahab and the meaning of his quest. The first occurs in Ahab's soliloquy following the "Quarter-

Deck" scene in which he has outfaced his crew and proved himself
their "match": "Like so many ant-hills of powder, they all stand
before me; and I their match." The remark that he "sleeps with
clenched hands; and wakes with his own bloody nails in his palms"
is almost certainly intended as a symbol of Ahab's self-cruci-
fixion. Similarly, Ahab's antagonism to God is reflected in Stubb's
remark on the extent of his captain's injury: "I never yet saw
him kneel." [23] There is a probable pun on "vice" in Ahab's exchange with the carpenter about the "pinch" and "grip" of his
tool; and Ahab certainly induces an ironic pun in forcing the carpenter's explanation that "faith" is "only a sort of exclamation-
like." [24] In Chapter 119, in which the corposants or lightning balls
play on the tips of the *Pequod*'s masts, the title, "The Candles,"
as well as a reference to the "trinity" of flames, gives the fire-
symbols a sacred implication, though the context makes them profane. Starbuck unquestionably intends the two puns he makes
with reference to Ahab — or his author intends them for him.
During the storm that caused the corposants Ahab's boat is
smashed in, and Starbuck grimly points out to Stubb that the
point of damage is precisely "where he is wont to stand — his
stand-point is stove, man!" And shortly thereafter Starbuck
makes explicit the meaning of Ahab's wanton destruction of his
instrument of navigation: "Has he not dashed his heavenly
quadrant?" Finally, Pip puns as he soliloquizes in Ahab's cabin
after the old man has rejected his redeeming love and has gone
on deck to tap nervously back and forth overhead: "Oh, master!
master! I am indeed downhearted when you walk over me." [25]

Two more puns of this type, though not directly related to
Ahab, provide even more striking evidence of the subtle linguistic virtuosity Melville had achieved in long anticipation of Joyce.
One of these is implicit in Ishmael's superficially humorous act
of making his will and locking it in his sea-chest after a particularly
harrowing chase. The safeguarding of the "will" within the
"chest" is of course capable of a double construction that hardly
needs explication. [26] The other is the pun with which Melville
concluded the episode of the skeleton-chapel in the Arsacides.
Having explored Tranquo's whale skeleton, both literally and
figuratively, from one end to the other, he comes at last to this
final paragraph on the great tapering spine, once more poetically

suggesting the fundamental figure of the church by way of preparing for the deceptively simple turn at the end:

There are forty and odd vertebrae in all, which in the skeleton are not locked together. They mostly lie like the great knobbed blocks on a Gothic spire, forming solid courses of heavy masonry. The largest, a middle one, is in width something less than three feet, and in depth more than four. The smallest, where the spine tapers away into the tail, is only two inches in width, and looks something like a white billiard ball. I was told that there were still smaller ones, but that they had been lost by some little cannibal urchins, the priest's children, who had stolen them to play marbles with. Thus we see how that the spine of even the hugest of living things tapers off at last into simple child's play.[27]

As an ordinary pun, "child's play" is good enough, neatly combining the two meanings (all that can be decently expected of a pun) of literal play by children and the common figurative equivalent of easy apprehension. What makes it so potently metaphysical is Melville's ability to endow it with a third level of meaning — the child-like simplicity of true religious faith. It is such extensions of comic technique, at once brilliantly imaginative and profoundly critical, that help to give the "linked analogies" of *Moby-Dick* their classic inexhaustibility.

# 8

# The Comic Vision

If comedy contributes to ambiguity of meaning in *Moby-Dick*, it contributes no less vitally to the ambiguities of attitude from which the ideas inherent in the story are viewed. Ideas are philosophical; attitudes, psychological. Hence the label I have assigned to the third major category of Melvillian comedy, the philosophical-psychological. The ideas it is concerned with are ideas of value, questions of distinction that were becoming more and more absorbing to Melville's skeptical intelligence. What was the truth about the qualities conventionally defined as merriment and gravity, madness and sanity, good and evil? In each case, he had decided once and for all in *Mardi*, the "question is more final than any answer." Circumstance and point of view are the only determinants with meaning. The spiritual impact of the whale's majestic "peaking of flukes" depends on "what mood you are in; if in the Dantean, the devils will occur to you; if in that of Isaiah, the archangels." Depending on the light in which it is seen, the diamond looks now like "the divinest symbol of the crystal skies," now "like some crown-jewel stolen from the King of Hell." [1] Thus on all questions of significance the prior question becomes: Seen by whom, in what mood, and in what light?

*Moby-Dick*'s philosophical ambiguities, insofar as they are explored by the comic spirit, are explored through three personalities organic to the novel: Stubb, Ahab, and Ishmael. Each of these reflects in his attitude, often by direct verbal echo, some aspect of the ambiguity of merriment and gravity set forth by Babbalanja in his demonic theory of humor. The book is thus shot through with the elusive perversity of Azzageddi; but it is happily

not unprovided with a criterion for evaluating the comic vision
of its principals. That criterion, based on Melville's primal sea–
land metaphor, is highly figurative but unmistakable in its application:

> The sun hides not the ocean, which is the dark side of this earth,
> and which is two thirds of this earth. So, therefore, that mortal man
> who hath more of joy than sorrow in him, that mortal man cannot be
> true — not true, or undeveloped. With books the same. The truest of
> all men was the Man of Sorrows, and the truest of all books is Solo-
> mon's. . . But even Solomon, he says, "the man that wandereth out of
> the way of understanding shall remain" (i.e. even while living) "in
> the congregation of the dead" . . . There is a wisdom that is woe; but
> there is a woe that is madness. And there is a Catskill eagle in some
> souls that can alike dive down into the blackest gorges, and soar out
> of them again and become invisible in the sunny places. And even as
> he forever flies within the gorge, that gorge is in the mountains; so
> that even in his lowest swoop, the mountain eagle is still higher than
> other birds upon the plain, even though they soar.[2]

Here, then, is a standard of sorts (though we can hardly hold
Melville to such an exact mathematical accounting): life is two-
thirds dark, one-third light; more sorrow than joy. And here are
standards by which to gauge the life-views of the three characters whose comic vision we are to examine. First we have the untrue or undeveloped man, the man "who hath more of joy than
sorrow in him"; that is Stubb. Next we have the man who is all
woe and therefore mad; that is Ahab. And finally we have the
balanced man, the man with the Catskill eagle in his soul: Ishmael. It is an alignment recognized in principle by Starbuck, himself the balanced agent of the tragic vision, as he ponders
amidships one night on the revelry in the forecastle and the
"unfaltering silence aft": "Methinks it pictures life. Foremost
through the sparkling sea shoots on the gay, embattled, bantering
bow, but only to drag dark Ahab after it, where he broods within
his sternward cabin, builded over the dead water of the
wake. . ."[3]

The life that it pictures, the essential thing of which Stubb,
Ahab, and Ishmael each has his vision, the thing with which each
must somehow come to terms, is of course the thing or complex of
things symbolized by the white whale himself: "outrageous
strength, with an inscrutable malice sinewing it"; "that intangible

malignity which has been from the beginning. . . all truth with
malice in it . . . all the subtle demonisms of life"; "the heartless
voids and immensities of the universe." [4] It is Stubb's role not to
understand this thing; or rather, to seek refuge in the negation of
thought and defend himself against tragic understanding by a
policy of determined levity. It is Ahab's role to understand the
thing and to fight it. It is Ishmael's role to understand it, accept
it for what it is, and adjust his conduct accordingly.

I

Melville introduces Stubb, his "happy-go-lucky," in his customary symbolic way, carefully using a symbol which he can
also apply to Ahab with directly opposite effect:

> What, perhaps, with other things, made Stubb such an easy-going,
> unfearing man, so cheerily trudging off with the burden of life in
> a world full of grave peddlers, all bowed to the ground with their
> packs; what helped to bring about that almost impious good-humor of
> his; that thing must have been his pipe. For, like his nose, his short,
> black little pipe was one of the regular features of his face. . . I say
> this continual smoking must have been one cause, at least, of his
> peculiar disposition; for everyone knows that this earthly air, whether
> ashore or afloat, is terribly infected with the nameless miseries of the
> numberless mortals who have died exhaling it; and as in time of the
> cholera, some people go about with a camphorated handkerchief to
> their mouths; so, likewise, against all mortal tribulations, Stubb's to-
> bacco smoke might have operated as a sort of disinfecting agent.[5]

This studious immunity to vexation and the sense of evil is soon
underscored in Stubb's observation on Ahab: "I guess he's got
what some folks ashore call a conscience; it's a kind of Tic-Dolly-
row they say — worse nor a toothache. Well, well; I don't know
what it is, but the Lord keep me from catching it. . . Think not,
is my eleventh commandment." [6]

After Ahab's revelation of the terrible purpose of the Pequod's
cruise, Stubb is characteristically the first to settle the whole matter
comfortably in his own mind, by reducing it to comic terms: "Ha!
ha! ha! ha! . . . I've been thinking over it ever since, and that ha,
ha's the final consequence. Why so? Because a laugh's the wisest,
easiest answer to all that's queer. . . I know not all that may be
coming, but be it what it will, I'll go to it laughing. Such a waggish

leering as lurks in all your horribles!" [7] This grotesque ambiguity in Stubb's vision is reflected emblematically in his behavior towards his men.

> He would say the most terrific things to his crew, in a tone so strangely compounded of fun and fury, and the fury seemed so calculated merely as a spice to the fun, that no oarsmen could hear such queer invocations without pulling for dear life, and yet pulling for the mere joke of the thing. . . Stubb was one of those odd sort of humorists, whose jollity is sometimes so curiously ambiguous, as to put all inferiors on their guard in the matter of obeying them.[8]

The ironic discrepancy is that the force of destiny which Stubb obstinately interprets as a hoax is in reality no more a hoax than the commands he so waggishly utters in the stern of his whaleboat.

As the tensions of the story draw tighter, the sterility of Stubb's vision becomes increasingly apparent. His reflections on the cabalistically marked doubloon, which is the symbol of the voyage's significance, are merely a clownish version of some familiar Shakespearean comic philosophy, and the "jolly" moral he draws from it is as inevitable in its way as that of Ahab, who finds it "stout stuff for woe to work on." [9] It is highly significant of the operation of Stubb's mind that he can eavesdrop with equanimity on all the doubloon's commentators except mad Pip, who, in describing him as "two bones stuck into a pair of old trousers, and two more poked into the sleeves of an old jacket," gives him an uncomfortable moment of insight into the spiritual scarecrow he is. "I can stand the rest," he mumbles, "for they have plain wits; but he's too crazy-witty for my sanity." The remark is a valuable contribution to the madness–sanity ambiguity that runs through the novel.

His reaction to the symbol of the sea, like his reaction to the symbol of the doubloon, is pathetic, almost terrible, in its comic uniformity. When the Pacific is mild and Starbuck is grasping at its quiet beauty to bolster his faith, Stubb "takes oaths that he has always been jolly." [10] When the ship is dashed about in a fearful electrical storm, Stubb insists "it's all in fun," and breaks into song. Even Starbuck's taunt that his tune was not quite the same when the corposants struck cannot reduce him beyond a certain querulous defiance of the true state of affairs: "No, no, it wasn't;

I said the corposants have mercy on us all; and I hope they will, still. But do they only have mercy on long faces? — have they no bowels for a laugh?" [11]

It is Ahab, finally, who with his diametrically opposite vision spells out the meaning of Stubb's fatal comic bias. Hearing with revulsion the ill-timed joking of his mate over the boat Moby Dick has chewed in the chase, Ahab cries, "What soulless thing is this that laughs before a wreck? Man, man! did I not know thee brave as fearless fire (and as mechanical) I could swear thou wert a poltroon." Soulless and mechanical, or untrue and undeveloped: that in the end is Stubb.[12] Even at the moment of death Stubb jests, once more in terms reminiscent of one of Azzageddi's diabolical paradoxes: "I grin at thee, thou grinning whale! Look ye, sun, moon, and stars! I call ye assassins of as good a fellow as ever spouted up his ghost. For all that, I would yet ring glasses with ye, would ye but hand the cup! Oh, oh! oh, oh! thou grinning whale, but there'll be plenty of gulping soon!" [13]

### 2

Ahab, too, is one to "laugh and hoot" at the gods, but whereas Stubb's laughter is a kittenish evasion of life, Ahab's is a profane challenge thrown in its teeth. The hellish apparitions in the cave of Hecate tell Macbeth to "laugh to scorn the power of man," but when Fedallah prophesies in close imitation of the Weird Sisters, Ahab's more terrible "laugh of derision" laughs to scorn the power of God.[14] This is the madness into which his surrender to woe has plunged him, and his own words, echoing Macbeth's, place him accurately in the scale of light and dark prescribed by his author: "So far gone am I in the dark side of earth, that its other side, the theoretical bright one, seems but uncertain twilight to me."[15] To make explicit the opposition of Ahab's view to Stubb's, Melville has Ahab throw away his pipe, again in a mood like Macbeth's: "What business have I with this pipe? This thing that is meant for sereneness, to send up mild white vapors among mild white hairs. . ." [16]

In his very tragic intensity, however, Ahab demonstrates Azzageddi's dictum that "woe is more merry than mirth." For, lugubrious as it is, Ahab has among his "humanities" a sense of humor

and makes a number of mirthless contributions to the comedy of
the book. As the *Pequod*'s workmen fashion him a new leg, it
suits his heavy facetiousness to conceive them as "manmaker" and
"Prometheus" and to invent a grim comic recipe for "a complete
man after a desirable pattern."

Imprimis, fifty feet high in his socks; then, chest modelled after the
Thames Tunnel; then, legs with roots to 'em, to stay in one place;
then, arms three feet through the wrist; no heart at all, brass forehead,
and about a quarter of an acre of fine brains; and let me see — shall I
order eyes to see outwards? No, but put a sky-light on top of his head
to illuminate inwards. There, take the order and away.¹⁷

A wicked Christian twist occurs to him, and he cynically plays
with the carpenter's bewildered replies.

Carpenter? why that's — but no; — a very tidy, and, I may say, an
extremely gentlemanlike sort of business thou art in here, carpenter;
— or would'st thou rather work in clay?
Sir? — Clay? clay, sir? That's mud; we leave clay to ditchers, sir.
The fellow's impious! What art thou sneezing about?
Bone is rather dusty, sir.
Take the hint, then; and when thou art dead, never bury thyself
under living people's noses.

It is in a final jesting exchange with the carpenter that Ahab
lays bare the fatal atheism and nihilism of his vision. The sight of
the carpenter converting Queequeg's coffin into a lifebuoy is irresistibly comical to his graveyard humor, and he once more uses
this uncomprehending colloquist to his own ends, as Poe's be-
reaved lover had used the raven.

"Art thou not an arrant, all-grasping, intermeddling, monopolizing,
heathenish old scamp, to be one day making legs, and the next day
coffins to clap them in, and yet again life-buoys out of those same
coffins? Thou art as unprincipled as the gods, and as much of a jack-
of-all-trades."
"But I do not mean anything, sir. I do as I do."
"The gods again. Hark ye, dost thou not ever sing working about
a coffin? The Titans, they say, hummed snatches when chipping out
the craters for volcanoes; and the grave-digger in the play sings, spade
in hand. Dost thou never?"
"Sing, sir? Do I sing? Oh, I'm indifferent enough, sir, for that; but
the reason why the grave-digger made music must have been because
there was none in his spade, sir. But the calking mallet is full of it.
Hark to it."

"Aye, and that's because the lid there's a sounding-board; and what in all things makes the sounding-board is this — there's naught beneath. And yet, a coffin with a body in it rings pretty much the same, Carpenter." [18]

### 3

When the ultimate catastrophe strikes the *Pequod*, death comes to both Ahab and Stubb, and comes in a way appropriate to each. Ahab dies violently, garroted by the superhuman force he so insanely taunted; Stubb, refusing to see in its final gesture anything more than a grin, drowns ignominiously in his drawers. Only Ishmael survives, buoyed up by that remarkable symbol of resurrection, the coffin-lifebuoy. The artistic reason for his survival lies in the careful balance of his comic vision between the fatal extremes of the two characters who are, in this respect, his foils.

The central statement of his comic philosophy — and that is to say the comic philosophy of the book — comes after the first chase of the voyage, a particularly reckless venture in which the high-spirited men virtually run up the whale's back in a storm and are rescued only after a damp and cheerless night in a swamped boat in the middle of nowhere. Ishmael's important reflections on that experience echo the Mardian theory of humor in three respects: the first is a verbal echo in the title of the chapter, "The Hyena"; the second is an echo of the philosophical concept that "life is an April day, that both laughs and weeps in a breath"; the third is an echo of the corresponding psychological concept that "mirth and sorrow are kin; are published by identical nerves."

There are certain queer times and occasions in this strange mixed affair we call life when a man takes this whole universe for a vast practical joke, though the wit thereof he but dimly discerns, and more than suspects that the joke is at nobody's expense but his own. However, nothing dispirits, and nothing seems worth while disputing. He bolts down all events, all creeds, and beliefs, and persuasions, all hard things visible and invisible, never mind how knobby; as an ostrich of potent digestion gobbles down bullets and gun flints. And as for small difficulties and worryings, prospects of sudden disaster, peril of life and limb; all these, and death itself, seem to him only sly, good-natured hits, and jolly punches in the side bestowed by the unseen and unaccountable old joker. That odd sort of wayward mood I am speaking of, comes over a man only in some time of extreme tribulation; it

comes in the very midst of his earnestness, so that what just before
might have seemed to him a thing most momentous, now seems but a
part of the general joke. There is nothing like the perils of whaling
to breed this free and easy sort of genial, desperado philosophy; and
with it I now regarded this whole voyage of the Pequod, and the great
White Whale its object.[19]

Superficially this attitude may seem to embrace both the inflexible levity of Stubb and the inflexible irreverence of Ahab
rather than to strike any sort of balance between them. An important distinction is that this mood is a flexible one, coming "only
in some time of extreme tribulation" as a kind of psychological
safety valve. It comes out of earnestness, whereas Stubb has no
earnestness; and the earnestness is grounded on faith, whereas
Ahab has no faith. The faith is not explicit in this purely humorous passage, but it is in another of Ishmael's mixed moods, the
one that comes on him as he sits pondering the memorial tablets
in the Whaleman's Chapel just before the *Pequod* sails.

Yes, Ishmael, the same fate may be thine. But somehow I grew merry
again. Delightful inducements to embark, fine chance for promotion,
it seems — aye, a stove boat will make me an immortal by brevet. Yes,
there is death in this business of whaling — a speechlessly quick chaotic
bundling of a man into Eternity. But what then? . . . Methinks my
body is but the lees of my better being. In fact take my body who
will, take it I say, it is not me. And therefore three cheers for Nantucket; and come a stove boat and a stove body when they will, for
stave my soul, Jove himself cannot.[20]

Ishmael saves himself from despair by laughing at what threatens
his body; Ahab dooms himself to it by laughing at what threatens
his soul. Ishmael's laughter is thus a psychological symbol of a
philosophical acceptance, long before a more solemn and less cred-
ible symbol was devised in *Billy Budd*.
   The voyage that for Ahab is a struggle for a definitive death is
for Ishmael a struggle for rebirth. That is the philosophical meaning of the favorite Melville joke with which *Moby-Dick* opens.

Whenever I find myself growing grim about the mouth; whenever
it is a damp, drizzly November in my soul; whenever I find myself
involuntarily pausing before coffin warehouses, and bringing up the
rear of every funeral I meet; and especially whenever my hypos get
such an upper hand of me, that it requires a strong moral principle to

prevent me from deliberately stepping into the street, and methodically knocking people's hats off — then, I account it high time to get
to sea as soon as I can. This is my substitute for pistol and ball.

The sober substratum in this notion is brought out as Melville
later applies it to Perth, the *Pequod*'s blacksmith, who, having
made a tragic mess of his life ashore, sought the sea as "another
life without the guilt of intermediate death." [21] Ishmael's mood,
of course, is only whimsically suicidal. Like a "sulky" whale he
once saw, he is merely "dispirited," and looking less for a new
life than for a fresh start on the old one.

The joke of the thing is that he should choose so radical a rem-
edy for his "hypos." He leaps from schoolmaster to sailor, from
the bosom of "an old established family" to the elemental society
of the forecastle. To make matters worse, he ships on a whaler;
and, as Redburn and White-Jacket had discovered before him, no
branch of the maritime profession was held in such uniform contempt as the "blubber-boilers." [22] The total abandon of any landsman who, like himself, would sacrifice comfort, safety, and respectability to go before the mast, especially in a whaler, never
failed to arouse in Melville an ambiguous excitement which
emerged sometimes in a tragic reflection, as in the case of Perth
or Bulkington, sometimes in a comic one, as in the case of Ishmael. The comedy of the situation, even when that aspect pre-
dominated in his mind, was never wholly unalloyed with the
sympathy that humanizes true humor. We have already remarked
the sympathy that lay behind the comic portrait of Rope Yarn in
*Omoo*, whose going to sea to repair his soul sounds so much like
Ishmael's: "Ropey went to the sign of the Pipe and Tankard; got
fuddled; and over his fifth pot meditated suicide — an intention
carried out; for the next day he shipped as landsman aboard the
Julia, South Seaman." And there is at least as much sympathy
mixed with the laughter when a friend of Redburn's writes of the
vanished Harry Bolton, "I cannot believe that his melancholy
could bring him to the insanity of throwing himself away in a
whaler." [23] This kind of humor, applied to and through the character of Ishmael, is an artistic balance wheel in *Moby-Dick* and
one of the symptoms of its spirit of renascence.

Another ambiguity in Ishmael's comic attitude is that it appears
to lead him to both acceptance and rebellion: acceptance in the

sailor's "genial, desperado philosophy," rebellion in the landsman's
urge to go around "methodically knocking people's hats off."
Both reactions have a certain reckless Pantagruelism in common,
both are deeply imbued with the demoniac temper of Azzageddi,
but they are not reactions to the same thing and therefore never
conflict. The distinction is related, as so much in Melville ultimately is, to the sea–land metaphor. The perverse hat-knocking
mood, in which Ishmael was so precisely anticipated by young
Redburn as he defied his supercilious fellow passengers on the river
boat — this essentially childish humor is a thing of the land, a
petulant revolt against the frustrations of orthodoxy. Redburn is
"afterward heartily ashamed" of it, Ishmael applies "strong moral
principle" to curb it, and both escape from it to the "open independence" of the sea, though of the two only Ishmael is mature
enough to recognize it as a compelling motive for that escape.
Once at sea, for him the symbol of physical and spiritual reality,
Ishmael's bitterness drops from him and he is ready to play the
game with whatever gods there be, in the highest good humor,
though he himself may very well be the butt of some "unseen
and unaccountable old joker."

This is the sane if somewhat pagan philosophy of "The Hyena."
It involves by definition the two ambiguities which most deeply
pervade the novel: the motivation of destiny, which is both diabolic and divine; and the reaction of man, which is both laughter
and terror. The latter is by now a familiar ambiguity, thematic in
all of Melville's books to date. Its recurrence in connection with
an occupation as hair-raising as whaling is understandably frequent. One of the standard perils of the chase, for instance, is the
whale-line, which is threaded in such murderous vicinity to every
oarsman as to make "the very marrow in his bones to quiver in
him like a shaken jelly." Yet "gayer sallies, more merry mirth,
better jokes, and brighter repartees, you never heard over your
mahogany, than you will hear over the half-inch white cedar of
the whale-boat, when thus hung in hangman's nooses." Another
"humorously perilous business" is being tied by the "monkey-
rope" to a blubber-cutting shipmate as he dodges the multiple
disasters of drowning, crushing, and shark-bite. There is mirth in
the face of death as Queequeg, in an access of fatalism, orders his
coffin and tries it on for size. And there is merriment before the

fires of hell as the crew, gathered at night before the symbolic try-works, exchange "their unholy adventures, their tales of terror told in words of mirth." [24]

Whatever force or forces direct the fate of this "merry-mad," "gloomy-jolly" *Pequod* are seen with a corresponding doubleness of vision. The fate that drove Pip mad acted through a sea that "jeeringly kept his finite body up," yet carried his soul "to wondrous depths" where "he saw God's foot upon the treadle of the loom." [25] The aftermaths of Ahab's demonic oaths remind us of Azzageddi's assertion that "there is laughter in heaven, and laughter in hell"; the Faustlike compact calls forth both. As Ahab passes the grog like the Eucharist to pledge his crew to the impious chase, Ishmael hears a low "subterranean laugh" from the hold; and afterwards, when Ahab plunges his barb into the blood of his pagan harpooneers to baptize it "in nomine diaboli," "a light, unnatural, half-bantering, yet most piteous sound was heard" — the mad laughter of Pip, who to Ahab is "holiness." [26]

These facts understood, all the ambiguities of Ishmael's comic vision and the middle course it finds between the polar nihilisms of Stubb and Ahab can be read in their subtle synthesis in a single passage:

Though amid all the smoking horror and diabolism of a sea-fight, sharks will be seen longingly gazing up to the ship's decks, like hungry dogs round a table where red meat is being carved, ready to bolt down every killed man that is tossed to them; and though, while the valiant butchers over the deck-table are thus cannibally carving each other's live meat with carving-knives all gilded and tasselled, the sharks, also, with their jewel-hilted mouths, are quarrelsomely carving away under the table at the dead meat; and though, were you to turn the whole affair upside down, it would still be pretty much the same thing, that is to say, a shocking sharkish business enough for all parties; and though sharks also are the invariable outriders of all slave ships crossing the Atlantic, systematically trotting alongside, to be handy in case a parcel is to be carried anywhere, or a dead slave to be decently buried; and though one or two other like instances might be set down, touching the set terms, places, and occasions, when sharks do most socially congregate, and most hilariously feast; yet there is no conceivable time or occasion when you will find them in such countless numbers, and in gayer or more jovial spirits, than around a dead sperm whale, moored by night to a whaleship at sea. If you have never seen that sight, then suspend your decision about the propriety of devil-worship, and the expediency of conciliating the devil. [27]

The genesis of such a vision is obvious enough. We have here in fact the predictable union of *Mardi*'s diabolism and the folk-comedy of hardship which set the tone of the early romances.[28] It is the artistically optimum combination of the two that strips the comic travesty of the narrative to its tragic core of terror and impending evil and death.

# 9

# The Heart of Comedy

In addition to being by turns a boisterous, a clever, and a profound book, *Moby-Dick* is a mythic omnibus of human life and death. Its observable patterns of comic attitude, figurative wit, and superficial jest are only parts of the inclusive comic pattern of the novel as a whole. That pattern is essentially a dramatic one. I have labeled it "dramatic-structural" because of the semantic limitations of the word "dramatic." Part of *Moby-Dick* is cast in a literally dramatic, or dramaturgic, form; and it must be borne in mind that the humor which plays through those strictly theatrical portions contributes no less to the enveloping structure of the novel, which is dramatic in a larger sense. In this sense the comic spirit illuminates the very heart of Melville's masterpiece.

### I

Readers of *Moby-Dick* are generally agreed that the moving literary influence behind it was Shakespearean tragedy.[1] With respect to comic technique the chief point of resemblance between Melville and Shakespeare, though it has been little noted, is fairly obvious. Both writers were given to having flashes of humor in the midst of their earnestness, or (as the case might be) flashes of earnestness in the midst of their humor. Both were profoundly indifferent to the theory and practice of genres and profoundly concerned with the theory and practice of life — a much more vital business, as Dr. Johnson long ago remarked, than anything conceived in the prescriptions of art.

Melville's comic method was of course not altogether Shakespeare's, even in *Moby-Dick* where the two are closest. Melville had largely from French tradition the critical humor that Shakespeare lacks; and he had largely from native tradition that profane and mocking view of "the rim or confines of things, the brink of the abyss, [which] was to Shakespeare dark and terrible altogether, lit up by no grim or ghastly ray of laughter." [2] But it is in the English tradition of Shakespeare (carried down through the works of Sterne and Lamb, whom Melville also admired) that Melville stands in his conception of comedy and tragedy as matters of degree, rather than of kind, as in the French tradition. It is a hallmark of the Shakespearean tradition for notes of agony or merriment to intrude into scenes of essentially opposite emotional tenor. Even tragic heroes like Hamlet, as E. E. Stoll has remarked, "give vent to their wit and their irony in the midst of their sufferings." [3] And Shakespeare's special talent for blending the comic and tragic is perhaps even more remarkable in those low-comedy interludes, such as the grave-digger scene in *Hamlet* and the porter scene in *Macbeth*, where a bloodcurdling irony is achieved through characters in ignorance of the tragic issue of the business they are being droll about. What the comedy appears to do in such scenes is to intensify the tragic potential of the play through the momentary illusion that life is less tragic than it really is. But the object in view, as one critic has put it, "is not so much to depict the confusion of exterior nature as the confusion of the soul at moments when tragic and comic seem to form one indivisible experience." [4] The words could pass for a paraphrase of Babbalanja's theory of humor.

Of the four or five Shakespearean tragedies with which *Moby-Dick* shows some points of affinity, *King Lear* has received the most attention, though a better case might very well be made for *Macbeth*. The point of resemblance that fascinates is the relationship of the madman and the fool to the tragic hero. In *Moby-Dick* the character of Pip was evidently conceived as a composite of the bedlam and the jester who support Lear in his adversity. In building his pathetic figure over those models, Melville passed over their Elizabethan comic surfaces and used their ambiguous dramatic power, as Shakespeare had done, "to emphasize, to contrast with, to comment on the tragic fate of his great protagonist." [5] Moreover, he did this in a conspicuously Shakespearean idiom, complete with stage directions and poetic soliloquies in the grand manner such as were never heard from Negro cabin boy, sane or crazed, on land or sea. The effect, despite the bolder and less sophisticated method, is not unlike that of Eugene O'Neill's New England transposition of the Agamemnon material.

This use of Pip is the key, in both purpose and method, to the use of more frankly comic persons involved in the tragic voyage of the *Pequod*. Ishmael, central though he is to the comic philosophy of the book, is conspicuously absent from the dramatic level of the story, standing aloof from the conflict as a commentator in the manner of a chorus, and coming in at the end almost as detached as Fortinbras to proclaim the continuity of life. But Stubb, like Pip, is an active participant in scenes which sketch the tragic progress of Ahab toward his damnation. At the dramatic heart of *Moby-Dick*, as on its surface, Stubb is Melville's principal comic agent, though here little of the old Yankee independence is left him. At carefully calculated intervals Melville converts him into a Shakespearean clown to cast the ironic light of comedy on Ahab and the somber meaning of his quest.

Ahab's first speech to Stubb — "Down, dog, and kennel!" [6] — seems a clear enough echo of the fool's speech in *Lear*, I, iv, which, to judge by the marking in his copy, impressed Melville as much as anything in the play: "Truth's a dog must to kennel." Melville's irony is the reverse of Shakespeare's in that the corrective role of the comic character, instead of being recognized by both parties, is recognized by neither. Since the irony is implicit in the allusion, it may even be missed by the reader; but one can hardly miss the explicit use of the dog metaphor in establishing the fatal excess of pride in Ahab and the fatal deficiency of it in his foil. Stubb's resentment has a fleeting moment of manly earnestness, then quickly collapses into comic rationalization, an attitude that makes him the ideal buffoon-commentator on Ahab's granitic immutability. In the same way, Stubb's comic superstitiousness about Fedallah ironically defines the diabolic influence at work on Ahab. As Vincent puts it, "The clown can see what the King will not; one is reminded of the insight of the fool as against the blindness of Lear." [7] Here again, of course, Stubb's irony proceeds less from true insight than from his fixed position of equal and opposite error.

Within the framework of this comic function Melville juggled Stubb's Shakespearean antecedents to suit his convenience. An evident resemblance to such prototypes as Bottom and Launcelot Gobbo has been seen in the highly derivative set-piece called "Queen Mab" (Chapter 31), in which Stubb relates to Flask his comical dream of symbolic capitulation to Ahab.[8] There is something of Falstaff, too, in Stubb's ingenious rationalization in that episode on the honor of being kicked by a great man. In the typhoon scene (Chapter 119) it is again the disarming bravado and "discretion" of the fat knight that are reflected in Stubb's frank disavowal of moral courage. And when Ahab speaks his final rebuke to Stubb ("What soulless thing is this that laughs before a wreck?"), we are reminded of the repulse of Falstaff by his former playmate, Henry V:

*I know thee not, old man: fall to thy prayers;*

. . . . .

*Reply not to me with a fool-born jest.*[9]

Stubb's great moment on the stage is a solo performance occupying most of Chapter 99 and investing him with a further variety of Shakespearean guises. This episode shows its genesis, in both style and situation, more clearly than any other in the book. It is a series of soliloquies before the symbolic doubloon by a succession of characters representing the gamut of opinion on the quest for the white whale — a series in which Stubb is himself a participant and on which he reports to the reader through the familiar Shakespearean expedient of eavesdropping and commenting within sight and hearing of the audience. As each man sees in the coin the reflection of his own point of view, so Stubb reads his philosophy in its zodiacal decoration, which he interprets Jaques-like as "the life of man in one round chapter." "There's a sermon now, writ in high heaven," he concludes, shifting lightly to the role of another philosopher in the same play, who had found sermons in stones. His comment on Flask's evaluation of the doubloon ("nine hundred and sixty cigars") is an impeccably antithetic Shakespearean witticism: "Shall I call that wise or foolish, now; if it be really wise it has a foolish look to it; yet, if it be really foolish, then it has a sort of wiseish look to it." Finally, the alternation of Pip's somnabulistic gibberish and Stubb's puzzled

asides results in a chilling travesty of the sleep-walking scene in
*Macbeth*. In a sense, Stubb's whole performance in this chapter
recalls the drunken whimsy of the porter in that play, who also
entertained himself with a series of character studies in a fixed
situation until the game palled on him. Melville may have had a
dozen or a score of Shakespearean scenes and characters in mind
as he constructed the episode; he certainly had in mind Shakespeare's controlling artistic purpose.

Whether he gained or lost by writing these scenes in so sedu-
lously Shakespearean a style is an arguable point. Certainly it must
be admitted that they are "lumbering enough . . . so derivative
in their conception that the humor runs thin." [10] Notwithstanding
the occasional advantage — even necessity — of representing
Ahab's foils in his own high-Shakespearean terms, it was far more
important that the comic structure of *Moby-Dick* remain firmly
rooted in its gross material fishery if the book was to escape being
the "monstrous fable," the "hideous and intolerable allegory" that
Melville wryly disavowed.[11] Accordingly, he was at some pains
to accomplish his dramatic purpose without consistently sacrificing the comic verisimilitude of his characters. Paradoxically,
the very scenes in which Shakespeare's idiom is abandoned are the
most finished tributes to the exemplar who introduced such figures as Bottom and Stephano into his airiest fantasies to "link the
imaginary with the real world." [12]

One case in point, "The Cabin Table" (Chapter 34), is a remarkable piece of comic counterpoint built on the rigid protocol
of the officers' mess, a device brilliantly calculated to illuminate
class levels and relationships in the microcosm of the *Pequod*.
Something of the sort had been attempted in Chapter 7 of *White-
Jacket*; the incomparably superior artistry of "The Cabin Table"
is one of the measures of a masterpiece. The playlet — for that is
what it is in all but form — begins with a brisk musical-comedy
stunt in which the principals successively move through the same
bit of stage business with increasingly hilarious effect, the clown
at the end getting his climactic laugh from a sudden incongruous
return to the sobriety with which the scene opened. On the heels
of this ridiculously mournful crew comes a new comedy team on
stage to a livelier tune — "the almost frantic democracy of those
inferior fellows the harpooneers." And binding these contrasting

acts into a firm comic unit is the burlesque figure of Dough-boy, the abject steward, whose existence, between "the standing spectacle of the black terrific Ahab, and the periodical tumultuous visitations of these three savages, . . . was one continual lip-quiver." Beneath all this "humorous obbligato," as Vincent calls it,[13] runs the ground-bass theme of Ahab's isolation, and the movement ends with Ahab in solitary, bearish possession of his gloomy cabin, an "alien" to "Christendom," like Shylock on the eve of the Christian festival, bidding Jessica

> *Let not the sound of shallow foppery enter*
> *My sober house.*

A similar contrapuntal intention is evident in "Leg and Arm" (Chapter 100), which displays Ahab in an even more incongruous musical-comedy setting. His foils, Boomer and Bunger, both sound and act like a vaudeville team, the one roaring contagiously at everything that is said, the other making his outrageous jokes with a straight face and a dry manner. Ahab is drawn into a "gam" with them when he learns that Captain Boomer has lost an arm to Moby Dick. As he swings onto the *Samuel Enderby*'s deck, he playfully crosses Boomer's ivory arm with his own ivory leg and greets his host with a heavy but well-meant Ahabian jest. What he does not know is that Captain Boomer has accepted his mutilation with good humor and has sensibly concluded to leave Moby Dick alone in future. The process of his finding out produces the striking antiphonal drama of the scene, Ahab withdrawing progressively into his furious impatience as Boomer and his surgeon Bunger wax merrier in their reminiscences. In the end the scene explodes when Bunger playfully attempts to draw off some of Ahab's "boiling" blood and is humorlessly dashed aside as his guest departs, "face set like a flint" to his monomaniac goal. Such scenes, though written in a strictly native and contemporary idiom, gain a massive Shakespearean force from theatrically induced tensions between low comedy and high tragedy.

2

The organic function of humor in *Moby-Dick* is not limited to the heightening of character impression in theatrical episodes.

Melville was aware of its larger dramatic utility, as to a lesser extent he had been in all his books. The student of *Redburn* notices his characteristic way of "balancing bitter or tragic scenes with humorous ones." [14] The same sense of balance, of dramatic alternation of moods, is observable in *White-Jacket*, where the sermons on naval abuses are framed in chapters of pure fun; it is observable to a naturally lesser degree in the more homogeneous *Typee* and *Omoo*; and it is observable with an almost mechanical regularity in *Mardi*, where comedy is periodically needed to offset the depressing visitations of the avengers and the heralds of Hautia. In *Moby-Dick* whole blocks of comic exposition or philosophy are built into the narrative where they will do the most good. Chapters 24 and 25, together constituting the first expository interlude, come strategically between the somber chapters on Bulkington and Starbuck. The two comic chapters on whale meat (64, 65) and the two on whaling history (82, 83) are effectively spaced to break up the intensive technological center of the book. A pyrotechnic display of five comic chapters (88–92) intervenes between the serious parts on "The Grand Armada" and the casting away of Pip; and the romantic-philosophical interlude of the "Bower in the Arsacides" (102, 103) lightly charms the reader before the final almost unrelieved rush to the tragic climax of the story. Such a pattern does not speak of mere whimsical divagation, full of Shandian charm signifying nothing. Melville knew what he was about. *Moby-Dick* is an uneconomical book, to be sure; but he rightly called its meandering "a careful disorderliness," and he rightly called it "the true method" of his enterprise.[15]

Within and beyond the blocks of comedy with which he paced his novel, Melville used humor as an oblique approach to the tragic and metaphysical meanings of his story. Many of *Moby-Dick*'s narrative and philosophical themes are first stated — sometimes solely stated — in comic terms. The method by which this is accomplished is usually Melville's characteristic analogical or contrapuntal technique: the juxtaposition of fact and symbol.[16] It is the ambiguous effect of humor in such passages at once to link the two planes of meaning and to obscure the connection between them. In Vincent's penetrating figure, "Melville employed flippancy as a screen, much as a magician through his patter masks

the fundamental machinery of his illusions." [17] How effectively
the masking was done is attested by posterity's lack of agreement
as to what is masked and by the continual discovery of new illusions under unsuspected masks. A case in point is the remarkable
(yet so far unremarked) passage in which Melville hid his description of *Moby-Dick* itself. His chosen symbol, transparently
enough, is another work of art: a painting which attracts Ishmael's attention as he enters the Spouter-Inn on the night his adventure begins.

On one side hung a very large oil-painting so thoroughly besmoked,
and every way defaced, that in the unequal cross-lights by which you
viewed it, it was only by diligent study and a series of systematic visits
to it, and careful inquiry of the neighbors, that you could any way
arrive at an understanding of its purpose. Such unaccountable masses
of shades and shadows, that at first you almost thought some ambitious
young artist, in the time of the New England hags, had endeavored to
delineate chaos bewitched. But by dint of much and earnest contemplation, and oft repeated ponderings, and especially by throwing open
the little window towards the back of the entry, you at last came to
the conclusion that such an idea, however wild, might not be altogether unwarranted.
   But what most puzzled and confounded you was a long, limber,
portentous, black mass of something hovering in the center of the
picture over three blue, dim, perpendicular lines floating in the name-
less yeast. A boggy, squitchy picture truly, enough to drive a nervous
man distracted. Yet was there a sort of indefinite, half-attained, un-
imaginable sublimity about it that fairly froze you to it, till you volun-
tarily took an oath with yourself to find out what that marvellous
painting meant. Ever and anon a bright, but, alas, deceptive idea would
dart you through. — It's the Black Sea in a midnight gale. — It's the
unnatural combat of the four primal elements. — It's a blasted heath.
— It's a Hyperborean winter scene. — It's the breaking-up of the ice-
bound stream of Time. But at last all these fancies yielded to that one
portentous something in the picture's midst. *That* once found out,
and all the rest were plain. But stop; does it not bear a faint resemblance to a gigantic fish? even the great leviathan himself?

In this oblique manner the "portentous" central figure of *Moby-
Dick* is itself anatomized in turn, its history, its habits, its features
all being exposed, simultaneously on physical, narrative, and metaphysical planes, through the catalytic agency of humor.[18]
   The artistic significance of Melville's thematic comedy is this:
that while the tone is frequently one of Rabelaisian irreverence,

the impelling motive beneath it is informed by respect for "the great inherent dignity and sublimity of the Sperm Whale," and, by extension, for the dignity and sublimity of what the Sperm Whale stands for.[19] This fact is the key to the structural function of comedy in *Moby-Dick*. None of it belittles; all of it, though it be like Falstaff a "gross mountain" of exaggeration, is nevertheless constantly at work increasing the stature of the subject. The *Pequod* is as real a ship as the *Dolly* or the *Julia* or the *Highlander* or the *Neversink*, but we hear no contemptuous witticisms about her biscuit or her coffee or her cockroaches; nor do we hear any contemptuous witticisms about her crew or her officers — no motley, drunken mob as in the *Julia*; no corrupt, incompetent hierarchy as in the *Neversink*. Above all, we hear no contemptuous witticisms about the whale. Melville's first literary whale is as appealingly comical as any in *Moby-Dick*, but it would have meant artistic disaster to the book. It is the whale, or school of whales, young Redburn sees on his outward voyage:

Can these be whales? Monstrous whales, such as I had heard of? I thought they would look like mountains on the sea; hills and valleys of flesh! regular krakens, that made it high tide, and inundated continents, when they descended to feed!

It was a bitter disappointment, from which I was long in recovering. I lost all respect for whales! and began to be a little dubious about the story of Jonah; for how could Jonah reside in such an insignificant tenement; how could he have had elbow-room there? But perhaps, thought I, the whale, which according to Rabbinical traditions was a female one, might have expanded to receive him like an anaconda, when it swallows an elk and leaves the antlers sticking out of its mouth.

Nevertheless, from that day, whales greatly fell in my estimation.

But it is always thus. If you read of St. Peter's, they say, and then go and visit it, ten to one, you account it a dwarf compared to your high-raised ideal. And doubtless, Jonah himself must have been disappointed when he looked up to the domed midriff surmounting the whale's belly, and surveyed the ribbed pillars around him. A pretty large belly, to be sure, thought he, but not so big as it might have been.[20]

In *Moby-Dick* the proportions of that particular whale are altered to the extent that "Jonah might have ensconced himself in a hollow tooth." [21]

The word for *Moby-Dick* is magnitude — and Miltonic, Shakespearean magnitude at that. Charles Olson suggests that Melville's inspiration for this aspect of his book was specifically *Antony and Cleopatra*, in which he marked such passages as

> *His legs bestrid the ocean; his rear'd arm*
> *Crested the world.*

But he adds that in translating this sense of tragic magnitude from classic Roman heroes to contemporary American whaling men, Melville "faced his difficulties." [22] These are the difficulties confronting every romantic artist who has made the revolutionary leap to realistic materials; historic difficulties still being wrestled with by the writers of opera, for example, who have abandoned persons of "quality" in favor of such proletarian figures as the housewife (*The Consul*), the fisherman (*Peter Grimes*), the common soldier (*Wozzeck*) — and the common sailor (*Billy Budd*). These difficulties are largely solved as Melville himself solved them in the original *Billy Budd* — without the aid of humor. Human dignity, after all, is human dignity. But how is it if the central figure of your tragedy, before whom all others are as pawns, is an animal, and the most grotesque, implausible animal in the world; and if the dignity to which you wish to raise that animal is the dignity of more than man — the dignity of God? Perhaps the only salvation of so mad a project is the one Melville successfully found: to accept the comic implications of the inherent incongruity and frankly cajole the reader into an acceptance, at first on purely comic terms, if necessary, of the intended scope and grandeur of the theme. It is a ticklish business, calling for an extraordinary literary magician with an extraordinary line of patter.

Thus it is that in the very act of expounding the greatness of his intent in *Moby-Dick* Melville clowns, defending the epic aspiration behind the laughing mask of frontier tall-talk:

> One often hears of writers that rise and swell with their subject, though it may seem but an ordinary one. How, then, with me, writing of this Leviathan? Unconsciously my chirography expands into placard capitals. Give me a condor's quill! Give me Vesuvius' crater for an ink-stand! Friends, hold my arms! For in the mere act of penning my thoughts of this Leviathan, they weary me, and make me faint with their outreaching comprehensiveness of sweep, as if to include the whole circle of the sciences, and all the generations of whales, and

men, and mastodons, past, present, and to come, with all the revolving panoramas of empire on earth, and throughout the whole universe, not excluding its suburbs. Such, and so magnifying, is the virtue of a large and liberal theme! We expand to its bulk. To produce a mighty book, you must choose a mighty theme. No great and enduring volume can ever be written on the flea, though many there be who have tried it.[23]

Thus the comedy which "mapped the outlines of *Moby-Dick* and shaped its form" [24] is not only compatible with its tragic theme but essential to it, and the characteristic mixture of the two becomes an organic feature of Melville's profoundest exploration of the ambiguity of life. "The stroke of the great humorist is worldwide, with lights of Tragedy in his laughter," George Meredith wrote.[25] By such a criterion, and in this book at least, Melville qualifies as a great humorist.

*Part Four*

# THE END OF COMEDY

# 10

# The Bright and the Dark

As an artist whose world appeared to him "half melancholy, half farcical," Melville was in uneasy possession of a secret all great humorists have shared:

> Duality of thought is the master condition of humor. More often than not the humorist smiles in silence over the apparently serious things he tells us; but we can also sometimes catch the quizzical or gently ironic turn of his lip while his face wears a mask of the most disarming innocence.[1]

Melville, at the height of his powers, knew how to make fun with a straight face, and also how to be earnest with a grin. In *Mardi* he had been moved to explore the curiously split personality of humor; in *Moby-Dick* he had developed its implications dramatically. In the writing that followed it was the ambiguity of humor that became the central problem of his artistic method.

I

*Pierre*, as its subtitle states, is a book about ambiguities. In it Melville made the fatal error of reversing the perfectly sound principle of humorous duality, that (in effect) ambiguity is the chosen vehicle of all smiles. Pierre's spiritual catastrophe begins when, contemplating the evil behind his father's cheerful portrait, he considers that a "smile is the chosen vehicle of all ambiguities."[2] The difference for both hero and reader is that by the former principle one detects a hidden meaning and smiles at one's discovery; by the latter one detects a sly smile and tortures oneself to discover the hidden meaning behind it. For Pierre it is the smiles of the world that are most fraught with terror. The dark face of Isabel comes to him "out of the heart of mirthfulness." The playful fiction of calling his mother "sister" only prepares him to accept the dreadful fiction of sister as wife, and thus "in sport he learnt the terms of woe." [3] For Pierre life becomes "a play, which begin how it may, in farce or comedy, ever hath its tragic end." Even White-Jacket had suggested that "if you begin the day with a laugh, you may, nevertheless, end it with a sob and a sigh"; but in Pierre's sorry world "the curtain inevitably falls upon a corpse." [4] Pierre is an Ahab, counterbalanced by a Stubb in the person of Charlie Millthorpe,[5] but there is no Ishmael in the picture. The result is neither good comedy nor good tragedy, but a kind of melodramatic frustration. The hysterical perversity of Pierre as he slaves over his defiantly unpopular book reminds us of Azzageddi and offers a suggestive insight into the inverted humor which Melville himself was writing into this book: "With the feeling of misery and death in him, he created forms of gladness and life. For the pangs in his heart, he put down hoots on the paper." [6]

At the opposite extreme is *The Confidence-Man*, that remarkable philosophical leg-pull, not a drama in any sense, but an extended conversation-piece in which Melville remorselessly teases the reader with ambiguities about which he is still serious but no longer tragic. Ambiguity is once again permitted to be the vehicle of smiles. Among the most deftly ironic passages in the book is a conversation in which the "cosmopolitan," an intellectual confidence man, demonstrates to his chance companion, Charlie Noble, a proposition about the nature of humor, while demonstrating to the reader, at Charlie's comic expense, its exact opposite. His false thesis, curiously enough, is one that Ishmael had presented as a true one: "that a good laugher cannot be a bad man." [7] Charlie has the insensitivity to laugh at cruelty and frown upon innocence, and the cosmopolitan nails him, all unconscious, to his ludicrous position. Their discussion of Shakespeare's humor in the following chapter (30) states the thematic ambiguity of *The Confidence-Man*; we read the book in miniature in the cosmopolitan's ironically puzzled description of Autolycus:

How is one to take Autolycus? A rogue so happy, so lucky, so triumphant, of so almost captivatingly vicious a career that a virtuous man reduced to the poor-house (were such a contingency conceivable), might almost long to change sides with him. And yet, see the words put into his mouth: "Oh," cries Autolycus, as he comes galloping, gay as a buck, upon the stage, "oh," he laughs, "oh what a fool is Honesty, and Trust, his sworn brother, a very simple gentleman." Think of that. Trust, that is, confidence — that is, the thing in this universe the sacredest — is rattlingly pronounced just the simplest. And the scenes in which the rogue figures seem purposely devised for verification of his principles.

In an earlier chapter (24), the cosmopolitan and the Missouri bachelor, representing philanthropist and misanthrope (though beneath the comic mask their roles are really reversed), discuss the familiar Melvillian dilemma of the comic versus the tragic view of life. The former tells a rakish tale to illustrate his notion that it is "sad business, this holding out against having a good time." "If I take your parable right," says the bachelor, "the meaning is, that one cannot enjoy life with gusto unless he renounce the too-sober view of life. But since the too-sober view is, doubtless, nearer true than the too-drunken; I, who rate truth, though cold water, above untruth, though Tokay, will stick to my earthen jug." It is Stubb and Ahab again; Melville makes certain that we do not miss the symbolic pipe of the cosmopolitan and the symbolic rifle of the Missourian. But this time there is an Ishmael in the picture: Melville himself, in his most Meredithian role, chuckling overhead as he pulls his slyly crossed puppet strings.

Many of the tales intervening between *Pierre* and *The Confidence-Man* are also concerned with the ambiguity of humor and the problem of the balanced view of life. Duality of thought is implicit in the very scheme of Melville's characteristically paired sketches. "Poor Man's Pudding and Rich Man's Crumbs" is a double satire, commenting ironically on confidence and charity respectively, in a kind of thematic preview of *The Confidence-Man*. In "The Paradise of Bachelors and the Tartarus of Maids" the light and shade are separated for contrast: the former has all the laughter, a jovial, roast-beef-and-claret humor reminiscent of Irving and Dickens, overlaid with an ambiguous sincerity; while the latter has the austere sincerity of Hawthorne, overlaid with an ambiguous humor devilishly built into its hidden biological allegory. In a significantly titled sketch from "The Encantadas,"

"Two Sides to a Tortoise," Melville explicitly resolves (at least in theory) the haunting dichotomy of dark and bright.

In view of the description given, may one be gay upon the Encantadas? Yes: that is, find one the gayety, and he will be gay. And, indeed, sackcloth and ashes as they are, the isles are not perhaps unmitigated gloom. For while no spectator can deny their claims to a most solemn and superstitious consideration, no more than my firmest resolutions can decline to behold the spectre-tortoise when emerging from its shadowy recess; yet even the tortoise, dark and melancholy as it is up the back, still possesses a bright side; its calipee or breast-plate being sometimes of a faint yellowish or golden tinge. Moreover, everyone knows that tortoises as well as turtles are of such a make, that if you but put them on their backs you thereby expose their bright sides without the possibility of their recovering themselves, and turning into view the other. But after you have done this, you should not swear that the tortoise has no dark side. Enjoy the bright, keep it turned up perpetually if you can, but be honest, and don't deny the black. Neither should he, who cannot turn the tortoise from its natural position so as to hide the darker and expose his livelier aspect, like a great October pumpkin in the sun, for that cause declare the creature to be one total inky blot. The tortoise is both black and bright.[8]

The resolution is more dramatically expressed in "The Fiddler," written the same year (1854) as "The Encantadas" and dealing directly with the artist's search for a perfect balance between the bright and dark views of life. In this allegorical tale, Helmstone, an unsuccessful and embittered author, is introduced by one Standard to a middle-aged man named Hautboy, a friendly, unassuming nobody in whom "good sense and good humor . . . joined hands."

It was plain that while Hautboy saw the world pretty much as it was, yet he did not theoretically espouse its bright side nor its dark side. Rejecting all solutions, he but acknowledged facts. What was sad in the world he did not superficially gainsay; what was glad in it he did not cynically slur; and all which was to him personally enjoyable, he gratefully took to his heart. It was plain, then — so it seemed at that moment, at least — that his extraordinary cheerfulness did not arise either from deficiency of feeling or thought.[9]

But despite his instinctive admiration for Hautboy, Helmstone decides that his good humor must be owing to docility and lack of genius, and he learns nothing from him until Standard reveals that he is a forgotten musical prodigy, once the toast of the civil-

ized world. "Next day," the story concludes, "I tore all my manuscripts, bought me a fiddle, and went to take regular lessons of
Hautboy." The striking contribution of both this piece and the
sketch from "The Encantadas" is the suggestion that the true
marriage of bright and dark, of the comic and the tragic views,
is brought about, not by chance, but by a continuous, creative act
of will.

Indeed, the lesson for the artist is that it *is* a marriage, not a
manic-depressive alternation of warring personalities. For all his
contemplation of the problem and for all his insight into it, it
seems to have been the hardest struggle of Melville's artistic
career to make that marriage work. Part of the interior story of
*Moby-Dick* is the story of that struggle blown up to epic proportions. Perhaps only the short story "Bartleby," written the
year after *Pierre*, represents in a finished work of art the perfect
balance of comedy and tragedy which Melville was coming to
understand.

Many readers of "Bartleby" who have savored it thoughtfully
have seen its ambiguous equilibrium as the principal cause of its
greatness.[10] Coming on the heels of *Pierre*, from which it evidently
takes its metropolitan, walled-canyon setting, and involving a relation between its narrator and its principal character not unlike
that in Poe's "Raven," "Bartleby" is something of a *tour de force*.
Neatly avoiding the dreary Gothicism latent in his materials, Melville gave controlled play to the comic aspects of the situation in
such a way as to bring to life one of the most unpromising figures
in fiction. One wonders what sort of wraith-like symbol Hawthorne would have made of the bloodless Bartleby. Melville con-
structs a substantial comic frame for his weird nihilistic drama
and surrounds his "motionless young man" with a bustling at-
torney and two ludicrously temperamental clerks — all minor
triumphs of solid Dickensian portraiture. Bartleby himself, thus
shored up, becomes a major triumph of ambiguous characterization. The ostensible quintessence of social absurdity, he nevertheless retains a massive dignity which is in clear contrast to the comic
discomfitures of his foils. In the light of the metaphysical pun in
the subtitle ("A Story of Wall Street")[11] it is more than possible
that only Bartleby, through his progressive "dead-wall reveries,"
has made a successful adjustment to the Melvillian world. The

narrator, uttering over Bartleby's body one of the noblest epi-
taphs in literature, seems to lay a wreath before the Sphinx:

"Eh! — He's asleep, ain't he?"
"With kings and counselors," murmured I.


2

The literary effect of Melville's comic ambiguity is difficult to
assess, ranging as it does between the polar modes of *Pierre* and
*The Confidence-Man*. It is helpful, however, to examine its most
evident sources of inspiration at those extremes. If *The Confidence-Man* is a more humorous book than *Pierre*, it is perhaps
because Melville adapted to its very different purposes the fanci-
ful touch of *Tristram Shandy*. Read as that book is read — as a
mordant but whimsical gambol with ideas and personalities, to
which progressive characterization, dramatic tension, and even
narrative consequence are irrelevant — *The Confidence-Man*
poses few of the solemn problems its critics have been prone to
labor over. The book begins and ends with a Shandian device and
is filled with Shandian echoes.

*The Confidence-Man* starts off with a Biblical text, the familiar
lines from First Corinthians about charity, which are posted on a
slate by a mute passenger aboard the steamboat *Fidèle*; and this is
followed by an anti-text, "No Trust," which the ship's barber
posts above his door. Early in *Tristram Shandy* (II, xvii) Cor-
poral Trim finds and reads to the assembled company a manuscript sermon which is highly suggestive of both the theme and
the tone of *The Confidence-Man*:

The SERMON
Hebrews xiii. 18
— *For we* trust *we have a good Conscience*

"Trust! — Trust we have a good conscience!"
Certainly, Trim, quoth my father, interrupting him, you give that
sentence a very improper accent; for you curl up your nose, man, and
read it with such a sneering tone, as if the Parson was going to abuse
the Apostle.
He is, an' please your Honour, replied Trim.

What follows in Melville bears similar atmospheric resemblance
to the manner and purpose of Sterne. There is the same high-

handed disregard of sequential action; the same whimsical treatment of dialogue; the same blithe tendency of the author to interrupt at any point in his own person; the same way of interpolating independent anecdotes, sometimes of grotesquely inappropriate proportions, when it suits his whim; the same striking trick of opening a chapter with a cryptic snatch of floating dialogue which gathers sense and relevance only after much leisurely backing and filling on the part of the author, who then, in his own sweet time, continues the conversation thus begun. Passage after passage might as reasonably be identified with the one book as with the other. Take from *The Confidence-Man* the opening of Chapter 33, for example, or the ending of Chapter 44:

> But ere be given the rather grave story of Charlemont, a reply must in civility be made to a certain voice which methinks I heard, that, in view of past chapters, and more particularly the last, where certain antics appear, exclaims: How unreal all this is! Who did ever dress or act like your cosmopolitan? And who, it might be returned, did ever dress or act like harlequin?

> In the endeavor to show, if possible, the impropriety of the phrase, *Quite an Original*, as applied by the barber's friends, we have, at unawares, been led into a dissertation bordering upon the prosy, perhaps upon the smoky. If so, the best use the smoke can be turned to, will be, by retiring under cover of it, in good trim as may be, to the story.

The very titles of these chapters have a Shandian air, notwithstanding their more literal resemblance, in default of chapter titles in Sterne, to those of, say, Fielding's *Tom Jones*: Chapter 33 — "Which May Pass for whatever it May Prove to be Worth"; Chapter 44 — "In Which the Last Three Words of the Last Chapter are made the Text of Discourse, which Will be Sure of Receiving More or Less Attention from Those Readers who do not Skip It."

The relationship to *Tristram Shandy* continues to suggest itself down to the very last line, a sentence that has consistently furrowed the brows of Melville's commentators: "Something further may follow of this Masquerade." This has been widely taken as prima-facie evidence that the book is unfinished; that Melville, after a brilliantly nervous performance, unflagging to the last page, suddenly grew weary of the whole business and threw down this sentence as he threw down his pen; that he per-

mitted the book to go to press with that mere detour sign at the
end of it, and to stand that way unaltered and unexplained through
the thirty-four remaining years of his life. Certainly the book with
such a conclusion is unfinished, but perhaps it is unfinished in a
more reasonable sense. Let us consider these last words of the book
in the light of its first words, which announce the exact date of the
story's action — the "first of April." And let us then add another
piece from the middle of the puzzle, the lines at the beginning of
Chapter 35 in which the cosmopolitan and Charlie Noble discuss
the interpolated story of Charlemont, the Gentleman-madman.

"Well, what do you think of the story of Charlemont?" mildly
asked he who told it.
"A very strange one," answered the auditor, who had been such
not with perfect ease, "but is it true?"
"Of course not; it is a story which I told with the purpose of every
story-teller — to amuse."

The cosmopolitan has, of course, an ulterior motive, but that is
the comic ambiguity of his remark. Seen in this light, the spirit
of Melville's conclusion may be very close to that of Sterne's:

L—d! said my mother, what is all this story about? —
A Cock and a Bull, said Yorick — And one of the best of its kind,
I ever heard.

As I read Melville's final words, they are far from being a symp-
tom of exhaustion, but are a calculated touch of infinitude to a
story which can have no end and which is therefore cut off at the
most equivocal and indeterminate point possible. A sense of
chronological accomplishment would have been inimical to the
purpose, which was to show that human relations are a theme with
variations, not sequential and climactic, but played together as an
ironic fugue — a *perpetuum mobile*, in fact. There is no development in the story and no end to it, and it is the whole ambiguously
humorous point of the book that there shall be none.[12]

*Pierre*, on the other hand, is nearly devoid of the whimsicality
of Sterne.[13] Its ambiguous comic quality is to be understood in
the light of two other Melvillian favorites, Carlyle and Shakespeare. *Sartor Resartus* is generally credited (or blamed) for the
conception of *Pierre*'s grotesque and ironic philosopher and for
the elephantine playfulness of style which is one of its most in-

sufferable blemishes. Its obvious central paradigm is *Hamlet*. Scholars and critics have amply exposed the debt on both the tragic and the low-comic levels.[14] But it was somewhere in between that Melville found and adapted the pivotal ambiguity that gives *Pierre* its controlling quality. What has been said of Hamlet's comic psychology can be applied with preternatural accuracy to both Melville and his self-imaging hero, Pierre:

> The relation between Hamlet's character and humour is an intimate and deep-laid one. . . The tragic predicament in which he finds himself forces upon him a policy of dissimulation. He must repress his feelings, hide his thoughts; and thus he is led to express nothing but under a veil, to use hints, riddles, puzzling and mystifying words. His mental life develops a double plane; and the duality of his consciousness is so persistent that it becomes as it were normal.[15]

The ambiguity thus cultivated is an attitude of simultaneous defense and challenge before the world, offering an orthodox interpretation with a built-in petard. Such pathological humor results less in the reader's amusement than in the hero's bitter delight in the physical stimulation of danger, the spiritual stimulation of covert honesty, and the intellectual stimulation of exercising his wit.

This extreme form of humor — tragic, morbid, repellent — characterizes both *Hamlet* and *Pierre*, but with one all-important difference. In Shakespeare the ironic mask is worn by the hero alone and is seen from the outside; in Melville it is worn by hero and author alike and must be seen from the inside. *Pierre* is a Chinese puzzle in which we have, literally, a man writing a bitter book about a man writing a bitter book about a man writing a bitter book. In the resultant mirror image the mood of Hamlet becomes the mood of *Pierre* the book as well as of Pierre the man. The final effect is self-mockery, a spectacle that must embarrass any but the most morbid reader.[16]

The ambiguous comic mood in question is most succinctly described in Redburn's word for it — "demonaic." In *Pierre* it is defined in these terms: "If fit opportunity offer in the hour of unusual affliction, minds of a certain temperament find a strange, hysterical relief in a wild, perverse humorousness, the more alluring from its entire unsuitableness to the occasion. . ." When we add to this mood its element of "wanton aggression," we have, in effect, the mad defiance of Redburn on the river boat, the "perversity" and "reckless contempt" of Harry Bolton, the hat-knocking temper of Ishmael in the opening chapter of *Moby-Dick*. In short, it is Ishmael's "genial desperado philosophy" shorn of its geniality.[17]

In the total context of Melville's work this humor of perversity has, in addition to its organic ambiguity, an ambiguous potential. It is capable of a positive and a negative expression, a constructive and a destructive, a bright and a dark. In one form or the other, or both, it appears like a signature in most of his writings, frequently marked by specific verbal echoes that return familiarly upon us. In *Israel Potter* the word "demoniac" keeps recurring in connection with the desperate humor it describes. When the luckless soldier of fortune, a satanic concentration of Israel Potter in *The Confidence-Man*, explodes in a burst of "milk-turning" laughter, Melville calls him both a "demoniac" and a "hyena," an epithet he had used for identical purposes in *Mardi* and *Moby-Dick*.[18]

Standing at the bright extreme of the demoniac mood, along with the chastened Ishmael, is the Ethan Allen of *Israel Potter*. "Scornful and ferocious" in captivity, he was yet full of "that wild, heroic sort of levity, which in the hour of oppression or peril seems inseparable from a nature like his; the mode whereby such a temper evinces its barbaric disdain of adversity, and how cheaply and waggishly it holds the malice, even though triumphant, of its foes!"[19] This is the true and admirable Pantagruelism, scornful of fortune but jealous of dignity. It was in this spirit that Melville remembered in his declining years the greatest hero of them all — Jack Chase. In *John Marr and Other Sailors* (1888) he called him "Jack Roy" because he was "king" of the crew, but he is the same manly captain of the main-top his admirer had celebrated in *White-Jacket*:

> . . . *a gallant, off-hand*
> *Mercutio indifferent in life's gay command.*
> *Magnanimous in humor; when the splintering shot fell,*
> *"Tooth-picks a-plenty, lads; thank 'em with a shell!"*
>
> . . . . .
> *Larking with thy life, if a joy but a toy,*
> *Heroic in thy levity wert thou, Jack Roy.*[20]

At the dark pole of perversity it is the self-derisive cynicism
of Hamlet that is indulged by Israel Potter, sharing "the reckless
sort of half-jolly despair" of the "dismal desperadoes" enslaved in
the brickyard, and by Pierre, refusing to proofread his book and
"jeering with himself at the rich harvest thus furnished to the
entomological critics." [21] Years later Melville wrote his own re-
morseful commentary on the unwholesome humor of *Pierre*:

> *Wandering late by morning seas*
> *When my heart with pain was low —*
> *Hate the censor pelted me —*
> *Deject I saw my shadow go.*
>
> *In elf-caprice of bitter tone*
> *I too would pelt the pelted one:*
> *At my shadow I cast a stone.*
>
> *When lo, upon that sun-lit ground*
> *I saw the quivering phantom take*
> *The likeness of St. Stephen crowned:*
> *Then did self-reverence awake.*[22]

### 3

Pierre's favorite books were *Hamlet* and the *Inferno*. The combination is significant, for the whole ambiguous problem of bright
and dark with which Melville wrestled so self-consciously from
*Mardi* on usually led him, quite unprotesting, straight to Hell.
It was the perfect commentary on his own tendencies that he read
and marked in "Rappaccini's Daughter" while he was at work on
*Moby-Dick*: "Blessed be all simple emotions, be they bright or
dark! It is the lurid intermixture of the two that produces the illuminating blaze of the infernal regions." [23] This was a fact that
both he and Hawthorne knew in their art and that Melville obviously enjoyed sharing with his friend in conspiratorial asides. It
is the Byronic romanticist who speaks in those hectic letters to
Hawthorne about "the Whale," which critics have so earnestly
seized upon as evidence of a tortured or atheistic soul: letters
which jest with theatrical irreverence about "the hell-fire in
which the whole book is broiled" and its diabolical "secret"

motto; which exult over the artistic catharsis of his "wicked" book, or the fact that his friend, penetrating to the "ugly Socrates" in it, "saw the flame in the mouth, and heard the rushing of the demon, — the familiar, — and recognized the sound; for you have heard it in your own solitudes." [24]

In the first flush of his enthusiasm for Hawthorne, Melville was carried away by his idol's romantic diabolism. In his gift copy of *Twice-Told Tales* he marked a paragraph of macabre comedy in "Chippings with a Chisel" in which the grisly conceit of a tombstone cutter "gnawing a pair of cross-bones and drinking out of a hollow death's head" is pronounced "humor . . . of the right sort." On a more philosophical plane, he based *Pierre* on one of Hawthorne's favorite themes, even then being reused in *The Blithedale Romance*: "the most awful truth in Bunyan's book of such, — from the very gate of heaven there is a by-way to the pit." [25] In psychology, too, Hawthorne had anticipated the wild, satanic humor of Pierre in the behavior of his own virtuous dupe-of-the-flesh, Arthur Dimmesdale, in *The Scarlet Letter* (1850).[26]

Religion was full of paradoxes and perplexities for Melville, as all his writings from *Mardi* to *Clarel* and *Billy Budd* attest. The flamboyant indomitability of Milton's Satan had a powerful appeal to the romantic freethinker who felt more derision than reverence for the pat orthodoxy of his respectable contemporaries.[27] Rightly or wrongly, he considered Hawthorne to be emancipated and disreputable like himself, and he took a kind of swaggering pleasure in writing him whimsical shockers like "We incline to think that God cannot explain His own secrets, and that He would like a little information on certain points Himself"; or, "You perceive I employ a capital initial in the pronoun referring to the Deity; don't you think there is a slight dash of flunkeyism in that usage?" [28]

In the same half-truculent humor he wrote into *Pierre* the suspiciously blasphemous epithet "Juggularius," a sardonic jest about the "hollow" of God's hand, and a tasteless conceit about displacing some of the omnipresent Spirit as one sits down. He attributed the onset of Pierre's Hamlet-like perversity to reaction against the irresolution of Christian blandness as personified in the Reverend Mr. Falsgrave.[29] And he likened his hero's spiritual anarchy to that of a priest he had heard of to whom, in the very act of administering the Sacrament, "the Evil One suddenly propounded . . . the possibility of the mere moonshine of the Christian Religion." For the most part, the diabolical humor of *Pierre* is sustained by the bare bravado of irreligion, a desperate stimulus which only accents the bombast of its melodrama and embarrasses the frequent soundness of its philosophy and psychology. In *Moby-Dick* the blending of bright and dark had produced the alchemic flame of which Hawthorne had written; in *Pierre* the mixture-as-before somehow merely curdled.

After *Pierre*, Melville's conjuring with his tragicomic devils regained some of its sureness in the sardonic ambiguity of "The Tartarus of Maids" and the ironic brimstone landscape of "The Enchanted Isles," then reached its climax in *The Confidence-Man*. In this masterpiece of equivocal Satanism the title character is clearly the Devil, gaily fleecing the world and even his own kind in various satiric disguises, most transparently that of an agent for the "Black Rapids Coal Company" who peddles his bogus stock in the very words of Milton's Satan.[30] Christ is by ironic implication a deaf-mute and a fool, God a benevolent capitalist on whose indiscriminate charity the Devil battens, the Bible a collection of news "too good to be true." In the end, innocent Humanity, in his dotage, girds himself with "Providence," which is a life-preserver in the form of a commode; and the Devil, in his suavest disguise, thoughtfully extinguishes the Light of the World, which has burned low and begun to smell bad. If this was Melville's April Fool's joke, it was a grisly one, but its humor is too muscular to be, like *Pierre*'s, a "death's head mockery." [31] Like "the Devil's Joke," the destination of the "flunkeying" sophist from the Philosophical Intelligence Office, *The Confidence-Man* is, one suspects, "a grotesquely shaped bluff."

#### 4

In the final analysis, Melville's mixtures of bright and dark in the period from *Pierre* to *The Confidence-Man* often result in such impenetrable ambiguities of tone that the reader attempting to extract serious meaning from his pages is in peril of finding himself, like Babbalanja's alchemist friend Atahalpa, endeavoring to hatch a fairy in a jar. Symptomatic of that peril is the problem of *Pierre*'s dedication — "To Greylock's Most Excellent Majesty." On the face of it there should be no more mystery about addressing a book to a mountain than about addressing one to a monument, as Melville did in the punning dedication to *Israel Potter*; yet one man reads it as a bitter comment on rejection by the world, and another finds it "playful rather than misanthropic." [32] The grotesque language of *Pierre*, too, presents a veiled front to the world, and the shrewd critic retreats to the position that "whether such language was to be read as an ironic parody or to be taken seriously was something for the reader to decide." [33] Like the great sperm whale, *Pierre* "has no face," and one "cannot completely make out his back parts." Conservatively, one must agree with Matthiessen: "It is hard always to be sure of its intention. . . The chief trouble is the lack of any norm." [34]

The same lack troubles *The Confidence-Man*, or at least its serious readers. The majority view is that it expresses "the cynical turn in Melville's attitude toward man"; that "he was in such a mood of Timonism that he was driven into writing the whole book as a satiric comment on the text from Corinthians." [35] But opposed to this are commentaries urging that it is to "misinterpret the book entirely" to read into it a satire on confidence; that it is, indeed, a subtle affirmation of faith in the philosophy of Corinthians.[36] One is reminded of the literary fact-of-life Mark Twain so amusingly documented in "The Petrified Man," a carefully camouflaged hoax about a fossil dug up with hands spread to nose in the classic gesture of derision. It was a fraud, Twain discovered, "altogether too delicate, for nobody ever perceived the satire part of it at all." Whether Melville erred in making these books "altogether too delicate" or whether he made them so for the express purpose of mystification — even this we must hesitate to decide. Books that no one would ever be able to figure out may have been precisely what Melville intended, if only as a magnificent nose-thumbing at a world of obvious tastes and easy answers.

Compounding the confusion are the inevitable puns. Though less numerous than in *Moby-Dick*, they are present in most of the writings of this period in sufficiently formidable profusion. Whether the more metaphysical of them, like "wall" in "Bartleby" and "bluff" in *The Confidence-Man*, are a guide or a trap for the

reader is a matter of opinion. Certainly they are a highly suggestive factor in the "Joycean art work" that Chase has found in
*Pierre*, particularly in its proper names; but even Chase's bold
conjectures are curbed by the reservation that "*Pierre* invites
many questionably occult readings." [37] *The Confidence-Man*
seems more transparently allegorical in such names as Frank
Goodman and Mark Winsome, and in such episodes as the story
of China Aster, where the idealistic hero is a candlemaker (note
the "eastern star" in his name) and the worldly villain, Orchis, is
a shoemaker, "whose calling it is to defend the understandings of
men from naked contact with the substance of things." Beneath
its easier narrative surface, however, *The Confidence-Man*
stealthily immures the reader in a ghostly forest of disassociated
hints, like "*Fidèle*," "advent," "lamb-like," "mass," and "member," which may be the punning instruments of an extensive
religious satire, or, conceivably, nothing of the sort.

For better or for worse, Melville was a punster of parts. No
mere juggler of verbal witticisms, he was at least as accomplished
at dialectical legerdemain as his mousy casuist from the Philosophical Intelligence Office, whose intellectual pea-rolling so con-
founds the Missouri bachelor:

> "But is analogy argument? You are a punster."
> "Punster, respected sir?" with a look of being aggrieved.
> "Yes, you pun with ideas as another man may with words." [38]

In a later day Melville would surely have been of the school of
Meredith, who held that "humorists are difficult: it is a piece of
their humor to puzzle our wits." Lacking the authority of Meredith, he invented his own preceptor in the person of Yamjamma,
the Mardian sage who "disdained to be plain; he scorned to be
fully comprehended by mortals." [39] At the placid end of his long
and unappreciated career, we catch a suggestive glimpse of the
author of *Pierre* and *The Confidence-Man* marking the following
lines in the translator's preface to a volume of Schopenhauer —
with what fraternal gleam in his eye we can only surmise: "His
irony is noteworthy; for it extends beyond mere isolated sentences, and sometimes applies to whole passages, which must be
read *cum grano salis*." [40]

# 11

# The Hornet's Nest

*Come on then, satire! general, unconfin'd,*
*Spread thy broad wing, and souse on all the kind.*
*Ye statesmen, priests, of one religion all!*
*Ye tradesmen, vile, in army, court, or hall!*
*Ye reverend atheists! . . .*

Sometime during or after 1856, the year of *The Confidence-Man*, Melville read and marked this passage in his copy of Pope.[1] That he should have felt a certain rapport with the Wasp of Twickenham is not surprising; the critical mind he exposed in print in the 1850's was itself "a hornet's nest of objectionable Truths." [2] These "Truths," as Murray has added them up, "either are shocking or depressing facts about man's hidden self, or scathing condemnations of civilization, or offensive references to Deity; or they are positive truths, in agreement with the Sermon on the Mount, which are 'ridiculous to men.'" The creative activity of a mind so oriented is bound to be largely negative, expending itself in reactions against orthodoxy.

One of the fundamental things Melville admired in Hawthorne was that "he says NO! in thunder; but the Devil himself cannot make him say *yes*." [3] Certainly Melville himself was a no-sayer, but those who accuse him of "Timonism" perhaps forget how violently negative one had to be to approach a balanced view of life amid the inflated optimism of nineteenth-century America. Whatever epidemic enthusiasm his contemporaries indulged in, Melville meant, like his happy fiddler Hautboy, to see the world "pretty much as it was," and "not theoretically espouse its bright side nor its dark side." When a British admirer sent him a copy of James Thomson's *City of Dreadful Night* in 1885, he wrote back: "As to pessimism, altho' neither pessimist nor optimist myself, nevertheless I relish it in the verse if for nothing else than as a counterpoise to the exorbitant hopefulness, juvenile and shallow, that makes such a bluster in these days — at least in some quarters." [4] It was the constitutional yea-sayers Melville was bitter about, and he turned on them with splenetic delight after he had finished his multiple saga of the sea.

I

It was men like Benjamin Franklin and Ralph Waldo Emerson who had shaped the righteous but repulsively confident personality of Melville's America — the "household Plato" and the "Plato who talks thro' his nose." [5] Of the two, Franklin was the simpler and more innocuous, a Yankee Pooh-Bah who was "everything but a poet." His brief portrait in *Israel Potter* is an affectionate caricature in which Melville paid his wry respects to a Founding Father who seemed to him half saint and half benevolent fraud. Even Franklin, with a good humor that Melville does not deny him, could scarcely have taken offense at the gentle rallying of his primness, frugality, and sentimentous pragmatism. Yet when we hear "words . . . from the wise man in the most graciously bland and flowing tones," we sense the characteristic sound of the Confidence Man; and when he utters himself in print we are sure of it.

"'So what signifies waiting and hoping for better times? We may make these times better, if we bestir ourselves. Industry need not wish, and he that lives upon hope will die fasting, as Poor Richard says. There are no gains without pains. Then help hands, for I have no lands, as Poor Richard says.' Oh, confound all this wisdom! It's a sort of insulting to talk wisdom to a man like me. It's wisdom that's cheap, and it's fortune that's dear. That ain't in Poor Richard; but it ought to be," concluded Israel, suddenly slamming down the pamphlet.[6]

Israel makes a pointed return to *Poor Richard* to ponder the saying, "God helps them that help themselves," and then goes forth to demonstrate through the remaining half century of his miserable existence that God does no such thing. Insofar as *Israel*

*Potter* is a satiric novel, it is a satire on this earliest American expression of the creed of Self-Reliance.

As Melville draws Franklin, there falls from him the faint shadow of George F. Babbitt. Long before Lewis, Melville was an articulate enemy of Babbittry, with its evangelical optimism, its Boosters Club geniality, its religious faith in established institutions, its brisk assurance of an American commercial Heaven. He had sketched his first Babbitt in the person of Charlie Millthorpe, Pierre's bourgeois chum, who boasts of his camaraderie with the Transcendentalists as though it were a membership in the Elks, and who breezily proposes "to stump the State on the Kantian Philosophy! A dollar a head, my boy!" In *The Confidence-Man* he completed his portrait of the pre-Babbitt American, not only in the foreground figures of Frank Goodman and Charlie Noble, who come close to the anti-Rotarian's concept of the Rotarian, but in a sparkling variety of lesser mutations as well.

Appropriately, it is his self-styled "golden boys," Frank and Charlie, whom he turns loose in praise of the indiscriminate fraternalism they so cynically exemplify. And it is to them that he assigns the militant espousal of the *status quo*, most delightfully concentrated in their indignant defense of freedom of the press against the "heart-breaking" aspersion that it is "on a par with *freedom of Colt's revolver.*" The smug hypocrisy of uncritical optimism he personifies in the oiliest of his charlatans, "the Happy Bonesetter," to whom Melville gleefully opposes himself momentarily in the person of the embittered soldier of fortune, who has "longed to get hold of the Happy Man, drill him, drop the powder, and leave him to explode at his leisure." [7]

Highest of all in comic quality is the solicitor for the Seminole Widow and Orphan Asylum, in whom Melville lampoons civic quackeries and the sophomoric commercialism of the national spirit. A combination of Autolycus and W. C. Fields, the agent proposes a "World's Charity," a kind of universal Community Chest, which would spell the end of poverty and paganism in precisely fourteen years through the collection and judicious redistribution of an estimated $11,200,000,000.

Eleven thousand two hundred millions; it will frighten none but a retail philanthropist. What is it but eight hundred millions for each of fourteen years? Now eight hundred millions — what is that, to average it, but one little dollar a head for the population of the planet? . . . Missions I would quicken with the Wall Street spirit. . . In brief, the conversion of the heathen, so far, at least, as depending on human effort, would, by the world's charity, be let out on contract. So much by bid for converting India, so much for Borneo, so much for Africa. Competition allowed, stimulus would be given. There would be no lethargy of monopoly. . . You see, this doing good to the world by driblets amounts to just nothing. I am for doing good to the world with a will. I am for doing good to the world once for all and having done with it. . . I am for sending ten thousand missionaries in a body and converting the Chinese *en masse* within six months of the debarkation. The thing is then done, and turn to something else.[8]

If the resemblance to Colonel Sellers is fleeting, still there is too much of Twain's sharp and genuinely funny satiric touch in such passages to justify the neglect in which Melville has lain as a satirist of American life.

Among the specific irritants to which he was exposed, none can have been more irksome to Melville than the literary Babbittries of his day. By the time he came to create his young author-hero Pierre in 1851 he was fed up with popular taste and professional opportunism to the point of satiric ignition. Perhaps he was a little *too* fed up; perhaps he already felt himself defeated by the tide of sentimental ephemera with which he was forced to compete. One can hardly read *Pierre* without sensing how painfully Melville must have been torn between a longing to burlesque this best-selling drivel and a temptation to reap some of the easy profit of its popularity. Apparently unable to make up his mind, he ended by dramatizing his own dilemma; but it is only as latent parody that the book makes sense against the background of contemporary fiction and its author's known quality of mind.

*Pierre* is in fact a compendium of all the diseases that had been accumulating for sixty years on the body of American popular fiction. It follows to the letter the formula prescribed by Susanna Rowson in 1794: "a sufficient quantity of sighs, tears, swooning hysterics, and all the moving expressions of heart-rending woe, . . . a duel, and, if convenient, a suicide." [9] The earliest ancestor of Pierre among the native votaries of Werther had shot himself when he discovered his fiancée to be his half-sister.[10] Seduction and the ruin of innocence were a "must," and Melville reinforced

the imminent fall of his principals with the ready-made wreckage
of Delly Ulver. He bowed dutifully, and grotesquely enough, to
the favorite fads: animal magnetism to increase the voltage of the
*femme fatale*, and the physiognomic trick of presenting women in
symbolic pairs — "blonde and brunette . . . seraph and sensual-
ist." [11] The Plinlimmon pamphlet strips to form the tractlike
quality of moral novels like the Reverend Sylvester Judd's *Margaret*, which Melville read in 1850;[12] and the irrational sacrifices
of Lucy and Pierre are in the last degree faithful to the tradition of
martyrdom as a prerequisite to perfect virtue in either sex. Heroes
and heroines were by definition perfectionists, they modeled
themselves consciously on Christ, and they came to predictably
melancholy passes. One contemporary of Pierre's became con-
vinced that he *was* Christ.[13] In all cases, the standard drama was
precisely that of *Pierre*; as the Reverend Mr. Judd put it in the
subtitle to *Margaret*: "A Tale of the Real and Ideal, Blight and
Bloom." The crowning achievement of the sentimentalists, their
sublime insipidity, Melville also mastered and surpassed. The style
of these books, invariably fustian, was capable of rising to an
orgiastic poeticism that defies travesty. Melville almost certainly
intended his worst writing in *Pierre* for satire, but there is no way
of proving it by the test of exaggeration.

Our only sure touchstone is a digressive section of the novel
entitled "Young America in Literature," where the satire on
vapidity becomes explicit and is effectively coupled with a comprehensive blast against the depraved state of contemporary criticism and publication.[14] When Pierre makes his literary debut with
a fluffy sonnet called "The Tropical Summer," he is instantly admired for his "genteelness" and acclaimed a superlatively "respectable" and "harmless" genius on the ground that "vulgarity and
vigor — two inseparable adjuncts — are equally removed from
him." His lionizing begins with a series of witless letters from
toadying mercenaries and admirers, such as the publishing house
of "Wonder & Wen," former tailors who retain the idiom of
their old trade. He receives endless requests to address lyceums
and clubs, such as the "Urquhartian Club for the Immediate Extension of the Limits of all Knowledge, both Human and Divine"
in a place called "Zadockprattsville." Melville could hardly have
foreseen that a mere six years later he would himself be lecturing

for pittances in a score of Zadockprattsvilles on "The South Seas" and "Roman Statuary." But most of his hero's comic conflicts in the literary arena are clearly based on his own experiences and personal crotchets. The ludicrous "bill-sticking" by which Wonder & Wen propose to embellish Pierre's title page reflects a tasteless custom particularly repugnant to Melville, who once wrote to his brother concerning a projected volume of poems, "For God's sake don't have *By the author of 'Typee' 'Piddledee' &c* on the title-page." [15] Pierre's refusal to let the "Captain Kidd Monthly" print his picture is a nearly verbatim repetition of Melville's capricious refusal to let his friend Duyckinck print his, on the ground that "almost everybody is having his 'mug' engraved nowadays." [16] In much the same way Melville must have reacted to the industrious compilers of biographical compendia who hound Pierre for everything from self-criticism to information on "the precise texture and hue of the first trowsers he wore." Small wonder, with such a view of his profession, that Melville refused to join the Author's Club. But the traits he saw beneath the mask were not limited to authors; he never joined any club. The Confidence Man wore many masks, but there was just one Confidence Man.

2

Beneath his masks the Confidence Man was not a "man," of course, nor even a concept that one could come cleanly to grips with. But there is an inspired portrait of him in Hawthorne's "The Celestial Railroad" that Melville could not have missed when he read and reviewed the *Mosses* in the summer of 1850:

At the end of the valley, as John Bunyan mentions, is a cavern where in his days dwelt two cruel giants, Pope and Pagan, who had strewn the ground about their residence with the bones of slaughtered pilgrims. These vile old troglodytes are no longer there, but in their deserted cave another terrible giant has thrust himself, and makes it his business to seize upon honest travelers and fat them for his table with plentiful meals of smoke, mist, moonshine, raw potatoes and sawdust. He is a German by birth, and is called Giant Transcendentalist, but as to his form, his features, his substance, and his nature generally, it is the chief peculiarity of this huge miscreant that neither he for himself nor anybody for him has ever been able to describe them. As we rushed by the cavern's mouth we caught a hasty glimpse of him, looking somewhat like an ill-proportioned figure, but considerably more like a heap of fog and duskiness. He shouted after us, but in so strange a phraseology that we knew not what he meant, nor whether to be encouraged or affrighted.

In his review Melville wrote that Hawthorne had "dropped germinous seeds" into his soul, and this story would seem to be one of them. Echoes of Giant Transcendentalist and his lair keep recurring in Melville's own sallies on the subject, and the conception of *The Confidence-Man* appears deeply indebted to the whole witty parable of the optimist's illusory trip to heaven.[17] Perhaps it was Hawthorne's Mr. Smooth-it-away who focused for Melville the central defect of transcendentalism, which he caught in the punning names of the characters through whom he satirized it: Blandmour, Merrymusk, Winsome, Plotinus Plinlimmon.[18] The common theme in all is confidence, in a sense which makes the term "confidence man" one of Melville's most penetrating puns.

The poet Blandmour in "Poor Man's Pudding" is the perfect Panglossian optimist. It is his dreamy belief that "through kind Nature, the poor, out of their very poverty, extract comfort," and that they ought to be grateful for their blessings. The narrator, however, tasting the moldy reality of "poor man's pudding," comes to the contrary conclusion that "of all the preposterous assumptions of humanity over humanity, nothing exceeds most of the criticisms made on the habits of the poor by the well-housed, well-warmed, and well-fed." Blandmour, though not an avowed Transcendentalist, is clearly one of Melville's "amiable philosophers of either the 'Compensation,' or 'Optimist' school, [who] deny that any misery is in the world, except for the purpose of throwing the fine *povertiresque* element into its general picture." [19] The reference to Emerson, however unjust, is unmistakable.

The woodcutter Merrymusk in "Cock-a-Doodle-Doo," complementing the figure of Blandmour, is the victim of that optimistic, compensatory philosophy. The villain, who is ironically made the hero of the story, is an extraordinary rooster whose irrepressible crow is "a perfect paean and *laudamus*." This Trumpet (that is his name) of victorious "self-reliance" belongs to the poverty-stricken Merrymusk, whose wife and children are all

dying, but who feels himself rich beyond measure in the possession of his "cheerer," who "crows through all; crows at the darkest." In the end, sick to death himself, Merrymusk yet stoutly
maintains that all is well, and as he and his family drop happily
dead one by one, the cock sounds their knell "in a rapture of
benevolent delight." Considering its ideological freight, the story
moves with a remarkable comic lightness and rewards even the
reader who is not attuned to parodic echoes of Emerson, Thoreau,
or Wordsworth.[20] To one who is, however, the fate of Melville's
pauper sawyer becomes a powerful ironic commentary on Hawthorne's "smoke, mist, moonshine, raw potatoes and sawdust."

In *Pierre* the burlesque is more direct and more strikingly reminiscent of "The Celestial Railroad." Pierre's residence in the city
is in the shabby old Church of the Apostles, now occupied on the
lower floors by lawyers and on the upper floors by a clique of
seedy philosophers known as "Apostles." In this absurd cabal
Melville neatly caricatured the so-called "Transcendental Club"
in which Emerson, Alcott, Margaret Fuller, and other leading
transcendentalists were associated in the 1830's and 1840's. The
mockery is cleverly conceived on several counts. The trick of
putting the doers on the ground floor and the theoreticians up-
stairs recalls Swift's telling division of the population of Laputa;
and the housing of philosophical "Apostles" in an abandoned
church echoes in less mythic terms the point that Hawthorne made
in putting his Giant Transcendentalist in the "deserted cave" of
Pope and Pagan. The mockery was accurate as well, to judge
from Alcott's pathetic admission:

> We are ghosts and spectres, chimeras, rumors, holding no known
> relation to the fields and houses where we are supposed or seen to
> abide; and our dealings with men have an aspect ridiculous and to be
> made game of at the bank and bar-room. Our very virtues are mytho-
> logical.[21]

And yet it was not their virtues that Melville was mocking. It
was rather

> that inevitable perverse ridiculousness, which so often bestreaks some
> of the essentially finest and noblest aspirations of those men, who dis-
> gusted with the common conventional quackeries, strive, in their
> clogged terrestrial humanities, after some imperfectly discerned, but
> heavenly ideals. . . Hardly a new-light Apostle, but who, in super-

addition to his revolutionary scheme for the minds and philosophies
of men, entertains some insane, heterodoxical notions about the econ-
omy of his body."

The principal offender in this respect was Bronson Alcott himself, whom Carlyle, out of his "hopeless unbelief in vegetables,"
dubbed "the Potato Quixote." [23] His long-suffering wife recorded
in her journal that their diet was "almost exclusively coarse bread
and water — the apples we have not being mellow." At Dove
Cottage, the forerunner of the famous Fruitlands, a winter day
began with a "cold-water sponging all over, and a rub with a
coarse crash linen towel," the water often frozen an inch over
and refreezing during the bathing; then on to a breakfast of
bread, apples, potatoes, and cold water.[24] Such was the regimen
at the Church of the Apostles, where Pierre daily glimpsed "many
a lean, philosophical nudity, refreshing his meager bones with
crash-towel and cold water," and where "a huge jug of Adam's
Ale, and a bushel-basket of Graham crackers were the only con-
vivials." Pierre himself is permitted to shiver, Alcott-fashion, in
"water thickened with incipient ice," but his creator amusingly
spares him the "Pythagorean dietings" he held so abysmal a substitute for "champagne and oysters."

Despite his fanatical veneration for Pythagoras, however, Alcott was far from the sole object of Melville's satire. Vegetarian-
ism, hydropathy, and other health fads were epidemic in mid-nineteenth century America. Most of the experimental utopian com-
munities that were springing up were vegetarian-abstinence
groups, and the chief pied piper of the day was Dr. Sylvester
Graham, inventor of the Graham cracker and "indefatigable
lecturer on matters of health." Bronson Alcott's cousin William
published two reform-and-health magazines in the mid-1830's
and no doubt influenced Alcott as he himself was influenced by
Graham.[25] A pair of jingles printed in a popular magazine about
the time of *Pierre* suggest that Melville and Hawthorne were
sniping at a potent enemy of common sense, and that they were
not alone in the battle.

> *Immortal Graham*! *As the ages roll,*
> *And changing nature decks thy lowly bed,*
> *Thy fame shall spread abroad from pole to pole,*
> *And Myriad throats take down thy Graham bread!*

> *It's water, water everywhere,*
> *And quarts to drink, if you can bear:*
> *'Tis well that we are made of clay,*
> *For common dust would wash away!*[26]

Such cultism was hardly basic to transcendental thought, but it was a common adjunct and irresistibly useful to the satirist as a peg to hang his ridicule on. The steam-baths with which some of the "advanced" Apostles refined their ritual soaking gave Melville the perfect opportunity for original play upon Hawthorne's "smoke" and "mist": "The smoke which issued from their heads, and overspread their pages, was prefigured in the mists that issued from under their door-sills and out of their windows."

As a focus for this broad burlesque of the rank-and-file, Melville invented the "Grand Master," Plotinus Plinlimmon. Plinlimmon is a cipher, characterized by "Inscrutableness" and "non-Benevolence." He is not so much a collection of characteristics as an absence of them. He reads nothing, writes nothing (his words are taken down by disciples), and "whence he came, no one could tell." He is neuter, having in him that which is "winning" and also that which "repelled." He is the ambiguous soul of transcendentalism and as such is the Confidence Man in person, his only mask — himself:

> Though the clothes worn by this man were strictly in accordance with the general style of any unobtrusive gentleman's dress, yet his clothes seemed to disguise this man. One would almost have said, his very face, the apparently natural glance of his very eye, disguised this man.[27]

His satiric meaning is summed up, not in his famous pamphlet, for which he is merely a convenient handle, but in a comic anecdote about a rich admirer who sent a gift of fine books and then found it unopened at the philosopher's door.

> "Missent," said Plotinus Plinlimmon placidly; "if any thing, I looked for some choice Curacoa from a nobleman like you. I should be very happy, my dear Count, to accept a few jugs of choice Curacoa."
> "I thought that the society of which you are the head, excluded all things of that sort" — replied the Count.
> "Dear Count, so they do; but Mohammed hath his own dispensation."
> "Ah! I see," said the noble scholar archly.

"I am afraid you do not see, dear Count" — said Plinlimmon; and instantly before the eyes of the Count, the inscrutable atmosphere eddied and eddied round about this Plotinus Plinlimmon.

Like Hawthorne's Giant, Plinlimmon resembles nothing so much as "a heap of fog and duskiness." Despite his titular resemblance to Emerson as "Grand Master," therefore, it is probably misreading Melville to identify him with any single personality as an intentional portrait.[28] The portrait of Emerson was yet to come, and there would be little doubt about the matter of identity when Melville went to work on Emerson.

### 3

Yet the satiric features of Plinlimmon and his Apostles can be clearly seen only in the light of Melville's opinion of Emerson. That opinion was suspicious, sometimes indignant, or incredulous; but it was not contemptuous or even altogether antagonistic. From first exposure he thought him "a great man," and he wrote a long letter to Duyckinck detailing his reactions.[29] He did "not oscillate in Emerson's rainbow," he protested, yet he thought him "more than a brilliant fellow," "an uncommon man"; if a humbug, then "no common humbug." He had even found his lecture "quite intelligible, tho' to say truth, they told me that this night he was unusually plain." All in all, he had been "very agreeably disappointed in Mr. Emerson." He had found him, at any rate, one of the world's "thought-divers," and it was Melville's way to "love all men who *dive*."

There was, however, a negative side to the picture. For one thing, he "could readily see in Emerson, notwithstanding his merit, a gaping flaw. It was, the insinuation, that had he lived in those days when the world was made, he might have offered some valuable suggestions." For another thing, it was a characteristic irritation to Melville that Emerson should be "above munching a plain cake in company of jolly fellows, & swigging off his ale like you and me. . . . His belly, sir, is in his chest, & his brains descend down into his neck and offer an obstacle to a draught of ale or a mouthful of cake." The asceticism which Melville made so ridiculous in the cult of the Apostles had an undeniable sanction of sorts from transcendental headquarters. "The sublime vision comes to the pure and simple soul in a clean and chaste body," Emerson wrote in "The Poet." "So the poet's habit of living should be set on a key so low that the common influences should delight him. His cheerfulness should be the gift of the sunlight; the air should suffice for his inspiration, and he should be tipsy with water." Melville could not refrain from registering a protest at this point in the margin of his copy.

There was in Emerson, as in Plinlimmon, something a little *too* sublime: "To crown all, a certain floating atmosphere seemed to invest and go along with this man." [30] As Matthiessen describes Emerson, there was in him "a serenity that had grown from no depth of experience but seemed to be constitutional." Matthiessen has spoken, too, of Emerson's ability to come out with an idea so "staggeringly innocent" as to make clear what Henry James, Sr., had meant in calling him his "unfallen friend." [31] It was this amputated insensitivity to reality that appalled and irritated Melville most of all. When he read in Emerson's "Prudence," "The drover, the sailor, buffets it all day, and his health renews itself at as vigorous a pulse under the sleet, as under the sun of June," he wrote in the margin: "To one who has weathered Cape Horn as a common sailor what stuff all this is."

Annotating another passage in "The Poet," he wrote: "His gross and astonishing errors and illusions spring from a self-conceit so intensely intellectual and calm that at first one hesitates to call it by its right name. Another species of Mr. Emerson's errors, or rather blindness, proceeds from a defect in the region of the heart." This was the defect he characterized in Plinlimmon by the term "non-benevolence." At its worst it was the sort of thing he found at second hand in a book which cited the tendency of "even the kindly Emerson" to utter unfeeling remarks about the common man: for example, "the worst of charity is that the lives you are asked to preserve are not worth preserving." [32] Melville's comment was: "These expressions attributed to the 'kindly Emerson' are somewhat different from the words of Christ to the multitude on the Mount." "Non-benevolence" was the word for it. It was, as in Plinlimmon, "neither Malice nor Illwill; but something passive." It was what Matthiessen called in Emerson "diffident blandness" as opposed to "satanic pride." [33] Satanic pride the author of *Moby-Dick* could have understood.

4

In *Pierre* and the stories that followed, Melville was feeling out
the transcendentalist position and its adherents. By 1856 he had
the range and in *The Confidence-Man* laid down a satiric barrage
of deadly accuracy on the ranking generals of the camp, Emerson
and Thoreau. A number of scholarly probing actions have been
fought over the ground since then in an indecisive effort to identify the bodies beyond cavil, but the inevitable consensus has been
that Mark Winsome and his disciple Egbert were, in all but name,
Emerson and his disciple Thoreau.[34]

The caricatures are sharply focused. Mark Winsome, billed as
"a mystic," appears to warn the cosmopolitan against Charlie
Noble, whom he suspects — a delightful irony — of being a confidence man. He is described as

> a blue-eyed man, sandy-haired, and Saxon-looking; perhaps five-and-
> forty; tall, and, but for a certain angularity, well made; little touch
> of the drawing-room about him, but a look of plain propriety of a
> Puritan sort, with a kind of farmer dignity. . . A neat, comely, almost
> ruddy cheek, coolly fresh . . . the colour of warmth preserved by the
> virtue of chill. Toning the whole man, was one-knows-not-what of
> shrewdness and mythiness, strangely jumbled; in that way, he seemed
> a kind of cross between a Yankee peddler and a Tartar priest. . .[35]

He has a "passionless air" and regards his new acquaintance with
"such a preternaturally cold, gemmy glance . . . that he seemed
more a metaphysical merman than a feeling man." He will accept
no entertainment but cold water ("Ice it well, waiter"), and sits
before it "purely and coldly radiant as a prism. It seemed as if
one could almost hear him vitreously chime and ring." In the next
chapter he introduces to the cosmopolitan "a well-dressed, com-
mercial-looking gentleman of about thirty . . . strikingly defer-
ential," whom he calls "Egbert, a disciple." "Egbert," he says,
"was the first among mankind to reduce to practice the principles
of Mark Winsome — principles previously accounted less adapted
to life than the closet." The reference to Thoreau, the pencil-
merchant, who practiced Emerson's self-reliance and noncon-
formity to a quixotic degree in Walden woods and even in the
Concord jail, is all but explicit.

But Melville is always closer to Voltaire than to Pope, and most
of the fun he has with his two philosophers is at the expense of

their ideas rather than their persons. The opening attack is aimed at the Emersonian concept of beauty, as set forth in Part III of *Nature*. Received by the cosmopolitan with a courtly flourish, Mark Winsome is moved to remark that he must have a beautiful soul — "one full of all love and truth; for where beauty is, there must those be." Emerson's exact words had been, "Beauty is the mark God sets upon virtue." Earlier in the same essay he had asserted that "there is no object so foul that intense light will not make beautiful," and he had added "the lion's claw" and "the serpent" as examples of the beautiful in nature. The cosmopolitan agrees with ironic suavity that "beauty is at bottom incompatible with ill," and cites "the latent benignity of that beautiful creature, the rattle-snake." It is an easy move from this gambit to the inevitable parody of Emerson's celebrated declaration in "Self-Reliance" that "a foolish consistency is the hobgoblin of little minds." Winsome's high-handed apology for self-contradiction is simply, "I seldom care to be consistent."

Characteristically, it was Melville's heart rather than his head that supplied the indignation behind his main attack. When the cosmopolitan requests the "favour" of enlightenment, following a Plinlimmon-like obfuscation, he gets instead a lecture on his unfortunate choice of a word which signifies to the mystic "some poor, unheroic submission to being done good to." The idea is Emersonian enough, but its most spectacular expression, possibly the one Melville had in mind, is Thoreau's remark in the first chapter of *Walden*: "If I knew for a certainty that a man was coming to my house with the conscious design of doing me good, I should run for my life. . ." Doing good to others proves just as repugnant to Winsome, who apparently feels, with Emerson and Thoreau, that philanthropy is "foolish" and a "greatly over-rated" virtue.[36]

This "non-benevolence," transcendentalism's "defect in the region of the heart," Melville found most egregiously displayed in the twin essays the Concord sages had written on friendship.[37] When pressed for an urgent loan by his "hypothetical friend," the cosmopolitan, Egbert refuses on the ground that "a true friend . . . should have a soul above loans"; and for authority he cites his "sublime master, who, in his Essay on Friendship, says so nobly, that if he want a terrestrial convenience, not to his friend celes-

tial (or friend social and intellectual) would he go; no: for his
terrestrial convenience, to his friend terrestrial (or humbler business friend) he goes." What the "sublime master" had said in his
"Essay on Friendship" did not, in fact, need a great deal of exaggeration for satiric purposes: "Why insist on rash personal relations with your friend? . . . Leave this touching and clawing.
Let him be to me a spirit. . . I can get politics and chat and
neighborly conveniences from cheaper companions." And what is
only implied in the master's essay Thoreau had made explicit in
his: "Friendship is not so kind as is imagined; it has not much
human blood in it."

It would be an oversimplification to say that Emerson is the
Confidence Man, for Mark Winsome and his disciple are only
two of the masks that the Confidence Man assumes. Their relatively minor role and late placement in the story might even per-
suade the reader that Melville did not, after all, attach much
thematic importance to them. Only his early manuscript notes,
which list the Winsome-Egbert chapters first, remain to demonstrate their germinal significance.[38] As the book took form, perhaps he came to see that Emerson himself was only another mask
for the general madness. The true villain was abroad in less tan-
gible form: "a false humanitarianism, an insensate optimism" —
"the greatest of all subjects for satire in Melville's time and place,
as bigotry and traditionalism had been . . . in Rabelais'."[39] In
*The Confidence-Man* he had found the perfect subject and the
perfect vehicle for his valedictory snort at the follies of his world.
As Meredith was later to discover, the comic spirit delights in
nothing so much as a masquerade, where at its own chosen moment it may expose in all its bathos "the striking discrepancy between the real and the false face."[40]

# 12

# Remembered Laughter

How sick was the author of *Pierre* and *The Confidence-Man*? Was he, as legend has it, almost psychopathically alienated from both the outer and the inner worlds that had fed his early popularity? How much do we surely learn from the occasional virulence of his later work, from his affected contempt for his early romances, from those moody posturings in his letters to Hawthorne?

It is admittedly tempting to view a great artist's letters as gospel revelations of the inner man, especially when they complain to another great artist of the unpopularity of truth, the venality of fame, and the ignominy of being remembered as a "man who lived among the cannibals." [1] Unfortunately, Melville was given to spiritual melodrama; before so flattering an audience as Hawthorne he was quite capable of picturing himself one moment as a tragic failure in whom "shortly the flower must fall to the mould," in the next as a budding genius to whom "Leviathan is not the biggest fish." [2] It is equally perilous to take at face value his scornful remarks about "Peedee, Hullabaloo & Pog-Dog." He was no more respectful about the sober "doggerel" of his maturest years, which he boasted to have sold at a bargain to a trunk-maker for linings, or even about *Clarel*, which he not inaccurately termed a "what not . . . eminently adapted for unpopularity." [3]

The truth of Melville's attitude toward his early work would seem to be, not so much that he considered it unworthy of him, as that he considered himself unworthy of it. Had this not been true or had Melville not understood it to be true, he could not have written as he did in *Pierre*:

In the inferior instances of an immediate literary success, in very young writers, it will be almost invariably observable, that for that instant success they were chiefly indebted to some rich and peculiar experience in life, embodied in a book, which because, for that cause, containing original matter, the author himself, forsooth, is to be considered original; in this way, many very original books, being the product of very unoriginal minds. Indeed, man has only to be but a little circumspect, and away flies the last rag of his vanity.[4]

It appears to have been perfectly clear to Melville that what his early writings lacked was not positive merit but an originality sufficiently independent of subject matter that the author could honestly take some credit for it. It was the sense of this lack — a somewhat exaggerated sense, posterity has agreed — that drove him to *Mardi* and *Moby-Dick*, that hounded him from *Pierre* to *The Confidence-Man*, and that, in all probability, accounts for his abrupt abandonment of prose for poetry thereafter. In any case, as another of these self-analytical passages from *Pierre* shows, he saw through his own affected disdain of his early work and related it with unimprovable accuracy both to the egoistic idealism that prompted it and to the crippling discouragement that resulted from it.

It is well enough known, that the best productions of the best human intellects, are generally regarded by those intellects as mere immature freshman exercises, wholly worthless in themselves, except as initiatives for entering the great University of God after death. Certain it is, that if any inferences can be drawn from observations of the familiar lives of men of the greatest mark, their finest things, those which become the foolish glory of the world, are not only very poor and inconsiderable to themselves, but often positively distasteful; they would rather not have the book in the room. In minds comparatively inferior as compared with the above, these surmising considerations so sadden and unfit, that they become careless of what they write; go to their desks with discontent, and only remain there — victims to headache, and pain in the back — by the hard constraint of some social necessity.[5]

What such insights make clear is that Melville's negativeness and ambiguity, however perverse they may have been, were not blind alleys. They were rather stages in a constructive search for those elements of merit and success in his early work capable of displaying the original character of his world and himself without the shallow appeal of exotic adventure. The inner turns and tensions of the search can only be guessed; we cannot even be sure that it was conscious. What we can see is an increasing recurrence, as Melville wrote himself out, of the two principal comic features that had distinguished *Typee* and *Omoo*. One is the mainspring of native and perhaps universal folklore — the complementary character pattern of the dupe and the trickster. The other is the mainspring of his own personal folklore — an exuberant sense of humor at play with the quirks of private memory and imagination.

I

Surprisingly, even *Pierre* proves to be radically related to the central theme of American folk humor: Pierre is a dupe, a "sucker." He is not, however, the Yankee comic sucker, victimized by a fast-talking pitchman. He is "the fool of Truth, the fool of Virtue, the fool of Fate." [6] As such he is what we are more likely to think of as the Cervantine or Meredithian comic sucker — the sentimentalist, whose exaggerated idealism provides the momentum for its own reduction to absurdity. In Melville as in Meredith, it is a comic absurdity only so long as the sucker fails to recognize his folly; the moment he comes face-to-face with it his absurdity becomes tragic. The essential paradox of Meredith's *The Tragic Comedians* is precisely that of *Pierre*: the hero indulges in an idealistic folly as a sop to his ego, and when his course comes to inevitable wreck against reality he turns at bay, stripped of illusions, and reverts to behavior as violently undercivilized as his previous conduct had been ludicrously overcivilized. In both cases the action is comic but the denouement is tragic. *Pierre* is not good comedy, even before the great awakening, because, unlike Cervantes and Meredith, Melville was emotionally involved in the very folly that doomed his hero.

Israel Potter, like Pierre, emerges as a tragicomic fool of Fate, gulled however by circumstance rather than by any fatal flaw in his character. Having none of the neurosis of Pierre, but a good deal of the comic shrewdness of the Yankee peddler, Potter is much closer to the traditional folk figure.[7] Except for his Puritan moodiness and sensitivity to moral principle, he could even be called a picaresque hero. Like Lazarillo de Tormes, whose adventures Melville had read in 1850,[8] he is dupe and trickster by turns and seems, for all his ingenuity, to suffer more than he gains from life. The moral principle, of course, by definition spoils him for a rogue, but he shares even with the unregenerate Dr. Long Ghost an instinctive adaptability and opportunism. His finest hour occurs when he rises to the formidable challenge of escaping detection in an enemy ship by concealing himself, like Poe's purloined letter, full in the public eye and persuading the perplexed authorities against their better judgment that he has been there all along. Equally brazen are the dodges he employs in other perilous situations — donning a dead man's clothes and stalking to freedom as an apparition, or posing as a scarecrow in the middle of a field and pointing woodenly at his pursuer. There is at times a wistful temerity about Israel Potter that seems less remarkable for its antecedents than for the immortal embodiment it has since received in the art of Charles Chaplin.

In *The Confidence-Man* Melville's use of the dupe and the trickster reached thematic proportions. Richard Chase, who is "tempted to call [it] his second-best book," bases his enthusiastic estimate on the premise that "it is a book of folklore"; and Matthiessen too has pointed out that its character types "were of the material which the frontier humorists were already quarrying, and which the local colorists were to discover after the civil war." [9] The fact is that Melville was himself one of the frontier humorists. If most of his materials had come from the sea frontier, still there were impressions enough from a single trip West in 1840 to yield him at least one book when he had found the way to use them.[10] What little we know of the journey suggests that it was the right kind for a future humorist and philosopher: precisely the vagabond junket by canal and lake to the great River itself that could best fill a man with a life and lore that were already crystallizing into comic mythology. The popular imagination was rapidly converting the swarming decks and cabins of the Mississippi steamer into a picaresque microcosm, populated by drifters and dreamers, by roughs and dandies, by sharps and yarn-spinners and the victims of both. By the time Melville began to chart the fabulous voyage of the *Fidèle* there were countless sketches in print to sharpen and color the pertinent recollections of what he had seen and heard.

A river boat had all the built-in advantages of a Canterbury pilgrimage, and the popular humorists of the forties and fifties had been quick to exploit them. T. B. Thorpe's classic tall tale, "The Big Bear of Arkansas," printed in 1841 and again in 1854, had been told on a river boat, as had many lesser tales contributed to *The Spirit of the Times* in those decades.[11] *The Confidence-Man*, different as it is from such sketches, is nevertheless carried by talk, by dialogue drifting from encounter to encounter along the moving deck. What continuity it might have had is cheerfully fractured again and again by the interpolation of oral anecdotes of a more or less "tall" variety. If the matter was new to Melville, the manner was old. He had learned to tell stories as his fellow practitioners had; he had merely learned to tell them on bigger ships.[12]

River boats were wonderful places for talk; they were also the best of all places to find human variety in a manageable package, and it was this feature that brought Chaucer's pilgrimage to mind as Melville set out to describe his *dramatis personae*. "All kinds of that multiform pilgrim species, man," cluster in the *Fidèle*, most of them "hunters" after one thing or another; but the kind that interested Melville here were the "still keener hunters after all these hunters." [13] Everywhere on the frontier and in the popular writings about the frontier were hunters of this stamp. Had he never met one, he might still have summoned a convincing cast from the myriad rogue portraits that were comic currency in those days. Johnson Hooper's famous anti-hero, Simon Suggs, whose adventures appeared in 1845, would have required only a little grooming to have served as a working model for Melville's confidence man. His philosophy, at least, is impeccable: "It is good to be shifty in a new country." Moreover, as his creator describes him, "the shifty Captain Suggs is a miracle of shrewdness. He possesses, in an eminent degree, that tact which enables man to detect the *soft spots* in his fellow, and to assimiliate himself to whatever company he may fall in with." [14] Ovid Bolus, Esq., the accomplished liar created by Joseph Baldwin in 1853, supplies the polish that Suggs lacks and narrows the gap between the frontier *picaro* and Melville's metaphysical thimblerigger:

He was strikingly handsome. There was something in his air and bearing almost princely, certainly quite distinguished. His manners

were winning, his address frank, cordial and flowing. He was built
after the model and structure of Bolingbroke in his youth, American-
ized and Hoosierized a little by a "raising in," and adaptation to the
Backwoods. He was fluent but choice of diction, a little sonorous in
the structure of his sentences to give effect to a voice like an organ.
His countenance was open and engaging, usually sedate of expression,
but capable of any modifications at the shortest notice. Add to this his
intelligence, shrewdness, tact, humor, and that he was a ready debater
and elegant declaimer, and had the gift of bringing out, to the fullest
extent, his resources, and you may see that Ovid, in a new country,
was a man apt to make no mean impression.[15]

Like the potent charlatan behind the Melvillian masks, this Winsome, Frank, Noble, sweet-voiced Ovid possesses a magical
"faculty of ubiquity" and a pious confidence in the efficacy of
"Faith, Hope, and Charity" in other people.

   Melville probably read such popular sketches and conceivably
took some ideas from them, but it is not necessary to suppose that
he did. The confidence man was not, after all, a literary invention,
but a fact no more distant than Pittsfield, Massachusetts, where
the local paper for December 8, 1854, reported the operations of
an imposter who had been selling sob-stories to clergymen under
assumed names.[16] Whatever his operational disguise, the confidence man was at heart a salesman — a Yankee peddler, as
Richard Chase has pointed out.[17] He was a shrewd and resourceful character whose naïve and fluid frontier market was, even
in Melville's day, a powerful inducement to the stretching of
profits. He traveled an ever-increasing circuit as the nation
expanded, hawking everything from clocks to Bibles, and among
his number were always those with the fraudulent commodity
and the philosophy of Barnum, along with some of his talent.
Bronson Alcott peddled books as a young man — honestly, it
need hardly be added; and James Whitcomb Riley, a generation
later, traveled with a medicine show and even set up as an independent confidence man, advertising himself as a blind sign-
painter.[18]

   The medicine show is of course the most famous confidence
game in American folklore, but self-accredited "doctors" traveled
independently as well, peddling herb concoctions, either natural
or patented, with distinctive names and a glib line of patter:
Bezoar Stone for snake bite, Seneca Snake Root, Turlington's

Original Balsam, Duffy's Elixir, and so on.[19] These quacks pretended to medical competence and, with a bluff ingenuity always guiltily admired by the American sense of humor, plied their brisk trade among the backwoods gullible. Jack Blunt, in *Redburn*, got his pills from such a doctor, "who by placards stuck on the posts along the wharves, advertised to remain standing at the northeast corner of Catherine Market, every Monday and Friday, between the hours of ten and twelve in the morning, to receive calls from patients, distribute medicines, and give advice gratis." And the "doctors" were far from alone in their Barnumism. According to one contemporary report, "Quack philosophers and quack philanthropists are plenty as quack ministers and quack doctors . . . Though the beach is strewed with the ribs of warning wrecks, we may see at this day squadrons of other quackeries on the broad bosom of public opinion breasting the billows." [20]

These were the charlatans that Melville knew and that his sense of humor transmuted into the cautious agent of the Black Rapids Coal Company, the sympathetic herb doctor with his Omni-Balsamic Reinvigorator and Samaritan Pain Dissuader, the pious solicitor for the Seminole Widow and Orphan Asylum, and the "flunkeying" representative of the Philosophical Intelligence Office. Members of the same clan, though without the beguiling nomenclature, are the man in mourning, the crippled "soldier," the scheming philanthropist, and the non-benevolent philosopher. All are explosive incarnations of the great American myth that something can be had for nothing, or of the great Christian myth that something ought to be had for nothing.

Transmuting this comic mythology into art is the pervasive structure of the masquerade. The very ambiguity of manner and tone is masquerade, the ironic equivocation that Mark Twain was to find at the heart of American humorous storytelling. The personalities of Melville's Yankee and backwoods prototypes were masked by the blank face, the submersion of emotion, the calculated assumption of legendary patterns of dress and behavior.[21] Their deliberate self-dramatizing was an invitation to mythic abstraction. Above all, there is masquerade in the duplicity of the trickster, who felled his headlong victims by a kind of psychological judo. As Baldwin described the moral scene, "Larceny

grew not only respectable, but genteel . . . Swindling was raised
to the dignity of the fine arts. Felony came forth from its covert,
put on more seemly habiliments, and took its seat with unabashed
front in the upper places of the synagogue." [22]

The mask that Melville deftly fitted to his protean trickster
was the ultimate mask of spiritual plausibility. With the scrupu-
lous delicacy of the pure-in-heart the Confidence Man probes for
the chink in his victim's armor and touches the nerve that delivers
the limp enthusiast into his hands. Where one approach occasionally fails, another is sure to succeed; no man's defenses are proof,
least of all against his own weaknesses. The collegian is repelled
by the moral insinuations of the man in mourning, but he pleads
to be bilked by the coal company agent, who affects to admire his
*savoir-faire*. The Missouri bachelor stands firm against the sticky
blandishments of the herb doctor, but he falls before the chop-
logic of the employment agent, who exploits his latent philanthropy. So, in his various disguises, the Confidence Man circulates
in the world, trading now on bereavement, now on sanctity, or
self-interest, or friendship, or reason, or the hope of salvation; and
his dupes fall prey to their own naïveté, or conceit, or fear, or
greed, or persuasion, or hope, or faith.

His most significant feature is the apparent insignificance of his
goals. It takes the cosmopolitan two full chapters to achieve — or
appear to achieve — a free shave in the ship's barber shop. Yet it is
just when the action seems lightest, because there is least at stake,
that its impact is most potent. Time and again we hear echoed the
sardonic taunt of the peg-leg: "How much money did the devil
make by gulling Eve?" [23] The ultimate motive of evil, we are
driven to reflect, may not extend beyond the deceiver's aesthetic
delight in the virtuosity of his own deception. Like Ovid Bolus,
"his genius and his performances were free from the vulgar alloy
of interest or temptation . . . What he did in that walk, was
from the irresistible promptings of instinct, and a disinterested
love of art." [24]

If *The Confidence-Man* is a unique book deserving of a higher
place in our literature than it has so far been accorded, it is because
no other American book has so trenchantly satirized the national
character — indeed, human nature in general — through the basic
figures of our comic folklore.

2

But *The Confidence-Man* does not wear its comic heart on its sleeve. We must read the last of Melville's shorter works as well if we are to savor the full triumph of his humor. As early as 1854 he had turned back with quiet assurance to his sailing days and pieced together some of his loveliest and funniest memories into the masterful sketches of "The Encantadas." In keeping with what the tortoise had taught him about "black and bright," he portrayed the geography and history of the blasted Galápagos with a comprehensive eye to their tragedy and their comedy and with a refreshing sense of the sovereign respect each owes to the other. No bitter laughter jars the delicate pathos of the Chola widow's fate, and no intrusive pity or desperation deflates the mock-heroic tale of the comic Emperor Jones on Charles's Isle, or the grotesque parody of the comic Caliban on Hood's Isle. Unlike Shakespeare's pathetically underprivileged fairy, the hermit Oberlus is so mythically vile that the incongruity of his human shape makes him consistently ludicrous.

When planting, his whole aspect and all his gestures were so malevolently and uselessly sinister and secret, that he seemed rather in act of dropping poison into wells than potatoes into soil. . . Indeed, the sole superiority of Oberlus over the tortoises was his possession of a larger capacity of degradation.

With Oberlus we are back in the salty world of *Omoo*, where the only respectable people were those "of an inferior order of rascality."

By the spring of 1856 the yarn-spinner and humorous essayist that had begun to reëmerge in "The Encantadas" was once more the ascendant Melville. Once again, for however brief a season, his writings recaptured the ebullient charm that has kept his young romances fresh. Yet to say that they have the old charm is not to say that they lack the new complexity, that they are totally devoid of the ambiguity that had constructively deepened his art since *Mardi*. It is to say that their sunny surfaces mask an inner stability — one would almost say serenity — rather than "the breaking heart" or "the bursting head." [25] Of the two sketches printed simultaneously in March by *Putnam's* and *Harper's*, "The 'Gees" is in fact the epitome of sunny surface, indistinguishable in matter and manner from *Omoo* and with no more depth of meaning in its comedy. The other, "I and My Chimney," though no less bright to the eye, supports and conceals a personal allegory as fabulous on its smaller scale as that of *Moby-Dick*.

The Melville of "I and My Chimney" is the whimsical, domesticated master of Arrowhead, that comfortable Pittsfield homestead with its fine old trees, which he delighted in "patting . . . on the back," and its massive central chimney, which on windy nights he fancied put "too much sail on the house," and its great sociable fireplace with the inscription: "I and my chimney smoke together." [26] This is the Melville that wrote: "I and my chimney, two grey-headed old smokers, reside in the country. We are, I may say, old settlers here; particularly my old chimney, which settles more and more every day . . ." The story he built around his chimney is a domestic farce, pitting a sentimentally conservative husband against a radically energetic wife who is bent on ridding them of the architecturally untidy chimney he loves, and who calls in an officious architect to plan the attack. The plot was unquestionably suggested to Melville by the well-meaning attempts of his family to alter the untidy architecture of his personality by consulting Dr. Holmes about his physical and particularly his mental health.[27] If the incident irritated him at the time, it no doubt amused him as well: he was continually having to remind people in his admittedly eccentric letters that he wasn't "crazy." In any event, the meaning of the incident for the story can hardly be more than Chase has unpretentiously stated it to be: "It is surely amusing to watch Melville dealing in his bantering way with the suspicions of his family." [28] Only by an act of imagination which substitutes the mood of *Pierre* for the mood expressed can one share Arvin's view that the story shows Melville's "deep resentment" against his wife and mother, who are "fused into a single image of intrusive and oppressive hostility." [29] The average, comic husband of the story, who is appalled at his wife's "terrible alacrity for improvement," is the average, comic husband of the Melville household, who wrote to his cousin Kate in the fall of 1868, "the apartment underwent a horrible cleaning & setting-to-rights, which means putting things where one can't find 'em." [30] The comic intranquillity between the "old smoker" and his more enterprising wife bears no more necessary relation to the inner life of Herman Melville than the tribulations of the Van Winkles to that of Washington Irving.

If the story has serious biographical meaning, it lies not in the domestic relations of the protagonist, but in the symbolism of his chimney. Read in the light of that symbolism, "I and My Chimney" becomes an important chapter in the spiritual auto-biography begun in *Mardi*, *Moby-Dick*, and *Pierre*, the profound-est theme of which is the struggle for self-knowledge. The com-mon madness of Taji, Ahab, and Pierre had been to dive reck-lessly within themselves in search of the mythical bedrock of Truth. The diving had killed them all. Only little Pip, whose more literal diving was ironically inadvertent, had touched bottom and emerged, mindless but not killed.

Rather carried down alive to wondrous depths, where strange shapes of the unwarped primal world glided to and fro before his passive eyes; and the miser-merman, Wisdom, revealed his hoarded heaps, and among the joyous, heartless, ever-juvenile eternities, Pip saw the multitudinous, God-omnipresent, coral insects, that out of the firma-ment of waters heaved the colossal orbs. He saw God's foot upon the treadle of the loom, and spoke it; and thereafter his shipmates called him mad. So man's insanity is heaven's sense. . .[31]

By 1856 Melville had evidently come to terms with himself and learned from all these deaths and madnesses to live with his enormous and tantalizing ego in a truce of mutual respect. There was no money in introspection, and no satisfaction, except the knowledge of mysteries the very exposure of which would topple the structure they supported. And, after all, his ego, like his chim-ney, was the "backbone" of his house. These are the riches of meaning a regained equanimity enabled him to translate with consummate skill into the comic idiom of "I and My Chimney," a few verbal echoes still faintly discernible from that magnificent passage about Pip:

Very often do I go down into my cellar, and attentively survey that vast square of masonry. I stand long, and ponder over, and wonder at it. It has a druidical look, away down in the umbrageous cellar there whose numerous vaulted passages, and far glens of gloom, resemble the dark, damp depths of primeval woods. So strongly did this conceit steal over me, so deeply was I penetrated with wonder at the chim-ney, that one day — when I was a little out of my mind, I now think

—getting a spade from the garden, I set to work, digging round the foundation, especially at the corners thereof, obscurely prompted by dreams of striking upon some old, earthen-worn memorial of that by-gone day, when, into all this gloom, the light of heaven entered, as the masons laid the foundation-stones. . .

In the closing lines of this most intimate of his sketches Melville seems to address himself to those critical mythologists who persist in finding twisted and painful levels in his maturest humor: "They think I am getting sour and unsocial. Some say that I have become a sort of mossy old misanthrope, while all the time the fact is, I am simply standing guard over my mossy old chimney; for it is resolved between me and my chimney, that I and my chimney will never surrender." Nothing remains of the defiant self-immolation of Taji and Pierre, who resolved in the face of "inevitable rocks" to "make a courageous wreck." [32] There is no death-wish in the Melville of 1856, though the mood had been real enough while it lasted, no doubt. As he wrote to his brother-in-law a few years later, "I once, like other spoonies, cherished a loose sort of notion that I did not care to live very long. But I will frankly own that I have now no serious, no insuperable objections to a respectable longevity." [33] With "I and My Chimney" the suicidal struggle for self-knowledge was conclusively past. He would return to the search in *Clarel*, but no longer to jeer at his failure, or at the world's failure to pay admission to the spectacle.

Two months later the same magazine, *Putnam's*, carried the last of his prose sketches, "The Apple-Tree Table, or Original Spiritual Manifestations." Using the same cast of characters — narrator, wife, and daughters — Melville wove around them a slight but entertaining plot dealing with the discovery, in his attic, of an old claw-footed apple-wood table which, when put into service before the fire, frightens everyone with mysterious noises until it is revealed that the heat has hatched out some dormant insects in the wood. It is at once a high-spirited and a profound work of art, deeply related to the theme and method of its predecessor, and containing in its subtitle, like "Bartleby," a striking metaphysical guide to the levels of its meaning. Superficially, "spiritual manifestations" simply points up the satire on spirit-rapping, which was a flourishing fad in Melville's day. Beneath that it is a reference to his recurrent theme of death and resurrection, which is rather remarkably embodied in the story without materially affecting its comic context. And beneath that (remember that they are "*orig-inal* spiritual manifestations") it is a reference to the symbolic account of his own artistic career, told in terms of the "satanic-looking little old table" he had hauled out of a long-unexplored "garret" to the vast discomfiture of himself and his family, who become reconciled to it only when they know that out of it has come a beautiful and living thing.

But the vehicle of this multiple allegory — the literal story — is jauntily designed, constructed with the tools of his most appealing craftsmanship and free from the creaking machinery of ambiguity that had marred even parts of *Moby-Dick* and "Bartleby." The discovery of the table, which opens the story, was conceived in the amusement Melville had felt during his first year in Pittsfield, when he reflected that the eggs he found laid in an old desk in the ancestral loft were rather emblematic of authors' desks, "especially those with pigeon-holes." [34] The humor that evolves from the discovery goes back beyond the Pittsfield days. As the long-suffering husband of a teetotaling wife, the narrator undergoes the familiar comic purgatory of having his sober alarms attributed to "a mind disordered, not by ghosts, but by punch." His own conviction is that he has been reading too much Cotton Mather by candlelight at a table which is, its animation persuades him, "rather too low for a reading table." The burlesque treatment of his inner "contest between panic and philosophy" is broadly Twainish, and there is something anticipatory of Thurber in his mad predicament when, having solved the mystery, he finds his evidence removed by the maid and is reduced to shouting at his uncomprehending wife, "The bug, the bug! . . . the bug under the tumbler." The meanings beyond the humor label the story as belonging to Melville's later work, but the comedy itself is as serene and unambiguous as it had been before Azzageddi led him down the sardonic road to self-ridicule.

3

To say, as the stories of 1856 seem to do, that Melville had come to terms with himself, is not to say that he had come to terms with God and man. The mordant satire of *The Confidence-Man* is ample evidence that he had an inexhaustible supply of religious

and sociological axes to grind. But the comic spirit had at last
mastered the self-consciousness that had negated its own function
in two of the three major books he had attempted. True, the very
self-consciousness of Ishmael's hyena-laughter had fused itself
into the organic wonder of *Moby-Dick*, but that was a miracle
not to be repeated. The comic spirit of 1856 had grown old
enough to stand apart and, like Meredith's aerial imp, shower
"volleys of silvery laughter" on what it saw. In the case of *The
Confidence-Man* there is nothing left behind when the comic
spirit has withdrawn; the whole book stands overhead laughing,
and the laughter, what we hear of it, includes us. Repelled by
what Matthiessen has aptly called its "diagrammatic abstraction" [35]
— which is in this case the totality of its comic detachment — the
majority of Melville's critics have condemned it as his dreariest
book and used it to perpetuate the legend of his almost psycho-
pathic misanthropy. Few have seen in it much of anything to
amuse them, and most would rebel at the suggestion that it stands
with *Omoo* as one of the terminal expressions of the art of
Herman Melville, humorist.

Perhaps, then, it is no very great mystery that Melville, for all
practical purposes, ceased to write humorously after 1856. When
he read Isaac Disraeli's article on Sterne in *The Literary Character* in 1862, he marked this passage with a double line in the margin: "I have frequently observed how humour, like the taste for
olives, is even repugnant to some palates, and have witnessed the
epicure of humour lose it all by discovering how some have
utterly rejected his favorite relish." Yet the abandonment of
comedy meant the abandonment of his true milieu, and it is possible that he came to realize this, too, if we can assign a self-
critical motive to his marking of another passage, this time in
Balzac's *Bureaucracy* (1889): "he aspired to something better,
but the fatal demon hiding in his wit hindered him from acquiring
the gravity which imposes on fools." Melville's demon had mercifully kept him from that fate. If it hindered his aspiration, it also
kept it pure and enabled him to accomplish the rare achievement
he so emphatically marked in Elizabeth Browning's "A Drama of
Exile," which was to

> *Strike with bold electric laughter*
> *The high tops of things divine.*

NOTES
BIBLIOGRAPHY
INDEX

## LIST OF ABBREVIATIONS

| | |
|---|---|
| CM | *The Confidence-Man* |
| IP | *Israel Potter* |
| M | *Mardi* |
| MD | *Moby-Dick* |
| O | *Omoo* |
| P | *Pierre* |
| R | *Redburn* |
| T | *Typee* |
| WJ | *White-Jacket* |

# Notes

## INTRODUCTION

1. Francis O. Matthiessen, *American Renaissance* (1941), p. 377.
2. Sidney Colvin, ed., *The Letters of Robert Louis Stevenson* (1899), II, 136.
3. Henry Clay Lukens, "American Literary Comedians," *Harper's New Monthly Magazine*, 80:783–797 (1890); Joseph Jones, "Melville: A 'Humorist' in 1890," *American Notes and Queries*, 8:68 (August 1948).
4. Raymond Weaver, *Herman Melville: Mariner and Mystic* (1921), p. 27.
5. Max Eastman, *The Sense of Humor* (1921), p. 21.
6. L. J. Potts, *Comedy* (1948), p. 20.
7. Arthur Tilley, *François Rabelais* (1907), p. 301; Louis Cazamian, *L'Humour de Shakespeare* (1945), p. 82.
8. Sculley Bradley, "Our Native Humor," *North American Review*, 242:351 (Winter 1937).
9. Cazamian, *L'Humour de Shakespeare*, p. 144; Thomas Marc Parrott, *Shakespearean Comedy* (1949), p. viii.
10. Melville to George Duyckinck, December 20, 1858, in Eleanor Melville Metcalf, *Herman Melville: Cycle and Epicycle* (1953), p. 172.
11. Letter of May 29, 1860, *ibid.*, p. 182.
12. Richard Tobias Greene ("Toby" of *Typee*) to Melville, January 4, 1861, in Jay Leyda, *The Melville Log* (1951), II, 632; Melville to Abraham Lansing, August 5, 1875, in Metcalf, *Herman Melville*, p. 232.
13. Melville to Evert Duyckinck, February 12, 1851, in Metcalf, *Herman Melville*, p. 99.
14. Leyda, *Log*, II, 524.
15. *R* 5:24, *MD* 101:444.
16. "Hawthorne and His Mosses," *The Apple-Tree Table*, p. 57.
17. Melville to Ellen Marett Gifford, October 5, 1885, in Metcalf, *Herman Melville*, p. 263.
18. *Journal up the Straits*, p. 97.
19. *MD* 32:131.
20. Balzac quoted by Eastman, *The Sense of Humor*, p. 228; *O* 8:34.

## CHAPTER I. THE COMIC MATTER

1. Albert Bigelow Paine, *Mark Twain, A Biography* (1912), I, 454.
2. *MD* 96:421.
3. *R* chap. 54, *O* chap. 10.
4. D. H. Lawrence, *Studies in Classic American Literature* (1923), p. 206; Constance Rourke, *American Humor* (1931), p. 184.
5. *T* 12:118.

6. Evert Duyckinck to Nathaniel Hawthorne, March 13, 1846, in Leyda, *Log*, I, 206; W. Clark Russell, "A Claim for American Literature," *North American Review*, 154:146 (1892).

7. *O* 3:12, *R* 8:48, *O* 41:183.

8. *WJ* 61:234.

9. *North American Review*, 242:356.

10. *O* 33:147–148.

11. *R* 2:13.

12. Letter of May 29, 1860, in Metcalf, *Herman Melville*, p. 182.

13. Philarète Chasles, "Voyages réels et fantastiques d'Herman Melville," [in translation] *Literary World*, 5:89 (1849). *T* 5:38–39.

14. *O* chap. 14. Cf. Melville to Hawthorne, June 29, 1851, in Metcalf, *Herman Melville*, p. 109: "I had rather be a fool with a heart, than Jupiter Olympus with his head."

15. Melville to Evert Duyckinck, December 14, 1849, *ibid.*, p. 71.

16. *R* 17:96.

17. *R* 28:150, *O* 37:165, *R* 28:151.

18. *WJ* 8:36, *T* 2:13, *R* 29:153, *WJ* 14:54, 91:365.

19. *WJ* 14:56.

20. *O* 15:61–62, 2:9, 17:66–67, 23:96.

21. Lewis Mumford, *Herman Melville* (1929), p. 53; Jean Simon, *Herman Melville, marin, metaphysicien, et poète* (1939), p. 254; Lawrence, *Studies in Classic American Literature*, p. 208; Matthiessen, *American Renaissance*, p. 378.

22. *O* 2:10–11.

23. *O* 72:314–316.

24. *O* chaps. 44, 45; *WJ* 38:147.

25. *O* 46:203, 47:207.

26. *Herman Melville*, p. 203.

27. *T* 24:213.

28. *O* 74:325.

29. *R* 9:53.

CHAPTER II. THE COMIC MANNER

1. In 1847 Melville did a series of unsigned and worthless parodies of Barnum for the comic weekly *Yankee Doodle*, a piece of hack-work uncharitably exhumed by Luther S. Mansfield, "Melville's Comic Articles on Zachary Taylor," *American Literature*, 9:411–418 (1938). See also the illuminating discussion of *Moby-Dick*'s "clear affinities to Barnum's showmanship" in Richard Chase, *Herman Melville: A Critical Study* (1949), pp. 75ff.

2. "Hawthorne and His Mosses," *The Apple-Tree Table*, p. 65.

3. *O* 79:344.

4. *T* 29:265.

5. *WJ* 47:189.

6. Metcalf, *Herman Melville*, p. 110.

7. Newton Arvin, *Herman Melville* (1950), p. 65.

8. *WJ* 6:28.

9. *WJ* 63:249.

10. Mumford, *Herman Melville*, p. 116.

11. Carl Van Vechten, "The Later Work of Herman Melville," *Double Dealer*, 3:10 (1922).

12. *WJ* 45:182.

13. Egbert S. Oliver, "Melville's Picture of Emerson and Thoreau in *The Confidence-Man*," *College English*, 8:64 (1946). More recently, Richard Chase has done some imaginative exploring on the subject in connection with *Pierre*. See below, p. 155.

14. Willard Thorp, "Redburn's Prosy Old Guide Book," *PMLA*, 53:1154–1155 (1938).

15. *WJ* 42:163.

16. *WJ* 19:77.

17. *American Humor*, pp. 192–193.

18. Simon, *Herman Melville*, p. 274; Carl Van Doren, "Melville Before the Mast," *Century Magazine*, 108:275–276 (June 1924).

## CHAPTER III. POINT OF DEPARTURE

1. Melville to Evert Duyckinck, December 14, 1849, in Metcalf, *Herman Melville*, p. 71; *Journal . . . to London*, p. 18.

2. "The Feegee simile would not have held good with respect to it. It was far from being 'tender as a dead man' " (*M* 14:37).

3. S. Foster Damon, "Pierre the Ambiguous," *Hound and Horn*, 2:109 (1929).

4. *M* 55:141, 57:145, 94:236.

5. *M* chap. 132.

6. *M* 124:317, 124:319, 136:356, 143:378.

7. *M* 164:448. The dream is not unlike Melville's own, in which, as he wrote to Hawthorne in the summer of 1851, "you and I shall sit down in Paradise, in some shady little corner by ourselves; and . . . smuggle a basket of champagne there (I won't believe in a Temperance Heaven), and . . . strike our glasses and our heads together, till both ring musically in concert" (Metcalf, *Herman Melville*, p. 108).

8. *M* 144:379, 84:212, 94:236, 95:241, 84:209.

9. Weaver, *Herman Melville*, p. 275.

10. Damon, *Hound and Horn*, 2:109.

11. The question of Shakespearean influence in *Mardi* is complicated by the fact that there is little external evidence of Melville's having read this or that play prior to its composition. The edition in which the marking in question appears was not acquired until early in 1849 (see Melville to Evert Duyckinck, February 24, 1849, in Metcalf, *Herman Melville*, p. 57), whereas at least the first draft of the book was completed as early as May 1848 (see Elizabeth Melville to Hope Shaw, May 5, 1848, *ibid.*, p. 53). However, there is a record of his having owned another edition as early as January of that year (Merton M. Sealts, "Melville's Reading: A Checklist of Books Owned and Borrowed," *Harvard Library Bulletin*, II–IV [1948–1950], no. 460a). In any event, the letter to Duyckinck in which he glories in the legibility of his new Shakespeare does not say that he never read him before, but only that the "vile small print" of "any copy that was come-atable" to him had kept his from "close acquaintance with the divine William."

12. *M* 163:446.

13. Enid Welsford, *The Fool — His Social and Literary History* (1935), pp. 80, 84.

14. *M* 114:287–288.

15. According to Howard Vincent in his introduction to *The Collected*

*Poems of Herman Melville* (1947), p. viii, "These poems should not be taken so seriously as some critics have seemed to, for they are the outpourings of the effusive Yoomy, Melville's ironic portrait of the romantic, long-haired poet whose verses are emotion recollected without tranquillity."

16. For an extended discussion of these characters as "humors," see Merrell R. Davis, *Melville's Mardi: A Chartless Voyage* (1952), chap. viii.

17. *M* 121:305.

## CHAPTER IV. THE PHILOSOPHIC VOYAGE

1. Albert Jay Nock and Catharine Wilson, *Francis Rabelais: The Man and His Work* (1929), p. 258.

2. Arvin, *Herman Melville*, pp. 96–97.

3. Reginald E. Watters, "Melville's Metaphysics of Evil," *University of Toronto Quarterly*, 9:171 (1940).

4. Arvin, *Herman Melville*, p. 98. Ralph H. Gabriel, "Melville, Critic of Mid-Nineteenth Century Beliefs," *The Course of American Democratic Thought* (1940), p. 70.

5. *M* chap. 171. In Arvin's opinion (*Herman Melville*, p. 91), Melville modeled his Doxodox on the double-talking Janotus de Bragmardo in the first book of Rabelais. For the low-comic mystification of Babbalanja he appears to have taken hints as well from the elaborately noncommittal philosopher Trouillogan, who leads Panurge into merry confusions in Book III.

6. However, Melville is not known to have read *Sartor Resartus* until 1850 (Sealts, "Melville's Reading," no. 123).

7. *M* chaps. 127–131.

8. *M* chaps. 138–142. Note another anticipation of Carroll in chap. 163: "They Converse of the Mollusca, Kings, Toad-stools, and Other Matters."

9. *M* chaps. 105–117. Isolated flashes of religious satire appearing elsewhere in *Mardi* are sometimes of interest. A clerical chameleon identified as "the good stranger" (chap. 99) is an embryonic forerunner of the Confidence Man; and the droll parable of Keevi, the god of thieves (chap. 92), is enhanced by a comic version of the Enceladus legend, which figures with such somber prominence in *Pierre*.

10. *M* 113:284–285, 114:290.

11. *M* 132:341–342.

12. *M* 116:295.

13. William Braswell, *Melville's Religious Thought: An Essay in Interpretation* (1943), p. 35.

14. Stephen A. Larrabee, "Melville Against the World," *South Atlantic Quarterly*, 34:416 (1935); Chasles, *Literary World*, 5:102.

15. *M* chap. 24; Carl Van Doren, *The American Novel* (1940), p. 87.

16. *M* 94:237–238.

17. *M* 89:222.

18. *American Renaissance*, p. 379n.

19. *Melville's Religious Thought*, p. 88.

20. *M* 103:258.

21. *M* 131:337–338.

22. *M* 138:364.

23. *M* chaps. 3, 60, 75, 97, 149, 181.

24. E.g., remarks on the history of Liverpool as treated in Redburn's

"prosy old guide book" (*R* 30:167), and White-Jacket's historical justification of noon dinners (*WJ* 7:32).

25. *M* 133:345.
26. *M* 104:260.
27. *M* 177:483–484.
28. *M* 95:239.

## CHAPTER V. DEVILS

1. *American Humor*, p. 193.
2. Maximilian Rudwin, *The Devil in Legend and Literature* (1931). The quotations which follow are from pp. 276, 277, 279.
3. *M* 66:164–165.
4. *T* 24:215.
5. Mumford, *Herman Melville*, p. 104.
6. *Ibid.*, p. 97.
7. Welsford, *The Fool*, pp. 76, 237.
8. The conviction is an important one. It becomes explicit in *Moby-Dick* — "man's insanity is heaven's sense" (*MD* 93:413) — and thematic in *Pierre*.
9. Mumford, *Herman Melville*, p. 104.
10. *M* 183:512, 126:324, 138:364.
11. *M* 183:511–512.
12. *Studies in Pessimism* (2d ed.; London, 1891), p. 84; *The Wisdom of Life* (2d ed.; London, 1891), p. 46; *The World as Will and Idea* (2d ed.; London, 1891), III, 152.
13. *M* 10:28, 180:490.
14. *M* 155:417.

## CHAPTER VI. THE FACE OF COMEDY

1. See Melville to Lemuel Shaw, October 6, 1849, and to R. H. Dana, Jr., May 1, 1850, in Metcalf, *Herman Melville*, pp. 67–68.
2. *MD* 32:131.
3. Weaver, *Herman Melville*, p. 154.
4. *MD* 5:29.
5. *Herman Melville*, p. 27.
6. *MD* 5:30.
7. *MD* chap. 81.
8. *MD* chap. 91; Joseph Jones, "Humor in *Moby-Dick*," *University of Texas Studies in English, 1945–46*, p. 65.
9. *MD* 101:442–444. The term "lubricated" is not of Melville's using; but he does speak in this connection of the Eskimo country, "where the convivial natives pledge each other in bumpers of train oil."
10. *MD* 101:441–442.
11. *MD* 92:407, 1:5.
12. *Journal to London*, pp. 71–72.
13. Matthiessen, *American Renaissance*, p. 384n. See also Howard Vincent, *The Trying-Out of Moby-Dick* (1949), p. 345, and Leon Howard, *Herman Melville: A Biography* (1951), p. 164.
14. Chase, *Herman Melville*, pp. 65ff., is useful on this point. See also C.

Merton Babcock, "Melville's Backwoods Seamen," *Western Folklore*, 10:126–133 (April 1951).

15. Sherman Paul, "Morgan Neville, Melville, and the Folk Hero," *Notes and Queries*, 194:278 (January 25, 1949), suggests the influence of the Mike Fink tradition on the conception of Steelkilt and calls attention to the tall-tale frame in which Melville's narrative method placed the whole *Town-Ho* episode.

16. *MD* 54:245.

17. *MD* 73:325–326.

18. *MD* 53:240.

19. "What I feel most moved to write, that is banned,—it will not pay. Yet, altogether, write the *other* way I cannot. So the product is a final hash, and all my books are botches" (Melville to Hawthorne, June 29, 1851, in Metcalf, *Herman Melville*, p. 108).

20. Modern Library edition (1927), p. 80.

21. *MD* 96:422–423.

22. *MD* 46:211.

23. There is some precedent for such a reading. Howard Vincent (*The Trying-Out of Moby-Dick*, p. 195) finds in this chapter Melville's symbolic apology for the "cetological center" of his novel. The two interpretations are perfectly compatible and even complementary.

## CHAPTER VII. LINKED ANALOGIES

1. *MD* 70:310. Notwithstanding Melville's frequent ridicule of Emerson and transcendental thought, this is a thoroughly Emersonian notion. Cf. *Nature*, Part IV: "The world is emblematic. . . The whole of nature is a metaphor of the human mind." Melville called his chapter "The Sphinx," and its meaning is very close to that of Emerson's poem of the same name, written ten years earlier:

> "Through a thousand voices
> Spoke the universal dame;
> 'Who telleth one of my meanings
> Is master of all I am.'"

2. *MD* 53:238.

3. *American Renaissance*, p. 126.

4. *The Trying-Out of Moby Dick*, p. 136.

5. Mumford, *Herman Melville*, p. 162.

6. *MD* 87:387 and note.

7. *MD* 88:391.

8. *MD* 45:205–206.

9. *MD* 57:270–271.

10. *MD* 65:299.

11. *MD* 2:9. One sly passage of such satire has been pointed out as an anticipation of Mark Twain—the *Bachelor*'s response when asked whether she has lost any men in the chase: "Not enough to speak of—two islanders, that's all" (*MD* 115:489); Jones, *University of Texas Studies in English, 1945–46*, pp. 62–63).

12. *MD* chap. 89.

13. *MD* 25:111, 90:399.

14. E.g., the reference to God as "King of the Cannibals" (*MD* 57:270),

and Queequeg's sour comment that "god wat made shark must be one dam Ingin" (*MD* 66:301).

15. Lawrance Thompson's minority reading of the sermon as satire is a *tour de force* supported, in the absence of conclusive evidence, by the general momentum of his imaginative thesis (*Melville's Quarrel with God* [1952], chap. vii). More reliable is the opinion of W. H. Auden, in *The Enchafèd Flood* (1950), p. 122, that the purpose of the sermon is "that we might know the moral presuppositions by which we are to judge the speeches and actions of Ahab and the rest."

16. *MD* 102:447–448.

17. *MD* 10:51, 17:81. The valedictory oration in Tom Sawyer's school "wound up with a sermon so destructive of hope to non-Presbyterians that it took the first prize"; and Tom remarks (in *Tom Sawyer Abroad*) that Jim "was a Presbyterian and had a most deep respect for Moses, which was a Presbyterian too, he said."

18. *American Renaissance*, pp. 443–444.

19. E.g., ridicule of the new study of comparative mythology in Chapter 82, "The Honor and Glory of Whaling" (Vincent, *The Trying-Out of Moby-Dick*, p. 276); and a gentle mocking of the current fad of phrenology in Chapters 79 and 80 on the head and skull of the whale (Tyrus Hillway, "Melville's Use of Two Pseudo-sciences," *Modern Language Notes*, 64:145–150 [March 1949]).

20. *MD* 78:343. Matthiessen's paraphrase: "Oblivion to cruel reality through idealism does not end in the transcendentalist's sweet vagueness, but in suffocation and death" (*American Renaissance*, p. 126).

21. There are at least 58 puns in *Moby-Dick*, as compared to a total of 56 for the earlier works.

22. Melville to Evert Duyckinck, August 16, 1850, in Metcalf, *Herman Melville*, p. 89. See, for example, the discussion of the pirate's presumed superiority over the whaleman: "It sometimes ends in uncommon elevation, indeed; but only at the gallows. And besides, when a man is elevated in that odd fashion, he has no proper foundation for his superior altitude. Hence, I conclude, that in boasting himself to be high lifted above a whaleman, in that assertion the pirate has no solid basis to stand on" (*MD* 53:239).

23. *MD* 44:199, 50:228.

24. *MD* 108:466, 127:520.

25. *MD* 129:526.

26. *MD* 49:227. This well-concealed pun has been pointed out by Vincent, *The Trying-Out of Moby-Dick*, p. 204.

27. *MD* 103:451.

## CHAPTER VIII. THE COMIC VISION

1. *MD* 86:375, 93:410.
2. *MD* 96:422–423.
3. *MD* 38:167.
4. *MD* 36:162, 41:181, 42:193.
5. *MD* 27:115–116.
6. *MD* 29:125.
7. *MD* 39:168. Cf. Azzageddi: "It is good to laugh, though the laugh be hollow; and wise to make merry, now and for aye. . . All ends in a shout. . .

Ha! ha! how demoniacs shout; how all skeletons grin; we all die with a rattle" (*M* 183:511).

8. *MD* 48:217.
9. *MD* chap. 99.
10. *MD* 114:487.
11. *MD* 119:499.
12. *MD* 133:545. W. H. Auden's otherwise admirable analysis of Stubb (*The Enchafèd Flood*, pp. 130, 132) is flawed by the unfortunate error of reading Flask into this scene in place of Stubb and then building a distinction between them on the strength of his erroneous reading.
13. *MD* 135:564. Cf. *M* 183:511 — "Ho! let us be gay, if only for an hour, and Death hand us the goblet."
14. *MD* 37:166, 117:492.
15. *MD* 127:520–521. Cf. *Macbeth*, III, iv:

> "I am in blood
> Stepp'd in so far that, should I wade no more,
> Returning were as tedious as go o'er."

16. *MD* 30:126. Cf. *Macbeth*, V, iii:

> "And that which should accompany old age,
> As honour, love, obedience, troops of friends,
> I must not look to have."

17. *MD* 108:466–467.
18. *MD* 127:519–520.
19. *MD* 49:225.
20. *MD* 7:36.
21. *MD* 112:481.
22. *R* 21:113, *WJ* 4:18–19.
23. *O* 14:59, *R* 62:351.
24. *MD* 60:280; chaps. 72, 110; 97:421.
25. *MD* 93:413.
26. *MD* 36:163, 113:484–485, 125:514.
27. *MD* 64:291–292.
28. When Constance Rourke writes (*American Humor*, p. 193) that "in *Moby-Dick* this many-sided diabolism reached an ultimate culmination," she unaccountably ignores the fatal predominance of that element in later books; but she does recognize its union here with the folk element in which she is primarily interested.

## CHAPTER IX. THE HEART OF COMEDY

1. All Melville scholars have made passing reference to the fact, and two have made partial and impressionistic studies of the Shakespearean influence: R. G. Hughes, "Melville and Shakespeare," *Shakespeare Association Bulletin*, 7:103–112 (July 1932); and Charles Olson, *Call Me Ishmael* (1947). A definitive study of the literary relations of Melville and Shakespeare has yet to be made.
2. E. E. Stoll, "The Comic Method," *Shakespearean Studies* (1927), p. 184.
3. *Ibid.*, p. 155.
4. Raymond M. Alden, "The Use of Comic Material in the Tragedy of

Shakespeare and His Contemporaries," *Journal of English and Germanic Philology*, 13:298 (1914).
5. Parrott, *Shakespearean Comedy*, p. 304.
6. *MD* 29:124.
7. *MD* chap. 73. Vincent, *The Trying-Out of Moby-Dick*, p. 250.
8. Vincent, p. 113.
9. *Henry IV, Part 2*, V, v. In connection with this passage it is interesting to note that Melville later wrote a humorous poem dramatizing Falstaff's probable rationalization of that repulse: "Falstaff's Lament over Prince Hal Become Henry V," *Collected Poems*, pp. 382–383.
10. Matthiessen, *American Renaissance*, p. 432.
11. *MD* 45:203.
12. Parrott, *Shakespearean Comedy*, p. 401.
13. *The Trying-Out of Moby-Dick*, p. 145.
14. William H. Gilman, *Melville's Early Life and Redburn* (1951), p. 207.
15. *MD* 82:359.
16. Essentially, this is the technique that Vincent has in mind when he speaks of Melville's "progression from deft exposition to humorous commentary, to serious statement whereby the expository information is brought into significant relationship with the theme" (*The Trying-Out of Moby-Dick*, p. 219). At its subtlest, however, the progression is vertical rather than horizontal, in the sense that the literal and figurative meanings develop simultaneously.
17. *The Trying-Out of Moby-Dick*, p. 270.
18. Among the most striking passages in this respect are the concluding paragraphs of Chapter 55 ("Of the Monstrous Pictures of Whales") and Chapter 86 ("The Tail"). The implications of such passages and the role of humor in bringing them out are admirably analyzed by Vincent in *The Trying-Out of Moby-Dick*, pp. 219, 293–294, 298.
19. *MD* 85:371. Of the most Rabelaisian and irreverent burlesque of all, the final remarks on the tail of the God-whale, Matthiessen writes: "The effect of that burlesque is to magnify rather than to lessen his theme; not to blaspheme Jehovah, but to add majesty to the whale" (*American Renaissance*, p. 431). In the presence of such explicit effects it is difficult to entertain the negative interpretations of Lawrance Thompson in *Melville's Quarrel with God*.
20. *R* 20:109–110.
21. *MD* 83:363.
22. *Call Me Ishmael*, p. 71.
23. *MD* 104:452.
24. Rourke, *American Humor*, p. 194.
25. George Meredith, *An Essay on Comedy and the Uses of the Comic Spirit* (1897), p. 78.

## CHAPTER X. THE BRIGHT AND THE DARK

1. Cazamian, *L'Humour de Shakespeare*, pp. 10–11.
2. *P* 4:98.
3. *P* 3:49, 10:208.
4. *P* 12:232, *WJ* 33:127.
5. "The whole world's a trick. Know the trick of it, all's right; don't know, all's wrong. Ha! Ha!" (*P* 23:376).
6. *P* 25:398.

7. *CM* 29:185.

8. *Piazza Tales*, p. 154.

9. *The Apple-Tree Table*, p. 261.

10. In a penetrating contemporary judgment, R. H. Dana, Sr., wrote to Evert Duyckinck, January 25, 1854, that the story "touches the nicer strings of our complicated nature & finely blends the pathetic & ludicrous" (Leyda, *Log*, I, 484). In our own time William E. Sedgwick has written that in "Bartleby" "a comic situation is sustained without jarring the delicate undertones of wistfulness and pathos" (*Herman Melville: The Tragedy of Mind* [1944], p. 182); and Richard Chase has described it as written with a simplicity "at once nakedly tragic and wistfully comic" (*Herman Melville*, p. 144).

11. The new edition of *Piazza Tales* (1948), edited by Egbert S. Oliver, for some reason omits the subtitle, but it appeared in the original publication, *Putnam's Monthly Magazine*, November and December 1853.

12. Charles Feidelson, Jr., has arrived at the same conclusion by way of an illuminating analogy with Gide. In *The Counterfeiters*, a self-imaging author-hero much like Pierre wishes to end his book, "might be continued." Feidelson suggests that Melville reasoned like Gide about such a book: "It must not be neatly rounded off, but rather disperse, disintegrate" (*Symbolism and American Literature* [1953], pp. 204, 209).

13. Melville borrowed once from *Tristram Shandy* but for noncomic purposes: The Plinlimmon pamphlet is found as casually and lost in precisely the same manner (through a hole in a coat pocket) as the sermon of Yorick which has been suggested as an influence on *The Confidence-Man*. Cf. *P* 14:242, 21:346; *Tristram Shandy* (Modern Library edition), pp. 105, 128.

14. Murray's notes point out numerous comic parallels: e.g., the gravedigger and the landlord of the Black Swan (*P* 13:238). The tragic relations are discussed by S. Foster Damon, "Pierre the Ambiguous," *Hound and Horn*, 2:107–118 (1929). See also Arvin's somewhat broader attribution of low-comic characters to Shakespearean influence: *Herman Melville*, pp. 227–228.

15. Louis Cazamian, "Humour in 'Hamlet,'" *Essais en deux langues* (1938), p. 133 (reprinted from *The Rice Institute Pamphlet*, July 1937).

16. Critics have toyed with this idea for years: see John Freeman, *Herman Melville* (1926), p. 111; and E. L. Grant Watson, "Melville's *Pierre*," *New England Quarterly*, 3:199 (1930). The definitive statements on the subject are by William Braswell: "The Satirical Temper of Melville's *Pierre*," *American Literature*, 7:424–438 (1936), and "Early Love Scenes in Melville's *Pierre*," *American Literature*, 22:283–289 (1950).

17. *P* 11:218–219, 9:195; *R* 2:13, 44:246. The contrasting moods of Ishmael and Pierre are brilliantly discussed in Sedgwick, *Herman Melville*, pp. 155–157.

18. *CM* 19:107.

19. *IP* 22:241.

20. *Collected Poems*, p. 185.

21. *IP* 23:251, *P* 25:400.

22. "Shelley's Vision," *Timoleon* (1891); in *Collected Poems*, p. 233.

23. Melville's review, "Hawthorne and His Mosses," appeared in *The Literary World*, August 17, 1850.

24. Metcalf, *Herman Melville*, pp. 111, 129.

25. In *Pierre*, in the words of the Plinlimmon pamphlet, "the absolute

effort to live in this world according to the strict letter of the chrono-metricals [i.e., divine precept] is somehow apt to involve those in-ferior beings eventually in strange, *unique* follies and sins, unimagined before" (*P* 14:249–250). Murray (Introduction to *Pierre*, p. lxxvii) has also noted this coincidence.

26. During his night of impotent expiation upon the scaffold of Hester's mortification (chap. 12) Dimmesdale is swept with a perverse urge to reveal himself to a passing Elder by some flippant remark. Later in the night, overcome by this "lurid playfulness," he "unawares, and to his own infinite alarm, burst into a great peal of laughter."

27. See his comments on the sovereignty of the individual "amid the powers of heaven, hell, and earth": Melville to Hawthorne, spring 1851, in Metcalf, *Herman Melville*, p. 105.

28. *Ibid.*, pp. 105, 109.

29. Was Melville thinking of the Reverend Mr. Shallow-Deep of "The Celestial Railroad" in Hawthorne's *Mosses?* Braswell (*Melville's Religious Thought*, p. 77) has suggested a possible pun in the name "Falsgrave."

30. *CM* 4:24. The parallel has been pointed out by Henry F. Pommer, *Milton and Melville* (1950), p. 31. Concerning the general diabolical symbol-ism of the title character, see John W. Shroeder, "Sources and Symbols for Melville's *Confidence-Man*," *PMLA*, 66:363–380 (1951).

31. Sedgwick, *Herman Melville*, p. 157.

32. Mumford, *Herman Melville*, p. 200; Matthiessen, *American Renais-sance*, p. 489.

33. Howard, *Herman Melville*, p. 190.

34. *American Renaissance*, p. 484. The reader will recall that it was Mel-ville's provision of a norm that made possible a positive estimate of *Moby-Dick*'s ambiguous comedy.

35. Braswell, *Melville's Religious Thought*, pp. 114–115; Matthiessen, *American Renaissance*, p. 411.

36. Reginald E. Watters, "Melville's 'Sociality,'" *American Literature*, 17:33–49 (1945); Gordon Beverly, "Herman Melville's Confidence," *London Times Literary Supplement*, November 11, 1949, p. 733. See also Chase, *Herman Melville*, p. 187n. Chase holds the former view but admits some validity in the latter.

37. *Herman Melville*, pp. 115ff, 122n.

38. *CM* 22:140–141.

39. Meredith, Prelude to *The Egoist*; *M* 104:260.

40. *The Wisdom of Life* (1891).

## CHAPTER XI. THE HORNET'S NEST

1. Vol. III, "Epilogue to the Satires," Dialogue II. The edition Melville owned was published in 1856.

2. Murray, Introduction to *Pierre*, p. xxx.

3. Melville to Hawthorne, spring 1851, in Metcalf, *Herman Melville*, p. 105.

4. Melville to James Billson, January 22, 1885, *ibid.*, p. 268.

5. *IP* 7:71; Melville to Evert Duyckinck, March 3, 1849, in Metcalf, *Herman Melville*, p. 59.

6. *IP* 9:81, 85.

7. *CM* chap. 30; 29:187; chap. 19.

8. *CM* 7:44–46.

9. Quoted in Herbert Ross Brown, *The Sentimental Novel in America,* *1789–1860* (1940), p. 156.

10. Harrington, the hero of William Hill Brown's *The Power of Sympathy* (1789).

11. Brown, *The Sentimental Novel in America,* p. 191.

12. Sealts, "Melville's Reading," no. 303.

13. In *The North and South* (1852) by C. Rush, cited in Brown, *The Sentimental Novel in America,* p. 183.

14. The state of affairs is helpfully sketched in Frank Luther Mott, *A History of American Magazines* (1938–39), I, 405–406.

15. Memo to Allan Melville, May 22, 1860, in Metcalf, *Herman Melville,* p. 184.

16. Letter of February 12, 1851, *ibid.,* p. 98.

17. The debt is specified in persuasive detail by Shroeder, *PMLA,* 66:363–380.

18. Plotinus: a Neoplatonic pagan idealist. Plinlimmon: a lofty Welsh mountain. There is a stimulating discussion of some possible implications of these names in Murray's note, *Pierre,* p. 475.

19. *P* 20:325.

20. The parallels to Thoreau's *A Week on the Concord and Merrimack Rivers* have been documented by Egbert S. Oliver, " 'Cock-a-Doodle-Doo!' and Transcendental Hocus-Pocus," *New England Quarterly,* 21:204–216 (June 1948). Leon Howard (*Herman Melville,* p. 210) has more recently asserted that the story is a parody on Wordsworth's "Resolution and Independence," to which it also bears undeniable resemblances. Oliver makes the stimulating suggestion that "Cock-a-Doodle-Doo!" was intended as a companion piece to "Bartleby" (they were the only things Melville published in 1853), the former ridiculing outward withdrawal as one extremity of the transcendental doctrine, the latter ridiculing inward withdrawal as the other. However, his formal attempt to prove "Bartleby" a similar satire on Thoreau ("A Second Look at 'Bartleby,'" *College English,* 6:431–439 [1945] ) is badly hampered by lack of facts and lack of decisive satiric tone in the story itself.

21. Odell Shepard, ed., *The Journals of Bronson Alcott* (1938), p. 205, entry for March 14, 1848.

22. *P* 22:352.

23. Letters to John Sterling, July 23 and August 29, 1842; Alexander Carlyle, ed., *Letters of Thomas Carlyle to John Stuart Mill, John Sterling, and Robert Browning* (1923), p. 257.

24. Odell Shepard, *Pedlar's Progress: The Life of Bronson Alcott* (1937), pp. 348, 351–352.

25. Alice Felt Tyler, *Freedom's Ferment* (1944), p. 441; Shepard, *Pedlar's Progress,* p. 440.

26. *Knickerbocker Magazine,* 39:278 (March 1852), 41:254 (March 1853); quoted in Mott, *History of American Magazines,* I, 479; II, 87.

27. *P* 21:341.

28. Henry A. Murray has contended, both in his excellent Introduction to *Pierre* (pp. lxxvii–lxxix) and in some very persuasive letters to me, that Plinlimmon is a secret portrait of Hawthorne. I like the argument in its parts, especially the ironic notion that Hawthorne was at the same moment writing Melville into the philosophic villain of *The Blithedale Romance*;

but I cannot reconcile the theory with the congruity of their interests, especially in the books in question, or with the fast friendship I believe to have persisted between them. On this latter point, so much debated, I was lately strengthened in my bias by reading Randall Stewart, "Melville and Hawthorne," *South Atlantic Quarterly*, 51:436–466 (1952).

29. Melville to Evert Duyckinck, February 24, 1849, and March 3, 1849; Metcalf, *Herman Melville*, pp. 58–59.

30. *P* 21:341.

31. *American Renaissance*, pp. 10, 4.

32. William R. Alger, *The Solitudes of Nature and of Man* (3rd ed., 1867), p. 110.

33. *American Renaissance*, p. 75.

34. The definitive article on the subject is Egbert S. Oliver, "Melville's Picture of Emerson and Thoreau in *The Confidence-Man*," *College English*, 8:61–72 (1946). Elizabeth Foster (Introduction to *The Confidence-Man*, pp. lxxiii–lxxxii) differs in viewing Egbert as a dramatized aspect of Emerson himself rather than as a literal disciple, but she defends the main contention without reservation. The lone dissenter is William Braswell, "Melville as a Critic of Emerson," *American Literature*, 9:319 (1937). No reasons are given for the skepticism of a scholar unusually well armed with the materials of conviction.

35. *CM* 36:212. One thinks at once of Lowell's famous remarks on Emerson in "A Fable for Critics" (1848): "A Greek head on right Yankee shoulders . . . / A Plotinus-Montaigne, where the Egyptian's gold mist / And the Gascon's shrewd wit cheek-by-jowl co-exist." Note also the "mist" of "Plotinus." Other parallels are similarly suggestive of Melville's having read Lowell with humorous appreciation and philosophic approval.

36. The epithets occur in "Self-Reliance" and *Walden* (chap. i) respectively.

37. Emerson's is a formal unit so entitled in his First Series, Thoreau's an untitled ramification of his loosely organized *A Week on the Concord and Merrimack Rivers* (pp. 371–394 in the Modern Library edition of *Walden*).

38. Foster, Introduction to *The Confidence-Man*, pp. lxxix–lxxxi.

39. Arvin, *Herman Melville*, p. 247.

40. Joseph Warren Beach, *The Comic Spirit in George Meredith* (1911), p. 126.

## CHAPTER XII. REMEMBERED LAUGHTER

1. Melville to Nathaniel Hawthorne, June 29, 1851, in Metcalf, *Herman Melville*, pp. 107–109.

2. Melville to Nathaniel Hawthorne, June 29, 1851, and November 1851, *ibid.*, pp. 110, 129.

3. Melville to Thomas Melville, May 25, 1862, *ibid.*, p. 198; Melville to James Billson, October 10, 1884, *ibid.*, p. 267.

4. *P* 18:304.

5. *P* 18:303.

6. *P* 26:422.

7. This aspect of Israel Potter has been well investigated by Richard Chase (*Herman Melville*, p. 177), who shows his relations to such figures as Brother Jonathan, Sam Slick, and Major Jack Downing.

8. Sealts, "Melville's Reading," no. 324.

9. Chase, *Herman Melville*, p. 185; Matthiessen, *American Renaissance*, p. 409n.

10. Howard, *Herman Melville*, pp. 31–37, 227. A close study of Melville's use of his observations in *The Confidence-Man* is John W. Nichol, "Melville and the Midwest," *PMLA*, 66:613–625 (1951). Readers who, like me, are prone to take Constance Rourke's *American Humor* as gospel, should beware of the misinformed judgment with which she concludes her consideration of Melville: "To have turned to the land — the western land — for heroic materials would have meant for Melville an unfamiliar element, even though a rich legendary material awaited him there."

11. Walter Blair, *Native American Humor* (1937), pp. 74, 84–85.

12. I am indebted to Walter Blair for the suggestion that Melville's style and narrative methods were influenced by oral "rehearsals" of his stories, particularly in *Typee* and *Omoo*, which he describes in his prefaces as having been "spun as a yarn" many times before being written down. A similar statement in the opening paragraph of "The 'Gees" (1856) makes it clear that the author of *The Confidence-Man* was a yarn-spinner still. See also Julian Hawthorne's comments on Melville as a storyteller in Metcalf, *Herman Melville*, p. 100.

13. *CM* 2:8.

14. Johnson J. Hooper, *Simon Suggs' Adventures* (1881; 1st ed., 1845), p. 26.

15. Joseph G. Baldwin, *The Flush Times of Alabama and Mississippi* (1853), pp. 6–7.

16. Leyda, *Log*, I, 494.

17. Chase, *Herman Melville*, p. 186.

18. Richardson Wright, *Hawkers and Walkers in Early America* (1927), pp. 17, 200.

19. *Ibid.*, pp. 57–58.

20. *Knickerbocker Magazine*, 17:362 (May 1841), quoted in Mott, *History of American Magazines*, I, 472.

21. Rourke, *American Humor*, pp. 11, 30, 43, 100, 211–212.

22. *The Flush Times*, p. 85.

23. *CM* 6:36.

24. Baldwin, *The Flush Times*, p. 3.

25. *P* 25:398.

26. Maunsell Bradhurst Field, *Memories of Many Men and of Some Women* (1874), p. 202; Melville to Evert Duyckinck, December 1850, in Metcalf, *Herman Melville*, p. 97; Richard Lathers, *The Reminiscences of Richard Lathers* (1907), p. 329.

27. Merton M. Sealts, "Herman Melville's 'I and My Chimney,'" *American Literature*, 13:142–154 (1941).

28. Chase, *Herman Melville*, p. 171.

29. Arvin, *Herman Melville*, p. 204.

30. Metcalf, *Herman Melville*, p. 210.

31. *MD* 93:413.

32. *P* 25:398. Taji's prayer had been: "Give me, ye gods, an utter wreck, if wreck I do" (*M* 169:461).

33. Melville to Samuel Shaw, December 10, 1862, in Metcalf, *Herman Melville*, p. 200.

34. Melville to Evert Duyckinck, August 16, 1850, *ibid.*, p. 88.

35. *American Renaissance*, p. 286.

# Bibliography

The following list includes all sources cited in the text except works of general literature which may be consulted in any convenient edition. An asterisk denotes a marked or annotated volume from Melville's library, and the following abbreviations designate the collections in which these books may now be found: HCL, Harvard College Library; YUL, Yale University Library; NYPL, New York Public Library.

Alden, Raymond M. "The Use of Comic Material in the Tragedy of Shakespeare and His Contemporaries," *Journal of English and Germanic Philology*, 13:281–298 (1914).

*Alger, William R. *The Solitudes of Nature and of Man*. 3rd ed. Boston: Roberts, 1867. HCL.

Anderson, Charles R. *Melville in the South Seas*. New York: Columbia University Press, 1939.

Arvin, Newton. *Herman Melville*. New York: Sloane, 1950.

Auden, Wystan Hugh. *The Enchafèd Flood*. New York: Random House, 1950.

Babcock, C. Merton. "Melville's Backwoods Seamen," *Western Folklore*, 10:126–133 (April 1951).

Baldwin, Joseph G. *The Flush Times of Alabama and Mississippi*. New York: D. Appleton, 1853.

*Balzac, Honoré de. *Bureaucracy; or, A Civil Service Reformer*. Trans. Katharine P. Wormeley. Boston: Roberts, 1889. NYPL.

Beach, Joseph Warren. *The Comic Spirit in George Meredith*. New York: Longmans, Green, 1911.

Beverly, Gordon. "Herman Melville's Confidence," *London Times Literary Supplement*, November 11, 1949, p. 733.

Blair, Walter. *Native American Humor*. New York: American Book Co., 1937.

Bradley, Sculley. "Our Native Humor," *North American Review*, 242:351–362 (Winter 1937).

Braswell, William. "Early Love Scenes in Melville's *Pierre*," *American Literature*, 22:283–289 (1950).

—— "Melville as a Critic of Emerson," *American Literature*, 9:317–334 (1937).

—— *Melville's Religious Thought: An Essay in Interpretation*. Durham: Duke University Press, 1943.

—— "The Satirical Temper of Melville's *Pierre*," *American Literature*, 7:424–438 (1936).

Brown, Herbert Ross. *The Sentimental Novel in America, 1789–1860*. Durham: Duke University Press, 1940.

*Browning, Elizabeth Barrett, *Poems*. 2 vols. New York: Francis, 1860. NYPL.

Carlyle, Alexander, ed. *Letters of Thomas Carlyle to John Stuart Mill, John Sterling, and Robert Browning.* New York: Stokes, 1923.

Cazamian, Louis. *L'Humour de Shakespeare.* Paris: Aubier, 1945.

—— "Humour in 'Hamlet,'" *Essais en deux langues.* Paris: Didier, 1938, pp. 131–140. Reprinted from *The Rice Institute Pamphlet,* July 1937.

*Cervantes, Miguel de. *Don Quixote de la Mancha.* 2 vols. Trans. Charles Jarvis. Philadelphia: Blanchard and Lea, 1853. HCL.

Chase, Richard. *Herman Melville: A Critical Study.* New York: Macmillan, 1949.

Chasles, Philarète. "Voyages réels et fantastiques d'Herman Melville" [in translation], *Literary World,* 5:89–90, 101–103 (1849).

Colvin, Sidney, ed. *The Letters of Robert Louis Stevenson.* 2 vols. New York: Scribner, 1899.

Damon, S. Foster. "Pierre the Ambiguous," *Hound and Horn,* 2:107–118 (1929).

Davis, Merrell R. *Melville's Mardi: A Chartless Voyage.* New Haven: Yale University Press, 1952.

*Disraeli, Isaac. *The Literary Character,* ed. B. Disraeli. London: Routledge, 1859. NYPL.

Eastman, Max. *The Sense of Humor.* New York: Scribner, 1921.

*Emerson, Ralph Waldo. *Essays.* 4th ed. Boston: Munroe, 1847. HCL.

* —— *Essays: Second Series.* 3rd ed. Boston: Munroe, 1844. HCL.

Feidelson, Charles, Jr. *Symbolism and American Literature.* Chicago: University of Chicago Press, 1953.

Field, Maunsell Bradhurst. *Memories of Many Men and of Some Women.* New York: Harper, 1874.

Freeman, John. *Herman Melville.* London: Macmillan, 1926.

Gabriel, Ralph H. "Melville, Critic of Mid-Nineteenth Century Beliefs," *The Course of American Democratic Thought.* New York: Ronald Press, 1940, pp. 67–77.

Gilman, William H. *Melville's Early Life and Redburn.* New York: New York University Press, 1951.

*Hawthorne, Nathaniel. *Mosses from an Old Manse.* New York: Wiley and Putnam, 1846. HCL.

* —— *Twice-Told Tales.* Vol. II. Boston: Munroe, 1842. HCL.

Hillway, Tyrus. "Melville's Use of Two Pseudo-sciences," *Modern Language Notes,* 64:145–150 (March 1949).

Hooper, Johnson J. *Simon Suggs' Adventures.* Philadelphia: Peterson, 1881.

Howard, Leon. *Herman Melville: A Biography.* Berkeley: University of California Press, 1951.

Hughes, R. G. "Melville and Shakespeare," *Shakespeare Association Bulletin,* 7:103–112 (July 1932).

*Irving, Washington. *A History of New York,* by Diedrich Knickerbocker [pseud.] Vol. I of *Works.* Philadelphia: Lea and Blanchard, 1840. HCL.

Jones, Joseph. "Humor in *Moby-Dick,*" *University of Texas Studies in English, 1945–46,* pp. 51–71.

—— "Melville: A 'Humorist' in 1890," *American Notes and Queries,* 8:68 (August 1948).

*La Bruyère, Jean de. *Works.* 2 vols. London: Bell, 1776. YUL.

Larrabee, Stephen A. "Melville Against the World," *South Atlantic Quarterly,* 34:410–418 (1935).

Lathers, Richard. *The Reminiscences of Richard Lathers*. New York: Grafton Press, 1907.

Lawrence, D. H. *Studies in Classic American Literature*. New York: Seltzer, 1923.

Leyda, Jay. *The Melville Log*. 2 vols. New York: Harcourt Brace, 1951.

Lukens, Henry Clay. "American Literary Comedians," *Harper's New Monthly Magazine*, 80:783–797 (1890).

Mansfield, Luther S. "Melville's Comic Articles on Zachary Taylor," *American Literature*, 9:411–418 (1938).

Matthiessen, Francis O. *American Renaissance*. New York: Oxford University Press, 1941.

Melville, Herman. *The Apple-Tree Table and Other Sketches*, ed. Henry Chapin. Princeton: Princeton University Press, 1922. Contents cited: "The Apple-Tree Table," "Hawthorne and His Mosses," "I and My Chimney," "The Paradise of Bachelors and the Tartarus of Maids," "Cock-a-Doodle-Doo!" "The Fiddler," "Poor Man's Pudding and Rich Man's Crumbs," "The 'Gees."

—— *Collected Poems*, ed. Howard P. Vincent. Chicago: Packard, Hendricks House, 1947.

—— *The Confidence-Man*, ed. Elizabeth Foster. New York: Hendricks House, 1954.

—— *Israel Potter, His Fifty Years of Exile*. Pequod Edition, ed. Raymond Weaver. New York: Boni, 1924.

—— *Journal of a Visit to London and the Continent, 1849–1850*, ed. Eleanor Melville Metcalf. Cambridge: Harvard University Press, 1948.

—— *Journal up the Straits*, ed. Raymond Weaver. New York: Colophon, 1935.

—— *Mardi, and a Voyage Thither*. Pequod Edition, ed. Raymond Weaver. New York: Boni, 1925.

—— *Moby-Dick; or, The Whale*, ed. Luther S. Mansfield and Howard P. Vincent. New York: Hendricks House, 1952.

—— *Omoo*. New York: United States Book Co., *c.* 1892.

—— *Piazza Tales*, ed. Egbert S. Oliver. New York: Hendricks House, Farrar Straus, 1948. Contents cited: "Bartleby," "The Encantadas."

—— *Pierre; or, The Ambiguities*, ed. Henry A. Murray. New York: Hendricks House, Farrar Straus, 1949.

—— *Redburn, His First Voyage*. Pequod Edition, ed. Raymond Weaver. New York: Boni, 1924.

—— *Typee*. World's Classics. London: Oxford University Press, 1924.

—— *White-Jacket; or, The World in a Man-of-War*. New York: Burt, *c.* 1892.

Meredith, George, *An Essay on Comedy and the Uses of the Comic Spirit*. New York: Scribner, 1897.

Metcalf, Eleanor Melville. *Herman Melville: Cycle and Epicycle*. Cambridge: Harvard University Press, 1953.

Mott, Frank Luther. *A History of American Magazines*. 3 vols. Cambridge: Harvard University Press, 1938–39.

Mumford, Lewis. *Herman Melville*. New York: Harcourt Brace, 1929.

Nichol, John W. "Melville and the Midwest," *PMLA*, 66:613–625 (1951).

Nock, Albert Jay, and Catharine R. Wilson. *Francis Rabelais: The Man and His Work*. New York: Harper, 1929.

Oliver, Egbert S. "'Cock-a-Doodle-Doo!' and Transcendental Hocus-Pocus," *New England Quarterly*, 21:204–216 (June 1948).

—— "Melville's Picture of Emerson and Thoreau in *The Confidence-Man*," *College English*, 8:61–72 (1946).

—— "A Second Look at 'Bartleby,'" *College English*, 6:431–439 (1945).

Olson, Charles. *Call Me Ishmael*. New York: Reynal and Hitchcock, 1947.

Paine, Albert Bigelow. *Mark Twain, A Biography*. 3 vols. New York: Harper, 1912.

Parrott, Thomas Marc. *Shakespearean Comedy*. New York: Oxford University Press, 1949.

Paul, Sherman. "Morgan Neville, Melville, and the Folk Hero," *Notes and Queries*, 194:278 (January 25, 1949).

Pommer, Henry F. *Milton and Melville*. Pittsburgh: University of Pittsburgh Press, 1950.

*Pope, Alexander, *Poetical Works*. Vol. III. Boston: Little, Brown, 1856. HCL.

Potts, L. J. *Comedy*. London: Hutchinson's University Library, 1948.

Rourke, Constance. *American Humor*. New York: Harcourt Brace, 1931.

Rudwin, Maximilian. *The Devil in Legend and Literature*. Chicago: Open Court Publishing Co., 1931.

Russell, W. Clark. "A Claim for American Literature," *North American Review*, 154:138–149 (1892).

*Schopenhauer, Arthur. *Studies in Pessimism*. Trans. T. B. Saunders. 2nd ed. London: Sonnenschein, 1891. HCL.

* —— *The Wisdom of Life*. Trans. T. B. Saunders. 2nd ed. London: Sonnenschein, 1891. HCL.

* —— *The World as Will and Idea*. 3 vols. Trans. R. B. Haldane and J. Kemp. 2nd ed. London: Trübner, 1888. HCL.

Sealts, Merton M. "Herman Melville's 'I and My Chimney,'" *American Literature*, 13:142–154 (1941).

—— "Melville's Reading: A Checklist of Books Owned and Borrowed," *Harvard Library Bulletin*, 2:141–163, 378–392 (1948); 3:119–130, 268–277, 407–421 (1949); 4:98–109 (1950).

Sedgwick, William E. *Herman Melville: The Tragedy of Mind*. Cambridge: Harvard University Press, 1944.

*Shakespeare, William. *Dramatic Works*. 7 vols. Boston: Hilliard, Gray, 1837. HCL.

Shepard, Odell, ed. *The Journals of Bronson Alcott*. Boston: Little, Brown, 1938.

—— *Pedlar's Progress: The Life of Bronson Alcott*. Boston: Little, Brown, 1937.

Shroeder, John W. "Sources and Symbols for Melville's *Confidence-Man*," *PMLA*, 66:363–380 (1951).

Simon, Jean. *Herman Melville, marin, metaphysicien et poète*. Paris: Boivin, 1939.

Stewart, Randall. "Melville and Hawthorne," *South Atlantic Quarterly*, 51:436–466 (1952).

Stoll, Elmer Edgar. "The Comic Method," *Shakespearean Studies*. New York: Macmillan, 1927, pp. 147–186.

Thompson, Lawrance. *Melville's Quarrel with God*. Princeton: Princeton University Press, 1952.

Thorp, Willard, ed. *Herman Melville: Representative Selections.* New York: American Book Co., 1938.
—— "Redburn's Prosy Old Guide Book," *PMLA*, 53:1146–1156 (1938).
Tilley, Arthur. *François Rabelais.* Philadelphia: Lippincott, 1907.
Tyler, Alice Felt. *Freedom's Ferment.* Minneapolis: University of Minnesota Press, 1944.
Van Doren, Carl. *The American Novel.* Rev. ed. New York: Macmillan, 1940.
—— "Melville Before the Mast," *Century Magazine*, 108:272–277 (June 1924).
Van Vechten, Carl. "The Later Work of Herman Melville," *Double Dealer*, 3:9–20 (1922).
Vincent, Howard P. *The Trying-Out of Moby-Dick.* Boston: Houghton Mifflin, 1949.
Watson, E. L. Grant. "Melville's *Pierre*," *New England Quarterly*, 3:195–234 (1930).
Watters, Reginald E. "Melville's Metaphysics of Evil," *University of Toronto Quarterly*, 9:170–182 (1940).
—— "Melville's 'Sociality,'" *American Literature*, 17:33–49 (1945).
Weaver, Raymond. *Herman Melville: Mariner and Mystic.* New York: Doran, 1921.
Welsford, Enid. *The Fool — His Social and Literary History.* New York: Farrar and Rinehart, 1935.
Wright, Richardson. *Hawkers and Walkers in Early America.* Philadelphia: Lippincott, 1927.

# INDEX

Characters from Melville's novels are identified by abbreviated titles. See the List of Abbreviations on page 186.